WHEN DOES HISTORY BEGIN?

HARJOT OBEROI

When Does History Begin?

RELIGION, NARRATIVE, AND IDENTITY
IN THE SIKH TRADITION

When Does History Begin? Religion, Narrative, and Identity in the Sikh Religion by Harjot Oberoi was first published by Permanent Black D-28 Oxford Apts, 11 IP Extension, Delhi 110092 INDIA, for the territory of SOUTH ASIA.

Not for sale in South Asia

Cover design by Anuradha Roy
Cover photo by Ricardo Gomez Angel, 2017 | Unsplash

Published by State University of New York Press, Albany

© 2021 Harjot Oberoi

All rights reserved

Printed in the United States of America

No part of this book may be used or reproduced in any manner whatsoever without written permission. No part of this book may be stored in a retrieval system or transmitted in any form or by any means including electronic, electrostatic, magnetic tape, mechanical, photocopying, recording, or otherwise without the prior permission in writing of the publisher.

For information, contact State University of New York Press, Albany, NY
www.sunypress.edu

Library of Congress Cataloging-in-Publication Data

Names: Oberoi, Harjot, author.
Title: When does history begin? : religion, narrative, and identity in the Sikh tradition / Harjot Oberoi.
Description: Albany : State University of New York Press, 2022. | Includes bibliographical references and index.
Identifiers: LCCN 2021018263 | ISBN 9781438487359 (hardcover) | ISBN 9781438487366 (ebook) | ISBN 9781438487342 (paperback)
Subjects: LCSH: Sikhism--History. | Sikhism--Historiography. | Sikhs--History.
Classification: LCC BL2017.6 .O248 2022 | DDC 294.609--dc23
LC record available at https://lccn.loc.gov/2021018263

10 9 8 7 6 5 4 3 2 1

for

David Strangway, Patricia Marchak,
and Kenneth Bryant

who exemplify virtues
at the core of the modern university

Contents

	Glossary	xi
	Preface	xv
	Introduction: After Affect – Poetry, Positivism, History	1
1	Brotherhood of the Pure: The Poetics and Politics of Cultural Transgression	30
2	Empire, Orientalism, and Native Informants: The Scholarly Endeavours of Sir Attar Singh Bhadour	79
3	Religious Protest: From Gurdwara Rikabganj to Viceregal Palace	103
4	The Ghadar Movement and Its Anarchist Genealogy	124
5	The Inner Life of Bhagat Singh and the Making of a Maximal Self	159
6	An Epic Without a Text: Imagining the Indian Diaspora	186
	Bibliography	206
	Index	221

It is as if a man is standing in a room facing a wall on which are painted a number of dummy doors. Wanting to get out, he fumblingly tries to open them, vainly trying them all, one after the other, over and over again. But, of course, it is quite useless. And all the time, although he doesn't realize it, there is a real door in the wall behind his back, and all he has to do is to turn round and open it. To help him get out of the room all we have to do is to get him to look in a different direction. But it's hard to do this, since, wanting to get out, he resists our attempts to turn him away from where he thinks the exit must be.

Ludwig Wittgenstein

Clichés, stock phrases, adherence to conventional, standardized codes of expression and conduct have the socially recognized function of protecting us against reality . . .

Hannah Arendt

Glossary

baoli	a large masonry or brick well with steps leading down to the water
bhai	lit. "brother"; honorific reserved for Sikhs of great piety and learning
bhana	divine will
bhut/bhoot	lit. "ghost"; non-human form; evil spirit
bida	farewell
dharma	moral and ethical obligations
din/deen	religion
diwan	congregation
ghazal	a poem made up of several couplets; often the couplets explore disparate themes
gurdwara	Sikh temple
hukam	divine order
iman	honesty; integrity
itihasa	history
izzat	honour
jajmani	system of allowing customary shares of the harvest to members of various castes (barbers, carpenters, agrarian labour, etc.) tied to particular cultivators in hereditary service arrangements
jathera	ancestral shrine

jhuth	lit. "false"; signifies all forms of impurity
kabar	grave
kavya	poetry
khanqah	Sufi hospice where a *pir* teaches disciples
langar	kitchen attached to every gurdwara; the provision of food to the needy regardless of caste or creed by such a kitchen
mahant	chief; head of a religious institution
mahakavya	epic poem
marhi	sacred cremation spot
masani	sacred area in cremation grounds
mastana	excited; possessed; emotionally charged
maulvi	title given to learned Muslim scholar
mazar	shrine or tomb of a saint
mazhab	religion
mleccha	barbarian; ritually impure; often used for people not indigenous to India
mukti-puris	Hindu sacred cities, like Benares, endowed with the power of salvation. In traditional accounts of Hinduism there are seven such cities
munshi	Hindu secretary or clerk; teacher of various subjects, particularly languages and religion
padshah	word of Persian origin used in India to designate an emperor
pandit	erudite person; address used for Brahmins
panth	community of followers (of a guru or doctrines)
pir	a spiritual teacher, often in the Sufi tradition
pirkhana	shrine of a Muslim *pir*

punya	merit
rasa	taste, emotions, aesthetics
rahit-nama	recorded version of the Khalsa code of discipline
sakhi	testimony; evidence; witness; narrative
samadh	tomb associated with Sikh and Hindu holy men
sati	burning of a widow on her husband's funeral pyre
seva	service; signifies devotion and charitable work
shaidi jatha	a band of martyrs
sher	a couplet in Urdu poetry
vimana	flying chariot

Preface

SOME BOOKS ARE born in the head, others are birthed in practice. The present volume emerged in part out of a senior seminar on British colonial rule in India that I taught for over two decades at the University of British Columbia. In the first decade the big question I urged my students to engage with was: What led to India's partition in 1947? In a way, because of some splendid historical scholarship and a rich archive of official sources, biographies, and oral testimonies, this was not a particularly challenging question. We counted British colonial policies of divide and rule, the decennial census starting in 1871, the various socio-religious reform movements that got entangled with questions of power and identity, the disintegration of the traditional ecumene because of evangelical fervour, the sabre rattling of a polemical vernacular press, the rising wave of religious separatism across the subcontinent, the well-documented rivalries between Gandhi and Jinnah, and finally the ineptitude of Lord Mountbatten.

But over the last couple of years I have had a nagging feeling that there was something important, something critical, missing from my big question for the seminar. Given the magnitude of the Partition tragedy – millions of people losing their homes overnight, tens of thousands slaughtered in well-planned campaigns of ethnic cleansing – it seemed incumbent on me as a professional historian to pose an alternative big question. And this new question, my inkling was, ought to ask all those enrolled in the course: Why bother at all to study the past? Yes, we teach history because in many critical ways our narratives and memories of the past shape our present, and our students ought to learn the protocols for verification and truth telling, particularly in this Age of False Narratives. But can history also provide us with something additional – a toolkit, or a sort of Swiss army knife – to deal with our daily lives? As a deliberative practice, history blends the humanities, philosophy, psychology, economics, politics, and biography, and this seemed to take me some way towards believing that analytical history can indeed provide a personal grand strategy to deal with the exigencies and contingencies that are part and parcel of our fragile human order – that the fog which envelops human societies can sometimes dissipate by pressing analytical history into service. Or was this line of thinking on the efficacy of history simply an illusion on my part? Had my nearly fifty years as a student of history made me excessively celebrate its potential virtues?

After a period of reflection and soul searching, my new big question for my senior seminar turned into this: Why could the human actors involved in the Partition not see, say as early as 1940, the looming tragedy? The question seemed necessary and logical, March 1940 being when Jinnah set out for the Muslim League his separatist agenda to fix what he saw as civilisational fault lines. Had Partition been foreseen as the epic tragedy it would soon develop into, August 1947 may have been forestalled from being as catastrophic as it proved. My new meta question did not show all that many leads within the annals of Indian historiography, and I felt compelled to re-educate myself in the intricacies of grand strategy, cognitive psychology, and behavioural economics.

If a grand strategy theorist was looking at the prospects of Partition, he would have instructed his pupils in the early 1940s to start investigating, first, what was going on at the high tables of the Great Powers (the Davos crowd of the time); then follow this up by reviewing what was going on in the subcontinent politically, culturally, and confessionally; and follow that up by examining similar trends at the regional level – say, political events in Bengal and Punjab; then excavate things at the district headquarters; and finally sift through the transcripts of village communities. The signs at the global level would have shown that the Great Powers had already ruthlessly used the tool of Partition when redrawing national boundaries during the Paris Peace Conference that followed the end of the Great War. The Treaty of Versailles in June 1919 was followed by several other significant treaties, plebiscites, and mandates that radically altered the map not only of central Europe but also of the Middle East, Africa, and East Asia. The intent to make the Germans pay exorbitant reparations meant they lost 13 per cent of their territories and that seven million Germans were uprooted – or if one prefers the Partition lexicon, made "displaced people". The Austro-Hungarian empire was permanently dissolved and from its ashes arose Yugoslavia, Czechoslovakia, and Poland. Russian intransigence was punished by allowing the independence of Finland, Estonia, Lithuania, and Latvia from the Slavic empire. The end of the Ottomans meant the new minting of nations like Iraq and Jordan. No one within elite establishments lost sleep over the fate of minorities such as the Kurds and the Yazidis. Cartographers in a hurry changed the colours and ethnic boundaries of the Middle East. In brief, then, much before the subcontinent was partitioned pell-mell by Cyril Radcliffe, the realpolitik exhibited by the Great Powers, particularly Britain, should have seemed a prognostication of the shape of things to come with the ending of the British Empire. Very little of the nightmare unleashed by the Great War was unknown to the Indian elites: India even had two eminent delegates at the Paris Peace Conference, Ganga Singh (Maharaja of Bikaner) and Lord S.P. Sinha, who had witnessed first-hand how the Big Four (Britain, France, the United States, and Italy) laid waste empires that had existed for centuries, turning myriad nations into provinces and provinces into new states. Partition, in brief, was a familiar phenomenon in recent history when it struck the subcontinent; only a couple of decades earlier, people all over Europe and Asia seemed to have gone to sleep at night in one nation and woken up next morning in another.

Having shown what happened because of Versailles in mid-1919, my proposal of deploying history as personal grand strategy would next have us look at what was going on in India at the national level. Jinnah was deeply embittered after the Congress denied him the spoils of power following the 1937 elections. In his role as "sole spokesman" of the Muslim community, he assured the colonial administration of unfettered Muslim support for the war. And then with the Lahore Resolution of 1940 and the failure of the Cripps Mission (1942), the political horizons turned increasingly dark.

Having noted the national mood, one should as a draughtsman of grand theory turn next to examining regions – provinces, districts, and the micro realities of villages. My own interest is in looking at undivided Punjab. In October 1937 Sikander Hayat Khan, the provincial premier, signed a pact with Jinnah that allowed Muslim members of his powerful Unionist party to simultaneously enrol as members of the Muslim League. Although the two parties had rather different agendas, this fusing of identities would unleash powerful new forces in the electoral arena. In the 1937 elections the League won only two seats for the Punjab legislature. After the pact, the League's fortunes soared. In 1946, it secured seventy-three of the eighty-eight seats reserved for Punjabi Muslims. Turning to the district level, the brutal Rawalpindi riots in February 1947 should have alerted everyone to the ethnic cleansing that was to follow in a few months.

Our final unit of analysis would be the villages dotting the Punjabi countryside. These housed tens of thousands of demobilised soldiers who had recently fought in Europe, Africa, and the Middle East. Virtually all of them had extensive training in the use of ballistics, firearms, and guerrilla warfare. Surely even an elementary sense of historical reasoning ought to have raised red flags among the people of the Punjab, warning them of being on the edge of a volcano about to burst.

But academic history – particularly one with a global and comparative sweep that would probe the constitution of power, ideology, and public sentiment – had no real roots in this part of the world. Modern historiography, with its distinct methodologies and technologies of truth telling, was a recent import into the Punjab, a small part of the project of colonial modernity. Under the auspices of this modernity the provincial administration had set up new curricula, schools, colleges, and universities in cities like Lahore and Amritsar. However, even with the inclusion of modern disciplinary history, the subject had not struck deep roots or won anything like a victory. Thinking historically and writing history in the modern way were, in fact, locked within a bitter and never-ending polemical battle with traditional ways of recounting the past.

Analytical history does not come naturally to anyone. We have to leave Plato's warm cave to get rid of flickering shadows and see the light. So, even in the best-case scenario – where modern historiography is widely available within public culture – it may still not prevent people from sleepwalking into a tragedy such as Partition. And the key reason for this resistance to history is the way people have, most generally, been hardwired through the course of human evolution. This was the lesson I grudgingly learned when exploring cognitive psychology and the world of neurologists while seeking to expand my understanding of historical ways of thinking.

The American-Israeli psychologist Daniel Kahneman, in his landmark book *Thinking, Fast and Slow* (2011), provides a road map of styles of thinking and of how core beliefs and judgements are arrived at. As a former recruiter of fighter pilots for the Israeli Air Force and the winner of a Nobel Prize in Economics in 2002, he knows a great deal about decision-making in uncertain times. Kahneman proposes that the long evolutionary history of humans has endowed them with a cognitive apparatus made up of two closely aligned components: one he calls *automatic thinking* and the other *effortful system*. The former allows us to tell a coherent story about ourselves within our respective habitats, and process myriad sensory and empirical data at lightning speed (so that we may live and enjoy life). Without nature's gift of automatic thinking we would turn into lugubrious beings. It is automatic thinking that endows us with "spontaneity", "intuition", "feelings", "cognitive ease", and "trust"; it banishes "doubts" and time-consuming questions relating to "vigilance". More concretely it is because of automatic or intuitive thinking that we speak effortlessly in our native language or immediately recognise friends that we may not have seen for very long.

Aligned to this primary mode of thinking is a second gift of nature, our mental machinery that allows us to be "slow", "doubtful", "deliberative", "logical", "orderly", "computational", and "sensitive to statistics". It is this second mode of thinking that Kahneman identifies in his mental mapping as our effortful system. A good illustration of effortful thinking is when we learn to drive or are asked to calculate, e.g., 373 times 279.

So far, to some degree, our story is simple. But as often happens with good stories, there is a twist. Unlike scholars in the humanities, most of Kahneman's work is conducted in well-furnished laboratories teeming with human volunteers at campuses such as Princeton. Having worked with thousands of volunteers and carried out hundreds of live experiments – often with some of the most gifted students and faculty members in the world – what Kahneman and his colleagues discovered is that, contrary to our optimistic view of human nature, the human mind is neither rational nor logical. As he puts it, humans are prey to cognitive illusions and errors, and the blame for this stems exclusively from the faculty of automatic thinking. The sage in Kahneman warns us against the traps that spring from our mental errors and badly coded cognitive systems.

Although he does not directly say so, Kahneman in a way affirms what the Greeks said about hubris. We are overconfident regarding our cognitive skills and judgements whereas outcomes in everyday lives and constantly updated twitter accounts demonstrate that most of us are regularly prone to error and a readiness to believe what is demonstrably false. We may not acknowledge our predisposition for intellecual infirmity or frame our propensity for the irrational in this fashion because we like telling ourselves comforting stories of humans being in absolute control of everything. Thus, for instance, when we are provided news of the catastrophic events that lie ahead with climate change, our response by and large is to deny their likelihood. We look out of the window and if it is raining or snowing it is easy or comforting to dismiss global warming. Scientists showing detailed charts of average temperatures since the industrial revolution and graphs of carbon emissions cut no ice: most of us are not inclined to this sort of deliberative inquiry. And much like we deny the complexities of weather systems, we tend to deny the complex historical narratives that historians of South Asia frame for us. We take refuge, Kahneman would say, in the automatic thinking which serves us well when reading edifying stories, responding to emotive content, and affirming knee-jerk group psychology.

Based on what I learned from cognitive psychology, scripting modern historiography as personal grand strategy proved a challenge. It was not simply a matter of turning certain mental switches on and others off: for history, to serve as grand strategy, needs to be acquired and crafted slowly by accumulating sources, facts, events, details, and technical methodologies. For my pedagogic purposes this visible epistemological tension between disciplinary history as grand strategy and what cognitive psychology suggests about our mental nuts and bolts was edifying. I wanted my students to encounter these intellectual tensions to decide for themselves the kind of adults they wanted to be: reliant on the beauty and seduction of automatic thinking, or alternatively on the hard labour of effortful systems. It was a difficult lesson to teach in a university setting – this argument that humans are, generally speaking, hardwired to be irrational and harbour illusions, and that modern historical narratives must be forged in order to counter the tendency to believe what is demonstrably untrue. In consequence, my new big question, or rather subject of debate, for the course which, in part, led to this book, included an in-built tension: that wisdom (in this case historical hindsight) and human cognitive capacities, particularly when they are gut-directed, often do not go together. I thought this a good lesson for students to learn, though it had the depressive elements of Greek tragedy built into it. Hegel, despite his innumerable obscurities, was correct: history does not lead to happiness. Throughout the book that follows, these tensions and ideas underlie the Sikh histories I narrate.

One more issue needs to be briefly addressed here. This has to do with how colonial modernity – a project that I shall review in one form or another in all the chapters that constitute this volume – permanently shattered indigenous life-worlds. Instead of approaching this in the abstract, as is often done, it is best to approach the question through the story of Max Weber (1864–1920), for outside the world of literature and novels there is no better guide when dealing with modernity than Weber. While in the first part of his life he was engaged with questions of trade and agriculture, in the latter part he turned to his widely known *Protestant Ethic and the Spirit of Capitalism* (1905).

His simultaneous engagement with religion and capitalism led him to think philosophically about rationality, social change, and life-worlds. One big hypothesis from this feverish intellectual journey was a very concise conclusion: we all now live in a disenchanted world. Having discovered his law of disenchantment, Weber, in his most famous speech, "Science as a Vocation", turned to his favourite theme of how modernity disenchants our world. He says disenchantment heralds four parallel processes:

(i) material and technological progress, including new techniques for organising human society through, say, the modern state and bureaucracy; (ii) the separation of facts and moral values; (iii) the retreat of the sacred from our lives; and (iv) rationality as the universal measuring yardstick. But even as the scholar in Weber charted social upheaval and the birth of new norms, at a personal level he was troubled by the consequences of a disenchanted world: it presented no possibilities for redemption. For most of his life he thought that redemption was to be had by investing in modern disciplines like sociology, economics, and the comparative study of world religions and history. But late in his life he began to wonder if there were no other alternatives to the "darkness" and "wintry" remit of disenchantment.

A hundred years on Weber points to an important aspect of intellectual life in our time. Much like the deep tension between disciplinary history and the neural networks of cognitive psychology, his life is a rich pedagogic resource illustrating how intractable our modern dilemmas remain. We look for wholeness and epistemological certitude, but the academy does not deliver. Perhaps this is all to the good since it prevents us from glib conclusions or a trade in clichés.

The maxim that it takes a village to raise a child applies to the writing of this book as well. My intellectual village is made up of many warm and generous colleagues, friends, and students. For over three decades the Department of Asian Studies at the University of British Columbia in Vancouver has been my home. During this time, I consider myself extremely fortunate to have a team of stellar colleagues, all of whom have shown boundless interest in my research interests. In particular, I would like to acknowledge Ken Bryant, Peter Harnetty, Dan Overmyer, Ross King, Sharalyn Orbaugh, Joshua Mostow, and Chris Rea. Among friends and students, I could always rely on enthusiasm and unwavering support from Doris Jakobsh, Van Dusenbery, Hugh Johnston, Roger Ballard, Vinay Lal, Douglas Ober, Gurharpal Singh, Nikki-Gurinder Kaur Singh, Peder Gedda, Sadhu Binning, Sukhwant Hundal, Harjeet Grewal, and Ajay Bhardwaj.

I would like to record my gratitude to Rudrangshu Mukherjee for including this volume in his acclaimed South Asian history series "Hedgehog and Fox".

It gives me immense pleasure to have this opportunity to thank my editor Rukun Advani for his judgement, feeling for prose, and warm embrace of the life of the mind. It was my good fortune to have him as my editor for my first book; twenty-six years later, not only is he my editor once again but has since become a mentor and friend. Few outside the world of writing and publishing realise the central role of an editor in the professional life of a writer. I am sure I speak for very many in South Asian Studies when I say that to have been edited and published by Rukun is to have experienced a quite special kind of pleasure – which he assures me is mutual.

Five of the six essays included in this book were previously published. The introductory chapter on the traditions of Indian historiography and the inner life of Bhagat Singh was especially written for this volume. All of the previously published essays have been substantially revised and enlarged. The venues of first publication are listed below:

"Brotherhood of the Pure: The Poetics and Politics of Cultural Transgression", *Modern Asian Studies*, vol. 26, 1992, pp. 157–97.

"Empire, Orientalism, and Native Informants: The Scholarly Endeavours of Sir Attar Singh Bhadour", *Journal of Punjab Studies*, vol. 17, 2010, pp. 95–114.

"From Gurdwara Rikabganj to Viceregal Palace: A Study of Religious Protest", *The Panjab Past and Present*, vol. 14, 1980, pp. 182–98.

"The Ghadar Movement and Its Anarchist Genealogy", *Economic and Political Weekly*, vol. 40, 2009, pp. 40-6.

"Imagining Indian Diaspora in Canada: An Epic Without a Text", in Bhikhu Parekh, Gurharpal Singh, and Steve Vertovec, eds, *Culture and Economy in the Indian Diaspora,* Routledge, 2003, pp. 181–93.

Introduction

After Affect: Poetry, Positivism, History

> The only thought which Philosophy brings with it to contemplation of History, is the simple conception of Reason; that Reason is the sovereign of the world; that the history of the world, therefore presents us with a rational process.
>
> **G.W. Hegel,** *The Philosophy of History*

> In the first place, beyond the rational there exists a more important and valid category – that of the meaningful which is the highest mark of being . . .
>
> **Claude Lévi-Strauss,** *Tristes Tropiques*

> What is truth? A mobile army of metaphors, metonyms, and anthropomorphisms; in short, a sum of human relations which have been enhanced, transposed and embellished poetically and rhetorically, and which after long use seem firm, canonical, and obligatory to a people.
>
> **Nietzsche, "On Truth and Lies in an Extra-Moral Sense"**

THE ESSAYS IN this volume are part of a larger argument that has long been in progress in the world of ideas, about the nature of truth and persuasion in historiography. But before I turn to these larger issues – which have centrally to do with facts and the nature of narratives that claim to be factual – let me begin with two stories. The first concerns the oeuvre of the Japanese filmmaker Akira Kurosawa (1910–1998). Within twentieth-century cinema, Kurosawa is as canonical as Sergei Eisenstein, George Lucas, Steven Spielberg, Oliver Stone,

Francis Ford Copolla, and Satyajit Ray. Over a fifty-year career of thirty films his key preoccupations can be summed up under five heads:

- exploring the honour codes of the Samurai warrior class
- the dialectic between the individual and the collective
- the elusiveness of truth
- human suffering, with almost no possibility of redemption
- despite the challenges of nihilism to constantly strive to expand the aesthetic dimension of cinematography

His 1957 film *Throne of Blood* was an adaptation of Shakespeare's *Macbeth*; two other adaptations followed, *The Bad Sleep Well* (of *Hamlet*) in 1960, and *Ran* (of *King Lear*) in 1985. In Japanese the word "ran" means chaos or turmoil. These three classics enhanced Kurosawa's stature, in no small part because, despite his core belief in the elusive nature of truth, he heroically sought throughout to capture "truthfulness" – or, to put it more truthfully, what his cinematic practice showed as the wide arc of truthfulness. Kurosawa is perhaps more internationally emblematic in this respect – in showing truth as a spectrum or arc – than anyone of comparable artistic repute in the modern world. A good illustration of this specific engagement with truth as something far from simple is Kurosawa's famous cinematographic innovation of simultaneously using three cameras for each take in his films. In his memoirs he reminisces:

> Working with three cameras simultaneously is not so easy as it may sound. It is extremely difficult to determine how to move them. For example, if a scene has three actors in it, all three are talking and moving about freely and naturally. In order to show how A, B and C cameras move to cover this action, even complete picture continuity is insufficient . . . The three camera positions are completely different for the beginning and the end of the shot, and they go through several transformations

in between. As a general system, I put the A camera in the most orthodox positions, use the B camera for quick decisive shots and the C camera as a kind of guerilla shot.[1]

Not only did Kurosawa use three cameras, each camera had lenses of different sizes and was positioned at a different angle from the others. The actors being filmed did not know which of the three cameras, at any given time, was working. It seems to me that even the very setting up of this elaborate cinematic framing scenario and related apparatus is to suggest that to arrive at what will be perceived as truthful is an entire enterprise; it is to say that truth is not something just existing out there in some natural state or obvious way; and to say that even with the best technology deployed, getting to the fact of the matter, or to the facts of a situation, is a complex exercise rather than some straightforward business that can be done and dusted.

If the pursuit of truth is an arduous task, that pursuit is best manifest in Kurosawa's most famous film, *Rashomon*.[2] While its plot is simple, overall the story line has interpretive challenges that are hard to disentangle. Roughly, this is the story: sometime in the twelfth century a Samurai and his wife are travelling through a forest outside the imperial city of Kyoto. A notorious bandit attacks the couple and in the resulting scuffle the Samurai is murdered. The dead man's body is discovered by a woodcutter who leads the local authorities to the scene of the crime. The police investigate the crime and the captured bandit is taken to be tried to a courthouse. The trial judge hears testimonies from four eyewitnesses at the crime scene: the bandit, the wife of the deceased, the woodcutter, and – since the Samurai is dead – a Shinto priest who acts as a medium to recover the warrior's voice.

[1] Kurosawa, *Something Like an Autobiography*, p. 194.
[2] Awarded the prize for Best Film at the Venice International Cinema Festival in 1950.

All four testimonies diverge greatly on what precisely happened. The bandit claims the Samurai died in a duel that had been spurred on by the deceased's wife. The wife claims she was deeply upset by slights against her by her husband, and, since she had fainted during a scuffle with him, it was strange for her dagger to be found lodged in his body. The Samurai, through the medium, conveys that he had felt dishonoured by his wife's romantic overtures to the bandit and so had committed ritual suicide. The woodcutter claims he discovered the dead body inadvertently and was only a bystander, but later confesses (to a set of acquaintances) that he was very much present at the scene of the crime and that all three protagonists were lying. The sequence of events, the woodcutter says, was completely different from what each of them had narrated to the judge.

What Kurosawa seems to be saying is that though only a single bloody event took place, the four subjective and alternative testimonies make it difficult to assert any single truth about a singular event. So, is the truth always relative and personal? Does each person always, as the *Rashomon* tale proposes, experience it differently? Is truth tied to our psychological and emotional states and to the burgeoning category of individual memory? How reliable are our memories? And what happens if there are more than four witnesses – say twenty? Do we then know truth as twenty different versions of an event? As twenty versions of recorded memories?

These are large, philosophical, and probing questions given memorable shape by Kurosawa. They concern judges, legal experts, psychologists interested in cognition – and, of course, the guild of historians. It is hard to write history without testimonies from the past. But if memories are malleable and governed by forgetfulness, self-interest, and our varied emotional states, how does one write history that can confidently be asserted as "objective"? The opening line in *Rashomon* is the disturbed voice of the woodcutter: "I don't understand, I just don't understand." The

INTRODUCTION 5

truth is in fact that understanding is a very tough nut to crack, even when one is equipped with three cameras and shoots each scene with different lenses and guerrilla placements.

For our second story, let us move from the forests of medieval Japan to the rich agrarian lands of early-modern Punjab. In the year 1843, just as the monsoon season started, Bhai Santokh Singh – a poet, scholar, exegete, and historian – was busy editing his monumental project entitled *Sri Gur Pratap Suraj Granth* (The Sun of Guru's Glory). This gigantic work is now more popularly known as *Suraj Prakash*. Written in the form of a mahakavya (epic poem), *Suraj Prakash* aims to provide a complete and authentic history of early Sikhism, focusing on the lives of the Sikh gurus and the great warrior-king Banda Bahadur. For close to two decades, starting in 1825, Santokh Singh was attached to the court of Raja Udey Singh, ruler of the princely state of Kaithal, a town close to the imperial city of Delhi. Certainly, the final product must have made the ruler a happy patron; even more certainly, without his extraordinary royal patronage Santokh Singh would not have had the luxury or even the means to write his magnum opus.[3]

Our enigmatic poet, Santokh Singh, has left us with an exhaustive history comprising 51,829 couplets within fourteen grand volumes. In total, he wrote over 250,000 lines of verse in various metres. When in the late 1920s a prominent publisher of Amritsar sought to turn the extant manuscripts into printed books, the printed volumes released between 1927 and 1935 weighed in as fourteen large-format books; if one is fortunate enough to locate the *Suraj Prakash* in a research library, an entire shelf is normally beheld as its lodgings. While Gibbon's

[3] See Macauliffe, *The Sikh Religion*, pp. 76–7. For some recent interventions on Bhai Santokh Singh, see Sagar, *Historical Analysis of Nanak Prakash*; Pashaura Singh, *Life and Work of Guru Arjan*, pp. 9–14; Jvala Singh, "Sourced Sikh History"; and Oberoi, *The Construction of Religious Boundaries*, pp. 132–4.

six-volume *Decline and Fall of the Roman Empire* is far broader in its geographical and chronological scope, for sheer size Santokh Singh's fourteen easily surpass Gibbon's.

Though in many ways Santokh Singh outshines a lot of the canonical historians, in one key dimension he is quite different from global historians, Herodotus down. Unlike the classical Graeco–Roman historians, or even those practising the historian's craft in, say, the Islamicate world or East Asia – most of whom wrote their chronicles in prose – Santokh Singh chose to write his monumental history as poetry. Why? Why did Santokh Singh write history as poetry, or as what in South Asia is called kavya? Why did this extraordinary scholar, fluent in Persian, Arabic, Sanskrit, Braj, and Punjabi, eschew the global trend of writing history in prose?[4]

As a preliminary, we can suggest that Santokh Singh in opting for poetry over prose was simply following the strong currents of cultural tradition in the subcontinent. Instead of choosing to open new conversations, say, with Persian prose chroniclers, Santokh Singh opted to follow classical Indic historians such as the Kashmiri historian Kalhana, whose *Rajatarangini*, a detailed history of the Kashmir region beginning in mythical times to the twelfth century, was finished in 1149. Given Kalhana's location close to the Silk Trade Routes of Central Asia and his considerable erudition, it is fair to assume that Kalhana was familiar with competing templates of global historiography: Graeco–Roman, Islamicate, and Sinic. But he seems to have ignored the dominant mode – prose – used by his contemporaries and predecessors in their narrations of the past, preferring to narrate his regional history as poetry. We get first-hand intimation of Kalhana's thoughts on how the past ought to be represented in the opening chapter of his pioneering history:

---

[4] For an outstanding survey of global trends in historiography and Indian contributions, see Thapar, *The Past Before Us*, esp. pp. 3–48.

Worthy of praise is that power of true poets, whatever it may be, which surpasses even the stream of nectar, in as much as by it their own bodies of glory as well as those of others obtain immortality. Who else but poets resembling Prajapatis [in creative power] and able to bring forth lovely productions, can place the past times before the eyes of men? If the poet did not see in his mind's eye the existence which he is to reveal to all men, what other indication would there be of his possessing divine intuition? . . . The noble-minded poet is alone worthy of praise whose word, like that of a judge, keeps free from love or hatred in relating the facts of the past.[5]

Clearly, for Kalhana "the facts of the past" ought to be narrated by a poet rather than a historian: only the poet has the "divine intuition" which allows him to see "in his mind's eye" existence in its totality.

Kalhana's view of the poet as divinely inspired arbiter of the past was widely shared across the subcontinent. What sort of cultural dynamics made this poet-historian so confident of what he acclaims as the "power of poets"? He seems not to be paralysed in any obvious way by what Harold Bloom, following Freud, calls "the anxiety of influence". In this view of historian as poet, the exceptional faculty of vision peculiar to the poet is key; it makes the poet-historian an analogue of the judge rendering justice to appellants. Like judges, poet-historians are capable of sifting through vast troves of materials and eyewitness accounts to provide fair judgment to an audience of what really transpired. For what transpired was never only at the superficial surface level of human experience – which secular history ordinarily reports – since it also transpired deep inside the human heart.

Following Sheldon Pollock, I would say Kalhana's supreme confidence and lack of methodological anxiety can be traced back to India's long classical tradition. Pollock argues that once Valmiki

---

[5] Stein, *Kalhana's Rajatarangini*, vol. 1, p. 2.

had finished composing the Ramayana, which happened at some point in the middle of the third century of the Common Era, the subcontinent, or at any rate the scholarly literati within it, came to possess a powerful new paradigm in the form of kavya, poetry that would be deployed for over a millennium in region after region to narrate the events, heroic deeds, betrayals, and archetypes of the past. Pollock does not use the word "paradigm" for this newly invented kavya, i.e. poetical history; he describes it as "a set of interpretive protocols".[6] And these protocols, he tells us, are made up of three interlocking rules: "Do not read *kavya* the way you read science, ancient lore, or the Veda; do not be concerned about a breach between what is said and what is really meant, about correspondence with an actual world, about information or injunction. And do not expect *kavya* to be like ordinary language; its purposes are different."[7] This classical protocol was often supplemented by categories of "indirection" and "imagination".[8] So, not exactly the science of history, as we understand the field today, but a vast cultural field made up of new coinages and imaginative strategies that would illuminate a body of known facts.

Ancient poet-historians did not therefore make a fetish of facts, as we moderns do, for the canon gave them plenty of leeway to alter facts. Pollock cites the example of Anandvardhana, a great theoretician of Sanskrit aesthetics, who explicitly instructed his followers, sometime in the late tenth century CE, to the effect that historical facts ought to be creatively altered to enhance the emotional outreach (rasa) of a text. His exact rules for how a poet-historian ought to go about these emendations are listed below:

> Another means by which a work as a whole may become suggestive of *rasa* is the abandoning of a state of affairs imposed

---

[6] Pollock, "Sanskrit Literary Culture from the Inside Out", p. 51.
[7] Ibid.
[8] Ibid., p. 56.

by historical reality, if it fails in any way to harmonise with the *rasa;* and the introduction, by invention if need be, of narrative appropriate to that *rasa*. No purpose is served by a poet's providing merely the historical facts. That is a task accomplished by historiography itself.[9]

So, while Anandvardhana is open to the idea that there are certain distinctions to be made between historiography proper (itihasa) and poetic history (kavya), particularly in the way facts ought to be treated, we know from actual cultural practices within the subcontinent that the preferred mode for representing the past for close to two millenniums was kavya. When Hegel speaks of the totality of history, this totality in South Asia was not to be attained via positivist historiography but by the aesthetic arrangement of already known facts within poetry. The two most major North Indian epics, the Ramayana and Mahabharata, are the Indian exemplars of such a totality. In both, such things as clan genealogies, individual biographies and aspirations, and histories of the imperium are subsumed under the grand banner of kavya. In other words, these two metatexts absorb historiography (itihasa) as well. As Pollock might put it, in South Asia – at least from within the tradition – facts, invented or known, serve poetry, and rarely does poetry serve facts.[10]

If we now turn back to Kalhana, we cannot be surprised by his choice of the kavya genre for by the first millennium of the Common Era Indic culture had developed sophisticated conventions on the scope and methodology of historical narrative. Kalhana in distant Kashmir apart, there are dozens of examples from various regions and historical epochs reiterating the distinctive

---

[9] Ingalls, *et al.*, *The Dhavanloka*, p. 440, cited in Pollock, *Literary Cultures in History*, p. 58.

[10] Pollock's exact words on this issue ought to be noted as well: "It remains the case, however, that historical fact constituted something of a problem for Sanskrit literary theory." Pollock, *Literary Cultures in History*, p. 57.

nature of Indic historical methodology. One prominent instance of poetry as history, or poetry as knowledge, is the text titled *Kanhadade-Prabandha*, written in a hybrid form of vernacular Rajasthani and Gujarati. This dates to 1455 and its author, an accomplished poet-historian named Padmanabha, was a Brahman by caste. Although much shorter than Kalhana's classic, this heroic poem of 1028 verses narrates the story of a Rajput clan of Chauhan rulers based in Jalor and Satal who offered stiff and glorious resistance to the expansive armies of the Delhi-based ruler Allaudin Khilji (1266–1316). Though the main objective of the Khilji campaign was the conquest of Gujarat, the Delhi ruler decided to punish the Rajput kings, who lay on his way, for not providing the imperial armies hospitality and smooth passage through Rajasthan, en route Gujarat, a major hub of international trade. The impasse between the imperial authorities and the Rajasthani ruler Kanhadade is narrated in considerable detail by this Brahman poet-historian, and an appreciation of his distinctive historiographical method requires quoting him at some length:

> On receiving the Sultan's orders, the Pradhans proceeded to Kanhadade, carrying with them a dress of honour sent by the Emperor. They presented the same to the Lord of Sambhar (Kanhadade) in his assembly, and spoke thus: "Know it well, your lordship, that the army of the Turks is on way to Soratha. Other routes have difficult passes. The Padshah, therefore, requests you to let the army pass this way." The Rair spoke out plainly to the envoys before the assembly, his words pregnant with truth and wisdom: "This is contrary to our *dharma*! The Kings do not give passage when by doing so villages are devastated, people are enslaved, ears of women torn (for ornaments), and cows and Brahmans are tortured. The Pradhans returned, their mission having failed. They were feeling much ashamed for it. Back home, they informed the Sultan that Kanhadade

had refused to acknowledge his authority. The Sultan realized that it would mean conflict, resulting in [the] destruction of many lives. He heaved a sigh, but then sent for Ulugh Khan, the renowned warrior, Mahmud Shah's main strength and his follower, a brave, persevering, and energetic noble. Farman was given to him to proceed with an army to Gujarat. The Sultan himself gave him bida [farewell] to undertake the campaign. Madhava Mutha, the influential Pradhan of Gujarat, was also sent with him. Senior Maliks and Amirs, Khojas and Khans were summoned and detailed to join the expedition.

Thus, we see that on one side was Allaudin – a mighty Padshah no doubt, and on the other side was Kanhadade Chauhana. Such was the confrontation, matching and terrible at the same time. I now relate how this led to the siege of Jalor, how wonderful defiance was offered to the Turks, and how Gujarat, Soratha and Somnatha experienced terrible times, how Raval Kanhadade, a warrior like the protecting portals, took a firm stand and won victory over Ulugh Khan's army.[11]

Having provided his readers with the context and historical background to the war, Padmanabha proceeds to provide detailed sketches of various battles and the concluding campaign, led by Allaudin Khilji in person, which culminated in the defeat of the key protagonist. A few vignettes from the war scenes are worth quoting as well – as illustrations of embellished historical method. Here is the poet-historian's description of the bravery of a great Rajput warrior, Batada:

> He stalked in front of the Sultan's army, with sword unsheathed and glittering. He saw the Turks ready and prepared to fight. But what of that! He had decided to fulfil his duty, having bid adieu to life. Angrily, he planted his foot in the battle,

---

[11] Bhatnagar, *Kanhadade Prabandha* (henceforth *KP*), pp. 3–4. The meaning of the phrase "protecting portals" is not wholly clear but can be inferred as denoting sturdiness and reliability.

determined to give way to the enemy only after his death. For about half to one hour, Batada plied his sword skilfully, but then young Turkish soldiers wearing armour angrily fell upon him. The Khan saw him falling after he had already killed a large number of *Mlechhas*. He praised Batada's bravery. In the heaven there were cries of "Jai", "Jai", as Batada went there seated in a vimana [mythological flying chariot].[12]

This description of a heroic warrior laying down his life is followed by a more encompassing description of Rajput deeds:

That a terrible and bloody contest was at hand, was clear to all. Presently, the vast host would set out, raising clouds of dust, darkening the sky, and making the figures indistinguishable. The sun would no longer be visible. Carrying thirty-six kinds of weapons, the Rajput warriors would move out, the bards reciting their deeds of fame. The brave warriors would fall upon the enemy, elephants dashing against elephants, horses against horses and foot soldiers locked up [*sic*] with foot soldiers. The hard and full-blooded blows of the swords, the thud of the strokes on the bucklers and shields, the sharp and swift passes of the shining blades, the loud twang of the bow strings, the sparks from the spear heads crashing and clanking, the hail of arrows – such would shortly be the scene, right as per martial traditions of the brave Rajput warriors.[13]

These passages from *Kanhadade* show history turning into an inexhaustible crucible perpetually fuelled by heroic deeds. The darkened sky, swirling clouds, steel weapons, war elephants and horses, blinding dust, bows and arrows, and bloodied warriors are all part of a dark symbolism preparing an intended audience for a clash of destinies and the unmasking of human fate. For

[12] Ibid., p. 6.
[13] Ibid., p. 22.

our purposes, noteworthy here is the emotive and passionate framing of the past. Similarly poetic text modes representing the past are to be found widely distributed over peninsular India.[14]

Santokh Singh, we can then argue, was well situated in a hoary historiographic tradition that, while deeply concerned with the standard items that appear within every historical repertoire – such as a temporal frame, the characterisation of historical agents, an emplotment of events, the causations and hidden meanings of the past – still chose to articulate the passage of time in large units of poetic utterance. Some of these poet-historians, in fact, put a huge effort into composing their narratives in the appropriate ragas and metres, so that when the text was recited it evoked the requisite moods of awe, joy, surprise, tragedy, and lamentation in their audience. The modern practice of silent reading would obviously have been a notion alien to the composers of such texts: what they were aiming for was a recitation that tilted hearts and minds towards specific affective structures and deep emotional states. It is instructive here to revisit the manual-like instructions that the author of *KP* provides on how his text ought to be handled, and what sorts of benefits would accrue to those who partook of his text:

> Those who listen to this account with attention, all their sins will be washed off. The reward which one gets by giving to charities, by taking a dip in the Ganges, the merit which one earns by undergoing austerities, or by beholding the Narbada river, by being truthful, by listening to the recitation of the Puranas, the reward which the ascetics receive, or the reward one earns by securing release of the captives, or by performing the Yagnas and pilgrimage to Prayaga, or the merit which one earns by making pilgrimage to Gangotri or Kedarnath, or the reward which one receives by a deep study of different branches

[14] For a highly sophisticated account of historiography in South India, see Rao, *et al.*, *Textures of Time*.

of knowledge, or the merit which one earns by taking a dip in the Godavari river, or by beholding Narayana himself, or by distributing charities at Kurukshetra, or the merit earned by courageous women who become *Sati*, or the reward which one gets by taking a dip in the Gomati river, or by residing for six months in Dvarika, or by a pilgrimage to Somnatha, or by residing in seven *Mukti-Puris*, verily the abodes of salvation, or by reciting the name of Lord Rama in the early hours of the morning, whosoever will recite *Kanhade-Charita*, or listen to its recital attentively, will earn the same merit (*punya*) which one will by the ways mentioned above . . . May the hopes and desires of all who recite it or listen to its recital be fulfilled.[15]

Pilgrimages, encountering gods, heading to sacred sites on the banks of rivers, and immersion in a historical sensorium are in the *Kanhadade* very similar activities. Why should an author propose ritualistic equivalences between sacred sites and his remembrance of the past in his kavya? His clues point quite transparently to the creation of a bedrock for the extension of Brahmanic hegemony: his narrative practices, he says, have to do with salvation and salvific desire, with the need for a populace to earn merit (punya). Much as pilgrimage can lead to punya and sometimes salvation, the act of hearing a poetic-historical narrative that adheres to the proper and prescribed Indic conventions can lead to merit and deliverance.[16] How could this be? What makes Padmanabha so confident when advancing such large metaphysical claims? My hypothesis is that this is because

---

[15] *KP*, p. 104.

[16] Many parallels can be cited from the Western literary-historical canon of this South Asian argument for the therapeutic and soteriological dimensions of poetic narrative, recommendations of the Bible as "the Good Book" being perhaps the most common. Chaucer's *Canterbury Tales* – specifically the Pardoner's Tale, the Monk's Tale, and the Parson's Tale – also come to mind as rough equivalents.

INTRODUCTION   15

Padmanabha firmly holds the keys to the doors of Indic theory of aesthetics or rasa (taste/emotional flavours). I cannot detail the rasa theory in all its intricacies and complexity here – it is a bit like string theory in quantum physics, defying easy or formulaic descriptions – but it is crucial for our purposes to note certain key features of the theory.

Pollock says Indian aesthetic theory took over a millennium and a half to fully evolve and represents one of the key contributions of Indian civilisation to global culture and discourses of discernment and taste.[17] All art forms – drama, painting, dance, poetry – are blended through the dexterous use of rasa. Indian intellectuals were initially unsure of how exactly rasa works, but eventually a consensus developed: rasa was inherent in every creative medium, and thus a reader or listener intensely engaged in or enraptured with an artefact was much like a fish able to draw breath from a surrounding element. The only difference was that what the reader or listener was drawing into his body was affect – a variety of emotions that then inhered in her consciousness.

The great minds of the classical era identified eight rasas: fear (Bhyanaka), laughter (Hasya), anger (Raudra), disgust (Bibhatsa), erotic love (Shingar), heroism (Veera), and compassion (Karuna).[18] In its denotative aspect, rasa was also argued as deeply transformative and capable of generating thirty-three different emotions.[19] Pollock has a sutra-like gloss on rasa, terming

---

[17] What follows on rasa theory here is based on Pollock, *A Rasa Reader*, pp. 1–46. I am deeply indebted to Sheldon Pollock – to his text and personal conversations – for my understanding of rasa theory. The extraordinary richness of his scholarly insights can benefit South Asian history even more than it has already.

[18] Some lists go on to include nine rasas, the ninth being peace/tranquillity (Shanta) rasa.

[19] For a list of these thirty-three emotions, see Pollock, *A Rasa Reader*, pp. 327–8. Also see Higgins, "An Alchemy of Emotions", pp. 43–54.

it an "emotional-aesthetic force".[20] It seems possible to unpack several layers in this useful gloss for a word conventionally translated as juice, taste, emotions, and aesthetics, but rarely as force.

What is striking about this system of emotions is that it encompasses not merely physiology or the senses. The physical element of emotions or passions is of course acknowledged, but the crowning achievement of this paradigm is that it moves beyond the sensorium and includes within its ambit matters of classification, evaluation, and judgement.[21] Thus, unlike the Cartesian mind–body split, where the mind orients our desires and feelings, rasa theorists persuasively argue that emotions and feelings drive the arc of our judgements. Cognition, then, is not merely a function of the brain, something that we have been told since the Enlightenment, but is deeply tied to feelings and emotions. And part of the DNA of human judgements stems from the texts under discussion: poetic epics and narratives produced by the creative classes in South Asia.

The second part of Pollock's gloss that we need to deconstruct is the term "aesthetics". What is being alluded to here is not just the dictionary usage concerning standards of beauty, but something much larger that would include such items as questioning, judging, refinement, surveillance, analysis, and pedagogic arrangements for learning and its transmission. It was through the touchstone of aesthetics that a culture decided what to include and exclude from its canon.

Finally, let us turn to the "force" aspect of Pollock's trinity. Here I see the rasa ensemble as a complex signalling device with the power to alter the homeostatic state. In other words, the uses and regulations of rasa generate an agenda, or action programme,

---

[20] Pollock, *A Rasa Reader*, p. 28.
[21] Here I am supplementing my reading of Pollock with Chatterjee, *et al.*, "Feeling Modern", pp. 539–57.

among those who imbibe the taste, the rasa, in which the artefact has been made available. And this agenda, these actions, are then recorded as history, a history of a cast of actors or a larger history of a community or region.

Thus, rasa cannot be deemed a passive variable; we become oblivious to both its generative and creative potency if we think of it in purely formal terms – as for instance we might think of ornamental adjectives, or the choice of a specific genre deployed for a particular kind of expression. Rasa is, by contrast with purely formal moulds or embellishments, capable of doing unanticipated things to humans, and in time great intellectuals, artists, and performers within the subcontinent acquired the skills and learning necessary for an expert handling of its capaciousness. Indian epics like the Ramayana and Mahabharata demonstrate the workings of rasa, and the fact that those who read or heard these epics went on to develop certain frames of behaviour and action ought not to surprise us.

Some concrete examples help in thinking this through. It is now commonplace to suggest that Indian ideas of gender, marriage, domesticity, kingship, statecraft, and politics are deeply influenced by these epics. If we think closely about why this is so, it becomes obvious that the influence is not merely because of the basic content of the stories narrated in them but very considerably because of an intricate deployment – which is inseparable from their bodies and their substance – of the eight listed rasas. Pollock's assertion, that rasa is an "emotional-aesthetic force" for action, cannot be disputed: one has only to recall the emotional intensity with which, over the centuries, geographically disparate South Asian audiences have been moved and inspired by the two Indian epics.

The life of Mahatma Gandhi, a lifelong reader of both epics, illustrates the emotive and inspirational action plan embedded in rasa aesthetics. When Gandhi proclaims Ram Rajya as the end goal of his politics, he is echoing his reading of the Ramayana;

he makes it clear he is keen to see the spirit of the epic translated into everyday politics in South Asia.

In brief, my argument is that starting from the time of Valmiki, to Kalhana and closer to Santokh Singh in our time, Indic culture has opted to render its history via poetry or more loosely via the use of poetic-literary tropes and strategies. Kalhana as poet-historian is not alone in asserting that the truth of the past can only be revealed in poetry. The assertion seems to have withstood the test of time: the obtuseness of James Mill and his ilk who saw the subcontinent as free of history is clear from the fact that the past never dies in South Asia, and has not in times past. Or we could rephrase this to suggest that the past never rests in South Asia. Rich offerings of it with the flavourings of rasa have allowed us to taste it in our everyday lives.[22] Even in the much-vaunted Persian histories of India, when Muhammad Qasim Farishta, as a court historian of the kingdom of Bijapur, wrote a history of Hindustan in the early-seventeenth century, he gave it the title *Naurasnama* (A Book of New Emotions/ Flavours). Much like caste, no one escapes rasa in South Asia.[23]

However, rendering the past in poetical frames in the form of a multi-media performance in front of a large body of people,

---

[22] I am aware that from time to time historians did choose to write about the past in prose, particularly for such things as lists of kings, clan histories, and land grants. This started with rock inscriptions, and once metals were introduced we begin to get prose histories on copper plates. For two recent works that closely examine prose histories, see Guha, "Speaking Historically", pp. 1084–1103, and Deshpande, *Creative Pasts*. And outside the Maharashtrian context we have the long history of Persian chronicles. For a survey of Persian histories, see Auer, "Persian Historiography in India", pp. 94–139. But as Sumit Guha – a votary of pre-colonial traditions of history in India – himself warns us, the existence of prose sources ought not to be conflated with historiography. As for Persian chronicles, we know next to nothing about the circulation of these texts and their impact on public consciousness.

[23] For a detailed analysis of Farishta, see Asif, *The Loss of Hindustan*, pp. 21–7.

almost as if the entire exercise of historiography were one vast emotional carnival of rasa theory, raises vexing issues for modern historians. Nor should we make the mistake of thinking that rasa theory provides a unified theory of everything to do with South Asian history and cultural production. Segregations of the imaginative and fanciful directions and capacity of poetry from mundane historical facts when creating the historical record have also long coexisted, specially for the past couple of centuries, with rasa-laden history. How can one get away with claims of historical fidelity when merging empirical facts and fanciful reconstructions – quite obviously, this too has been a perennial question in historical assumptions distinguishable from those of the rasa history tradition. From the time of Plato, we have been told that poetry and knowledge do not mix well at all – everyone knows Plato thought it best to ban poets from his proposed ideal Republic. It is never hard to detect the ire of modern historians with poetry as a form of knowledge. Max Macauliffe, the famous British historian of the Sikhs, has this to say about Santokh Singh's endeavours: "He was unquestionably a poet . . . the consequence was that he invented several stories . . . some of his inventions are due to his exaggerated ideas of prowess and force in bad as well as in a good cause – a reflex of the spirit of the marauding age in which he lived. His statements accordingly cannot be accepted as even an approach to history."[24] This juxtaposition of fact and imagination also, as is generally known, gave rise to the cliché, particularly within Orientalist circles, that Indians lacked a sense of history or historical consciousness.

Given this context of undervaluing the past, or at least rendering it in a different register from other civilisational systems of knowledge, the oft-quoted statement of the eleventh-century Muslim ethnographer Al-Biruni is hardly surprising: "Unfortunately, the Hindus do not pay much attention to the historical

---

[24] Macauliffe, *The Sikh Religion*, p. 77.

order of things, they are very careless in relating the chronological succession of kings, and when they are pressed for information and are at a loss, not knowing what to say, they invariably take to tale-telling."[25] In another passage he notes:

> Besides, the scientific books of the Hindus are composed in various favourite metres, by which they intend, considering that the books soon become corrupted by additions and omissions, to preserve them exactly as they are, in order to facilitate their being learned by heart, because they consider as canonical only that which is known by heart, not that which exists in writing. Now it is well known that in all metrical compositions there is much misty and constrained phraseology merely intended to fill up the metre and serving as a kind of patchwork, and this necessitates a certain amount of verbosity. This is also one of the reasons why a word has sometimes one meaning and sometimes another. From all this it will appear that the metrical form of literary composition is one of the causes which makes the study of Sanskrit literature so particularly difficult.[26]

What Al-Biruni wrote about Sanskrit literature applies to classical Indian historiography. Literary texts overlapped with historical narratives, and often there was no difference between the two. Clearly, Indian historiography was not for the faint of heart and was rather far removed from the canons of world historiography.

Fortunately, where Al-Biruni gave up, others persisted. For the stakes in answering the question why South Asians rarely wrote prose histories are very high. Some of the most gifted historians of recent times have devoted extraordinary professional energies to answer this vexing question of form: Why narrate the past in

---

[25] Sachau, *Alberuni's India*, vol. 2, pp. 14–15.
[26] Ibid., vol. 1, pp. 21–2.

poetical metres? The best hypothesis proposed so far is that the poetical form of Indian historiography ought not to distract us. Poetry was simply a genre, the actual intent was history.[27] Yet despite considerable and cogent assertions of this view, it has proven hard for contemporary historiographers to square the circle. The answer to the question why men like Kalhana, Padmanabha, Santokh Singh, and dozens of others took to writing history in verse rather than prose may in the end be a very simple one. But to arrive at this simple answer, we need to take an etic detour and call upon the assistance of Nietzsche.

Among the moderns it was Nietzsche who first identified passion as a major engine of history. This finding of his was strikingly different from that of the other great masters of knowledge. If we were to sketch an inventory of alternatives to Nietzsche on the motors of history or on what leads to human dynamism (some call it progress), the list would read something like this: for Aristotle the key was mimesis; the Roman historian Tacitus zeroed in on imperium; the polymath Arab scholar Ibn Khaldun preferred the dialectic between the steppe and the city; the Scottish founder of modern economics Adam Smith chose the invisible hand of free markets; the Berlin professor Hegel fetishised reason; for the utilitarian James Mill it all came down to legislation; the legal luminary Macaulay preferred education; the Rhinelander Marx gutted all previous assumptions by choosing class, only to be outwitted by Freud who settled on the unconscious; and finally Weber, with the advantage of historical hindsight, opted for the Protestant ethic and its ascetic disposition. Nietzsche ignored them by turning back to the ancient Greeks and excavating for us unrestrained passion as the key emotion in the making of human history. He came to this conclusion largely by mining two epics, *The Iliad* and *The Odyssey*, as well as the Greek tragic playwrights, particularly the tragedies of Sophocles and Euripides. Although

---

[27] For one such suggestion, see Rao, *et al.*, *Textures of Time*.

the Nietzschean celebration of raw emotions and passion can be detected in several of his key texts, for our purposes an essay he published in 1874, entitled "On the Uses and Disadvantages of History for Life", is most illustrative.[28] While acknowledging at its beginning that the study of the past has some advantages – particularly if done under the rubric of monumental, antiquarian, and critical strains of historiography – towards its concluding parts he expresses deep dissatisfaction with the discipline of history. For him the writing of history simply denudes humans of any instinct or capacity to start grand projects. The human agent reading historical narratives, instead of turning into a lively and joyous actor undertaking new adventures, suddenly turns away from the arc of human agency. "We want to serve history only to the extent that history serves life," writes Nietzsche, "for it is possible to value the study of history to such a degree that life becomes stunted and degenerate."[29] In other words – and as we also learn from *Hamlet* – it is often important to forget in order to act. Nietzsche's essay has to be read as a therapeutic effort to bring the excitement of the human will, desires, raw emotions, and passions back into focus when scripting the human drama. The originality of its argument can be seen in this:

> With an excess of history man again ceases to exist, and without that envelope of the unhistorical he would never have begun or dared to begin. What deed would man be capable of if he had not first entered into that vaporous region of the unhistorical? This condition – unhistorical, anti-historical through and through – is the womb not only of the unjust but

---

[28] This essay was proposed as part of a total of thirteen essays. However, Nietzsche did not complete the proposed number and only published four. Initially, each essay was published independently but later all four appeared as a collection. For a fine introduction to the series and the essay on history writing, see Breazeale, *Untimely Meditations*.

[29] Ibid., p. 59.

of every just deed too; and no painter will paint his picture; no general achieve his victory, no people attain its freedom without having first desired and striven for it in an unhistorical condition. As he who acts is, in Goethe's words, always without a conscience, so he is also without knowledge, he forgets most things so as to do one thing, he is unjust towards what lies behind him, and he recognises the rights only of what is now come into being and no other rights whatever.[30]

Instead of welcoming historical consciousness, Nietzsche unabashedly declares we ought to hate it, for it is "instruction without invigoration".[31] His unrelenting critique of both historical consciousness and the historian's craft reopened a wound that had been stitched and healed in antiquity by men like Socrates, Plato, and Aristotle. As classical philosophy and early historiography took root, a conscious effort was made to exorcise raw emotions not only from human affairs but also from foundational texts meant for educating the young. In the field of historiography the most celebrated exorciser of all had been Thucydides (the "father" of history). In his famous account of the war between Athens and Sparta, he denigrates poets and others like Herodotus who celebrated passion. His takedown is worth citing:

> On the whole, however, the conclusions I have drawn from the proofs quoted may, I believe, safely be relied upon. Assuredly they will not be disturbed either by the verses of a poet displaying the exaggeration of his craft, or by the composition of chroniclers that are attractive at truth's expense: the subjects they treat of being out of reach of evidence, and time having robbed most of them of historical value by enthroning them in the region of legend. Turning from these, we can rest satisfied with having proceeded from clearest data, and of having

[30] Ibid., p. 64.
[31] Ibid., p. 59.

arrived at conclusions as exact as can be expected in matters of such antiquity. The absence of romance in my history, I fear, detracts somewhat from its interest; but if it be judged useful by those inquirers who desire an exact knowledge of the past as an aid to understanding of the future, which in the course of human things must resemble if it does not reflect it, I shall be content. In fine, I have written my work, not as an essay which is to win the applause of the moment, but as a possession for all time.[32]

A similar sentiment is expressed by Plato, when in his utopian *Republic* he seeks to exile all poets, for he accuses them of kindling passions and derailing all rational endeavour. But as Freud taught us, the repressed inevitably returns – as it does with Nietzsche's critique of classical and Enlightenment rationality. Despite the odds, given the weight of tradition, he succeeds in reintroducing passion into the domain of historiography.

In this sense Nietzsche provides us with the key to decipher a major strain of Indian historical writings. The fact that the Ramayana and the Mahabharata and the compositions of men like Kalhana and Santokh Singh were written in verse has much to do with generating what we might describe as a panoply of emotions within those who savoured these texts. In Indian civilisational praxis, poetic history on an epic scale was indubitably the way to generate the right telos.

While Nietzsche has helped us unlock a major triumph of Indian historiography – the past as passion – we are still left with a blind spot. Rasa theory's infiltrations into historical narrative also, paradoxically, compel us to confront the truth that the past cannot be understood by emotions alone. While in the western context a Nietzschean correction was much needed, in the Indian context we have had an overabundance of emotions,

---

[32] Thucydides, *The Peloponnesian War*, pp. 15–16.

so that emotively charged narratives of the past have merged into and bolstered hierarchical projects in the domain of myth and religious belief. In the popular domain, particularly within the confessional milieu (but also Bollywood), history has become all about feelings and sentiments: the reliance on rasa to narrate the past has been selective, agenda-driven, and responsible for massive distortions of the past. The superfluity of emotions involved in the traditional toolkit of historical narration quite obviously needs to be tempered by a reason-based toolkit, i.e. modern critical historiography. This toolkit was invented by historians like Thucydides and modified, refined, and expanded by historians operating in the Graeco–Roman, Sinic, and Islamicate worlds. While some of the trends they began did filter into India, particularly during the Mughal epoch, much Indian historiography continued in its imbrication with human passion. It took British colonialism for many in South Asia to acknowledge Hegel's dictum that there is "reason in history".

An institutional habitus for history as a discipline was only established in India in 1919, when the University of Calcutta set up a postgraduate department dedicated to teaching and researching history.[33] Gradually, other metropolitan campuses followed and set up similar intellectual centres. The close ideological affiliation between Indian nationalism and historical excavations of the past further boosted the modern fortunes of the discipline. Indian elites and masses both wanted, if one may adapt Nehru, to discover India. This then led some professional historians into looking like minor celebrities, Jadunath Sarkar being probably the best known, with others including R.G. Bhandarkar, G.S. Sardesai, and R.C. Majumdar. Their Punjab analogues were Ganda Singh, Harbans Singh, and V.N. Dutta. These modern historians, like their professional colleagues elsewhere,

---

[33] For my account of the institutional growth of history in India here, I am indebted to Chakrabarty, "The Public Life of History: An Argument Out of India", pp. 169–90.

distinguished their praxis from impassioned history by cultivating all of the key ingredients of modern historiography: deep knowledge of the archives, critical evaluation of sources and primary materials, verification protocols, and vigilance when acknowledging what exactly constitutes facts. "Among themselves," says Dipesh Chakrabarty,

> they debated "scientific" ways of studying the past, but they were all votaries of the new science of history. The idea that history could be a subject of "research" and the very conception of "research" itself were new. This demand in public life for "research knowledge" of the past had something to do both with European administrators' enthusiasm for discovering "Indian" history and with the cultural nationalism of nineteenth-century Indian intellectuals, many of whom subscribed to the supposedly universal ideals of Empire.[34]

The rise of this new modern history, at least within elite circles, ended the long knowledge regime of poetry as history, or history as kavya and rasa.

Notwithstanding the regime change, if we may call it that, a dilemma arose. The Indian public largely refused to acknowledge the epistemic shift: the "truths" discovered by historians were not generally palatable to an audience attuned to history as passion. Moreover, this new method of recording the past was politically manipulable by those with a vested interest in perpetuating myth as history, in whose argument it was an import within the baggage of colonial conquest and therefore Christian, elite-controlled, and suspect.[35] What the public called for was still a rasa-infused historiography.

Given this large indifference to a radical change in ways of writing the past, and the widespread refusal of the Indian public

---

[34] Ibid., p. 171.

[35] This dilemma is astutely explored in Bhattacharya, "Predicaments of Secular Histories", pp. 57–73.

to be persuaded, historians bred in the new episteme were continuously compelled to make a choice between the emotional and the epistemological. The emotional, despite Nietzsche's plea, had to be discounted. Professional historians cannot make up and embellish facts, as some rasa theorists might want. Myth, folklore, confessional histories, self-interested testimonies, and chronicles written on behalf of the state or sponsored by elites need to be critically evaluated and subjected to rigorous post-Enlightenment protocols, regardless of how strongly they are opposed and sought to be relativised or discarded by the proponents of passion and propaganda. Emotions too need to be historicised. As Isaiah Berlin persuasively argues, ours is an awkward lot, for we humans have to constantly make choices in the domain of values, clashing alternatives, and incompatible goals. "What is clear," he says,

> is that values can clash – that is why civilizations are incompatible. They can be incompatible between cultures, or groups in the same culture, or between you and me . . . The notion of the perfect whole, the ultimate solution, in which all good things coexist, seems to me to be not only merely unattainable – that is a truism – but conceptually incoherent; I do not know what is meant by a harmony of this kind. Some among the Great Goods cannot live together. That is a conceptual Truth. We are doomed to choose, and every choice may entail an irreparable loss.[36]

Deeply aware as I am of the dilemmas of choice and the sadness of loss – emotional and communitarian – the essays that are included in this volume are all based on a historiographical choice: a deconstruction of emotions. The book comprises six essays, chronologically covering the period of colonial modernity and its post-colonial aftermath. Each essay grapples with historical

[36] Berlin, *The Crooked Timber of Humanity*, pp. 12–13.

episodes constituted by powerful emotional drives. The opening essay, on the Kuka movement, reports on the emotive role that the sacrality of the cow plays in the inner lives of Kuka Sikhs, and how Sikh metaphysics prepares these historical actors to turn into martyrs.

This is followed by an intervention on the emotions of knowledge. The exemplar here is Sir Attar Singh Bhadour (1833–1896), a colonial subject who opts to turn into a "native informant" on behalf of his British patrons.

Subsequently, I examine the centrality of holy spaces and the critical role such spaces play in the making of the Sikh community.

Parallel to the political campaigns launched to save a sacred wall in the imperial capital of Delhi in the age of Lutyens, Punjabis living in the far-off Pacific Coast of Canada and the United States launched the Ghadar movement that, in part, was fuelled by the emotional registers of vernacular poetry. The moral and political arc of the Ghadar movement leads us directly into examining the inner life of the nationalist icon Shaheed Bhagat Singh.

I conclude by reflecting on how the diasporic experience unleashes new emotional energies and how, at times, such untamed energies lead to ruptures and new psychological articulations. So, while I address the role of emotions in the making of history and community formation, in my capacity as a cultural historian trained in modern historiography I have had no temptations to make emotions the central engine of my analysis. In other words, while important lessons can be learned from rasa aesthetics and our classical poet-historians on how to find our way out of the labyrinths of dry-as-dust history, the purpose here is to treat emotions as only one variable among many. Equally, if at times not more so than emotions, are things of importance such as political power, state apparatuses, class alignments, cultural hegemony, socio-economic transformations, and individual choices anchored in secular and religious ideologies.

Taking into account all these extrinsic factors and producing complex transcripts of the past can at times extract a terrible toll, both for those practising the historian's craft and those who consume such chronicles. This toll is best summed up by a Russian proverb that, loosely translated, states: if we write histories, we lose an eye but if we do not write histories we lose both eyes.

1

Brotherhood of the Pure
The Poetics and Politics of Cultural Transgression

> Purity and impurity are principles of evaluation and separation.
> The pure must be kept uncontaminated by the less pure.
>
> **Mary Douglas**

THE SPRING MONTH of Magh heralds festivals, pilgrimages, and popular rituals in the North Indian countryside. In 1872 a small village, Bhaini, in Punjab's Ludhiana district, was the scene of feverish activity. Participants in a millenarian community popularly known as Kukas had collected there on 11 and 12 January in connection with the coming spring festivities. They had, however, very little to celebrate. In the preceding four months nine of their number had been hanged by the colonial authorities on charges of attacking slaughter-houses and killing butchers, others had been imprisoned, and many more subjected to increased surveillance and restrictions. British officials had nervously shifted their views of the Kukas. Earlier seen as religious reformers within the Sikh tradition, they were now deemed political rebels.[1] Those present will have felt

---

[1] This perspective is clearly reflected in Memorandum on Ram Singh and Kukas by J.W. Macnabb, Officiating Commissioner, Ambala Division, 4 November 1871, reproduced in Nahar Singh, *Goroo Ram Singh and the Kuka Sikhs*, vol. 1, pp. 143–52 (hereafter *KS*). Nahar Singh's is a very useful

the heavy gaze of colonial suspicion on them, so the atmosphere at Bhaini will have been tense and unnerving.

On 13 January, the day of the traditional festival of Lohri (signifying the approach of spring), a party of Kuka zealots left their leader's village to mount an attack on Malerkotla, the capital of a small Muslim principality of the same name, approximately thirty miles south of Ludhiana. The next day, en route to their destination, the Kuka crowd raided the fort of Malodh, the residence of a Sikh aristocrat related to the Maharaja of Patiala, possibly to avenge through his affine the anti-Kuka policies of the maharaja, and to equip themselves with arms and horses. The insurgents found little material success. Next morning, on 15 January, when a band of approximately 120 Kuka Sikhs attempted against all odds to invade the town of Malerkotla, they were repulsed by trained and well-armed state troops. The same afternoon, an armed contingent from the Sikh principality of Patiala succeeded in capturing sixty-eight of the raiding Kukas. They were brought to Malerkotla, where L. Cowan, the officiating deputy commissioner of Ludhiana district, following the hardened traditions of the Punjab school of administration, had forty-nine of them blown to their death from guns, without the niceties of a legal trial. The next day, T.D. Forsyth, commissioner of the Ambala division, on joining his subordinate, had sixteen more Kukas blown from guns, this time after the formalities of a brief trial. These drastic measures earned the Kukas a hallowed place in the textbooks of modern Indian history and made them a part of the "heroic" Sikh tradition.

Why did a small party of Kuka Sikhs attack the state of Malerkotla? What was the source of their confidence – a self-assurance so blindingly supreme that it made them feel invincible against a greatly superior political-military power? Answers to

---

three-volume compilation of British official documents on the Kukas available at the National Archives, New Delhi.

these questions have not been lacking ever since the Kuka movement reached its climax on the parade ground of Malerkotla. The first to respond were British officials, who proposed a simple and straightforward theory to vindicate their own actions and the fair name of English justice. In British eyes, the kingdom of Maharaja Ranjit Singh had been a Sikh state. Its annexation by the British a decade after Ranjit Singh's death in 1839 had meant the Sikhs had lost their superior status in the Punjab; a proud community had been humiliated. To avenge their disgraceful defeat and regain past glories, Sikhs had been constantly on the lookout for an opportunity to overthrow British rule and the Kuka movement, under the leadership of Ram Singh, was a direct manifestation of this basic urge. By suppressing it in time the authorities believed they had prevented this evil design from materialising and protected the interests of civil society.[2]

A second interpretation of the Kuka actions is advanced by nationalist historians, for whom the Kukas provided fine clay for a nationalist mould: here was one more straightforward illustration of Indian communities waging war against British imperialism almost immediately after their territories had been unjustly annexed. The Kuka struggle, in line with 1857, was a heroic battle within the larger war for freedom from British oppression.[3]

In retrospect, it is not hard to see through the ideological justifications of British apologists as much as through the persistent efforts of nationalist historians to incorporate all sorts of social movements under the nationalist banner. But in fact no alternative perspective was available until the historian W.H. McLeod re-examined the available materials. With refreshing vigour, McLeod broke clear of existing orthodoxies to offer an alternative explanation. He showed how the Kuka movement constituted a millenarian response emerging from specific socio-economic

[2] For this interpretation, see Macnabb's memorandum cited above.

[3] This line of thought is clearly seen in Bajwa, *Kuka Movement*; Ahluwalia, *Kukas*; and Joginder Singh, *Kuka Movement*.

circumstances, particularly a tremendous rise in the Sikh population, the failure of a harvest that had led to a famine, and the growth of a discontented peasantry – features characteristic of most millenarian uprisings: McLeod himself noted the striking similarities of the Kuka movement with millenarian stirrings in other parts of the world.[4]

While these strands – the colonial, the nationalist, and the millenarian – on the Kukas have clarified various facets of their movement, specially its political dynamics and close connection with social conditions, all three strands are broadly in line with the dominant historiography of Indian nationalism. This is because their exploratory and analytic focus has been on what might be called the "pragmatic" aspects of the movement – on themes connected with material disaffection and rebellion and their nationalist import – rather than on the movement's semantic and symbolic aspects. The existing historiography has helped us grasp the underlying causes of the movement and define its character – an essential task – but given us precious little on what the movement meant to the participants themselves. To interpret the actors' objectives, their own structures of consciousness and experience, is as crucial as locating the major causes and features of a social movement. Such an exercise requires a study of imagery, symbols, metaphors, and codes of behaviour that take us beyond socio-political circumstances. If we neglect the semantic and the symbolic it is hard to adequately comprehend the discourses of Ram Singh and the statements of his followers.

In a letter to his disciples, Ram Singh prophesied: "on a Sunday midnight locks will open and two suns shall appear on the horizon, one on the left and the other on the right. A white elephant will descend on earth . . ."[5] The message loaded with

---

[4] McLeod, "The Kukas", pp. 85–103.

[5] Reproduced in Ganda Singh, *Kukian d Vithia*, letter no. 4, p. 25, my translation (hereafter *Vithia*).

symbolic language is meaningless without semiotic analysis. Kaisra Singh, a Kuka Sikh, recorded this before he was blown away from a gun at Malerkotla parade grounds:

> I went to Bhainee for the Maghee Mela [fair]. I sat near where Heera Singh and Lehna Singh were. They did not advise me to join in any enterprise. *God put it into my heart to go with them* . . . I left Bhainee with them. We went together to Ruboo, and from Ruboo to Malodh. God ordered me to go there. No one else told me . . . I had not even a stick. I then came with the party [to] Kotlah. I came inside the town to the palace gate. I was in [a] fight before the treasury, but had no arms . . . We came to Kotlah by *God's order to kill the slayers of kine* . . .[6]

Kaisra Singh was hardly an exception among the Kuka insurgents. Their ranks were crowded with men who shared similar views, staunchly believing in the justness of their power to challenge the alien Raj and its collaborators: God was on their side, he spoke to them, they were following his directives.

Here I examine the phenomenology of such deeply held beliefs in order to answer such questions as: What convictions made people die for their religion? How does religion play a role in resistance? Why are apocalyptic visions believed? What evokes the moral indignation of communities?

In Pursuit of Holiness

Holiness, a fundamental concern of religions, is a concept difficult to define. Broadly speaking, it seems a compound of notions drawn from folk belief and mythology, theology and eschatology, and ideas of salvation and sacredness. The concept

---

[6] Examination of the accused number # 3, Kaisra Singh in "Copy of the Correspondence, or Extracts from Correspondence, Relating to Kooka Outbreak", *Parliamentary Papers*, vol. 45, 1872, p. 43. Emphasis added.

endows individuals, texts, times, places, institutions, and communities with a distinctly powerful hold over the human mind and emotions, making it distinguishable from others in circulation within civil society. The term holiness subsumes the meanings of "sacred" – in common parlance the two are synonymous – but holiness also subsumes within itself a moral code that informs the values, beliefs, concepts, and symbols through which a community conceives what is just, legitimate, and virtuous. With this encapsulation within itself of a moral order, holiness enables a community to distinguish the pure from the impure, the right from the wrong, and the sacred from the profane, thereby establishing codes of individual and collective conduct.[7]

Those who violate standards of holiness are usually subjected to the intense rage and indignation of the community, expressed through words, gestures, rumours, signs, and occasionally weapons. These traditional expressions of outrage against transgressors of a "holy order" – or a socially constructed common sense of holiness – were easily communicated and comprehended in local society but not as easily decoded by external observers: British officials, for instance, saw in many of the Kuka actions a primitive mind at work, while for the community its punitive acts were derived from a storehouse of expressive tradition. The argument which follows places this specific idea of a holy order and its defence at the centre of analysis of the Kuka movement.

The Kukas did not create the holy order they so zealously chose to pursue – they were only extending and interpreting it. The evolution of the Kukas into a "sect" within the Sikh tradition and their singling out in British files have heavily coloured readings of the early history of the Kukas. Consequently, it

---

[7] On the importance of a moral order for peasant societies particularly in the "economic" domain, see Scott, *The Moral Economy of the Peasant*. For its ramifications in the Indian sphere, see Metcalf, *Moral Conduct and Authority*, pp. 1–22. Although she surveys the importance of the moral order in Islam, her study can illuminate similar concepts among other Indian traditions.

occasionally appears as if their ideology suddenly materialised out of nowhere and was without deep roots in their society. This view is erroneous. The argument is useful for the orthodox Sikh tradition – which views Kukas as a marginal sect that went astray – but it is historically erroneous, especially if we look at Kukas in relation to larger Sikh society. Kuka cosmology concerning a holy person, purity, right conduct, dress, food taboos, and sacredness had a long history, both within the Sikh tradition and in the larger framework of Indic culture.[8]

In 1708 Guru Gobind Singh, shortly before his death that year, decided to make the Guru Granth Sahib the eternal future Guru of the Sikhs, thereby endowing the young community with a source of both cohesion and potential differences. Solidarity was achieved because the community was left with a common object of veneration and a scripture to guide the faithful, particularly in periods of trial, but powerful differences were also a possibility for hundreds of pages of verse in the holy book were open to differing interpretations. The evolving tradition was partially saved from this fundamental source of interpretive differences by the important tradition of the Bhais, dating back to the early Sikh movement.

Etymologically, the word bhai means brother, but within the early Sikh tradition the word was also used as an honorific for the holy men of the panth.[9] To qualify for the title, a person had

---

[8] I have often used the term Kuka Sikhs here because the difference between the Kukas and the Sikhs had not fully crystallised in the nineteenth century and the two categories often overlapped. This is one reason why the British authorities found it so hard to judge the exact number of Kukas in the Punjab. At the same time, it must be acknowledged that there were certain differences between sectors of the Sikh tradition and the Kukas, particularly doctrinal ones, which came to a head when Ram Singh visited the Anandupr Sahib shrine.

[9] The Sanskrit word "panth" (lit. path or road) is used to designate groups in India who follow particular teachers or doctrines. The early Sikh community was thus known as the Nanak-panth, meaning the "followers of

to demonstrate a capacity to interpret the Guru Granth Sahib, communicate the wisdom of the Gurus enshrined in it, and be publicly recognised for his piety. If in addition he could work miracles, heal the sick, and give succour to the distressed, he was sure to occupy a position of considerable reverence and authority within the community. Such fully realised men were sometimes also honoured with the appellation "Baba". However, it must be noted here that in the nineteenth century the honorific Bhai was also used for those who acted as professional readers of the Guru Granth Sahib.[10]

The concept of "bhai" is as old as the Sikh faith. Among the first to earn the title and respect of a Bhai, probably the progenitor of the whole Bhai tradition, was Bhai Buddha (1506–1631). A disciple of Guru Nanak from the time of the Kartarpur community, he was a contemporary of seven Sikh Gurus and installed four of them to the guruship. It appears he was also consulted during the compilation of the Guru Granth Sahib. Equally important, if not more crucial, for the foundation of the Bhai tradition was Gurdas Bhalla (1551–1636). Well known for his work as a scribe, and amanuensis of the Guru Granth Sahib, he also authored commentaries on the compositions of the Sikh Gurus. The latter task he performed so well that his exegetical works are known as "the key to Guru Granth Sahib", i.e. to the Sikh scripture. Possibly since the days of Gurdas Bhalla, popularly known as Bhai Gurdas, the faculty of expounding on the teachings of the Sikh Gurus has been woven into the definition of a Bhai, and Bhais have been honoured as embodiments of the holy.

In the chronicles of the Sikhs, after Bhai Gurdas the following are prominent: Bhai Nand Lal, a poet closely associated with the

---

Nanak". Later generations increasingly dropped the prefix, with the result that the community came to be known as simply "the panth". This remains the preferred title now in English usage, as also in Hindi and Punjabi.

[10] Temple, "Honorific Class Names in the Punjab", p. 118.

tenth Sikh preceptor; Bhai Mani Singh, a renowned martyr; Bhai Vasti Ram, famed for his miraculous powers to heal the sick; Bhai Sant Singh, a tutor of Maharaja Ranjit Singh; Bhai Ram Singh, at one time a prime minister of the Lahore state; Bhai Gobind Ram, a member of the Lahore court; Bhai Gurmukh Singh, a confidant of Maharaja Sher Singh; Bhai Bir Singh, a guide to the Sikh nobility and subalterns alike; and Bhai Maharaj Singh, a resolute opponent of the British. The holiness of Bhai Vasti Ram and his grandson Bhai Ram Singh elevated them to the position of chief arbiters in the affairs of the Sikh state.

Maharaja Ranjit Singh believed he owed his kingdom to the blessings of Bhai Vasti Ram, a figure of phenomenal piety and learning in the eighteenth century.[11] Ranjit Singh's conviction not only illustrates the centrality of a holy person in the Sikh tradition but also exemplifies another key concept of the Sikh community: blessings. Blessings from a holy man could rectify worldly misfortune, ward off evil, and help overcome human shortcomings. In 1799, when faced with the combined forces of leading Sikh chieftains outside the city of Lahore, the maharaja turned to Bhai Vasti Ram for advice and blessings. Victorious in the battle, his conviction of Vasti Ram's holiness was further confirmed. The Bhai's death in 1803 cut short his career, but his progeny amply enjoyed the bounties of the state. Bhai Ram Singh, a grandson, was shown such great deference that he was among a handful of persons allowed a seat in the presence of the maharaja. He was a scholar of Sanskrit, proficient in Persian, had ample skills in medicine, and his counsel was sought on a variety of issues: the politics of the court, the policy towards the British, the treatment of Sikh feudatories, and the crowning of Ranjit Singh's heirs. Under Kanwar Nau Nihal Singh this Bhai was made prime minister, and six months before he died in October 1847 Bhai Ram Singh was among the signatories of the

---

[11] The above account is based on Kirpal Singh, *An Historical Account*, p. 9.

fateful treaty between the British government and the state of Lahore.

Another famous Bhai lineage in central Punjab was that of the Bhais of Bagarian, an old Sikh family dating back to the time of the Sikh Gurus. Of humble Tarkhan origins, their close association with the Sikh Gurus greatly enhanced their social standing and earned them much religious merit. In the seventeenth century they were given the title Bhai by Guru Hargobind, the sixth Sikh Guru, for their exemplary service and unflinching devotion to the Sikh cause. The family was renowned in Malwa for its piety, works of charity, and propagation of Sikhism.[12] The *rites de passage* for the Sikh princes were conducted by the head of the Bagarian family. He was also approached in the eighteenth and nineteenth centuries by the princes for religious instruction and blessings. The Bagarian Bhais endowed one of the largest langars in the province in their ancestral village at Ludhiana; it fed a constant stream of travellers, pilgrims, and the rural poor regardless of caste or creed.[13] From the time of Bhai Gurdas, a poet and scribe to the Bhais of Bagarian and the religious and political mentor of maharajas, the tradition of the Bhais, although never canonised, had become deeply rooted and attracted wide veneration. An average Sikh in the nineteenth century considered the person of a Bhai holy, sacred, and inviolable. But Bhais were not only born to established families, they could be recognised, exalted, and endowed by the Sikh public.

Ram Singh, the leader of the Kuka Sikhs in the second half of the nineteenth century, became a leading representative of this ancient Sikh tradition and effectively harnessed it to launch a powerful millenarian movement. Although the Kukas today use

---

[12] The Malwa region lies south and south-east of the Sutlej river.

[13] Account based on Walker, *Final Report on the Revision of Settlement 1878–83 of the Ludhiana District*, p. 61 (hereafter *Ludhiana Report*); and idem, *Chiefs and Families of Note in the Punjab*, vol. I, pp. 203–9; and *Khalsa Akhbar*, 14 April 1888, p. 7.

the honorific Guru for Ram Singh, the prefix employed by Ram Singh himself was Bhai.[14] Placed outside the ambience of this hallowed lineage, historians are hard pressed to explain how the humble Ram Singh, a one-time carpenter and soldier, succeeded in making tens of thousands flock to his standard. The legitimacy of his prophetic utterances, the power of his person, and his drive to reorder the world around him stemmed from a process which his contemporaries understood very well and openly offered to support. Having outlined the paradigm of the Bhais – without reference to which it is hard to enter the world the Kuka Sikhs constructed for themselves – I will try to reconstruct the world according to Bhai Ram Singh.

Very little is known about the early life of Ram Singh.[15] He was born in 1816 in a humble rural family – his father was a carpenter in the village of Bhaini in Ludhiana district. Assisting his father in the daily chores, the boy grew up memorising several compositions from the Guru Granth Sahib, reciting from the scriptures, and acquiring a working knowledge of Punjabi. He may have received some formal education at the hands of a local learned man. By the time he was twenty he, like many young men of his age, left his village to join an army regiment named after Prince Nau Nihal Singh, the grandson of Ranjit Singh. During his service years he met Bhai Balak Singh, whose personality, convictions, teachings, and vision so impressed him that he became an ardent disciple. Although Bhai Balak Singh had been influenced by another teacher, Jawahar Mal, for the Kukas the line of their masters only starts with Balak Singh, who is considered in a sense the founder of the movement.

---

[14] Ganda Singh, *Vithia*, p. 6.

[15] This brief biographical note is based on Ganda Singh, *Vithia*, and Nahar Singh, *Namdhari Itihas* (hereafter *Itihas*). Both these works have made extensive use of primary sources in Urdu and Punjabi, particularly the literature produced by the Kukas themselves. For instance, Santokh Singh, *Satgur Bilas*; Dhian Singh, *Sri Satguru Bilas*; and Alam, *Jug Paltau Satguru*.

Just before the Anglo–Sikh war of 1845, Ram Singh left the army and returned to his native place to work as a sharecropper. In his thirty-fourth year he again left Bhaini, this time for Ferozepore, to work for an uncle who had undertaken to repair a fort and various other buildings. Legends of his stay there record his power to work miracles. According to one account, on a Sunday when Ram Singh was employed to put a roof on a poor man's house in Ferozepore city, one of the beams proved a foot too short and the owner begged Ram Singh to remedy the defect without obliging him to buy a new beam that he could not afford. Ram Singh thereupon miraculously extended the beam by a foot. According to Flora Annie Steel, who recorded the legend, "hundreds of persons in Ferozepore will attest the above tale, many being eye-witnesses and the house can be shown to the curious."[16] The legend concludes that on the day of this miracle Ram Singh obtained five hundred followers. Clearly, in popular sentiment a connection existed between miracles, the sanctity accorded to Ram Singh as a Bhai, and his teachings. Recognising the elements of holiness in Ram Singh was seen by many as a means of earning religious merit: this is a claim he never explicitly makes but is granted by others. This process of recognition by the Sikh masses is acknowledged by Ram Singh in a letter: "first Sikhs generally recognised Bir Singh, then Maharaj Singh and now me."[17]

The uncharted domain of miracles has much to tell us about faith, beliefs, and consciousness in nineteenth-century Punjab. To some of us today, with the arrogance of our intellectual assumptions, miracles appear to be inventions, or seem signs of credulity; for those who believed in them, they possessed a rationality of their own and functioned within a system of cultural references they understood. In their conception, Ram Singh was

---

[16] Steel, "Folklore in the Punjab", p. 42.
[17] Ganda Singh, *Vithia*, letter no. 44, p. 302.

no ordinary mortal, so he could do what common men could not. Miracles ascribed to him gave credence to his prophetic status. When he was absorbed in early morning meditation, it was believed a bright light could be seen circling his head.[18] A halo, or other form of aura around the head, has for long in histories of religions indicated personal holiness.

Two years before the great uprising of 1857, Ram Singh returned to his native Bhaini and started a shop which shows him as both ironmonger and grain seller. At the same time, he collected around him a core group of associates and disciples, most of whom were demobilised soldiers from former regiments of the Lahore state. From this nucleus were to emerge many prominent Kukas of the future. For the benefit of a growing number of adherents who visited Bhaini, Ram Singh, in line with Sikh tradition, set up a langar. In 1862, when Bhai Balak Singh died at Hazro, Ram Singh emerged as one of his three successors.[19] By now he manifested the major characteristics of a Bhai: piety, the ability to expound on the scriptures, and a demonstrated capacity to work miracles. These features confirmed to his followers that Ram Singh was a holy man whose rise had in fact been predicted in prophecies then current.

Let us now turn to what Ram Singh preached to his growing following, and to the nature of his message.

If one were looking for a single dominant theme in Ram Singh's teachings, it would be his emphasis on the opposition between what is pure and impure.[20] This recurrent concern may seem novel because interpretations of the Sikh movement always emphasise Sikhism as having already freed itself of ritual concerns by, in part, discounting ideas of purity and impurity. While it is true that questioning the caste-Hindu polarity of purity and

---

[18] Nahar Singh, *Itihas*, p. 46.
[19] Ganda Singh, *Vithia*, pp. 17–18.
[20] On how the pure–impure antinomy has influenced different cultures, see Douglas, *Purity and Danger*.

impurity as the organising principle of society was a defining feature of the Sikh movement, this cannot obfuscate the fact that Sikhs themselves have always paid great attention to notions of ritual purity, both individual and corporate.[21] The third Sikh Guru, Amar Das (1479–1574), constructed a baoli at Goindwal which became a pilgrimage site for Sikhs to bathe in and rid themselves of impurity. All major Sikh shrines, including Amritsar's Golden Temple, continued this tradition of an attached water tank for purificatory immersion, the obvious analogue being the Hindu tradition of acquiring merit by immersion in the Ganges. Mircea Eliade notes several features associated with water in religious thinking: it breaks and dissolves all forms, does away with the past, purifies and regenerates; in short, it is a symbol of renewal.[22]

All visitors to a Sikh shrine were required – from very early in the history of the panth but certainly by the nineteenth century – to shed footwear, then wash their feet and hands before entering, spaces outside the shrine being thought dirty, unclean, impure. This notion of dirt and impurity in the world outside seeks to purify the devotee by his very entry into the pure confines of a shrine. The concept of purity at work here has obviously less to do with the shrine as eliminating the mundane and material impurity of soil, excrement, and germs, and more to do with a culturally embedded notion of spiritual purity in spatially designated locations. Given the relevance, and in fact the importance, attached to ideas and notions of purity in Sikhism, the insistent emphases in Ram Singh's teachings on avoiding life-polluting

---

[21] Sikh concerns with purity and pollution are clearly reflected in the *Sau Sakhian* anthology circulated within the community in the nineteenth century. In a list of sixty-four injunctions in the anthology, several are concerned with the maintenance of purity. For an English translation of the original text, see Attar Singh, *Sakhe Book*, pp. 18–24.

[22] Eliade, *Patterns in Comparative Religion*, p. 194, cited in Douglas, *Purity and Danger*, p. 16.

impurities are far from surprising: they are in accord with his own religious heritage and mesh with the beliefs of the larger society of which he was a part.[23]

The state of purity is a desirable ideal, but in many holy orders the belief is that the organic processes of the human body, as well as man's social surroundings, make attainment of the ideal difficult. Impurities arise in a variety of areas: from bodily emissions, from menstruating women, during rites of passage such as birth and death, in certain kinds of food and material, and within anomalous social situations. To negate these polluting forces Ram Singh elaborated a cluster of rituals which would generate purity of body, speech, food, dress, and action. What were these rituals?

According to the hagiographic literature, one of the first ritual acts Ram Singh performed was the initiation of five Sikhs at Bhaini in 1857.[24] In itself this was a minor occurrence, but it marked an important departure in the practice of the initiation ritual. Candidates for initiation mostly visited four or five large Sikh shrines, such as the Golden Temple. Ram Singh changed this. He literally brought the possibility of the ritual to the doorstep of those who wanted to participate in it. The literature records how, in his extensive tours of central Punjab, Ram Singh conducted the initiation ritual in innumerable villages.[25] In his teachings he was insistent on the need for and importance of initiation. How is this insistence on the initiation ritual connected to ideas of purity and impurity? The uninitiated were perceived as being in a state of religious liminality, for while they were nominally Sikhs they had not confirmed their allegiance and were therefore liable to the dangers of impurity. In the nineteenth century this condition could be connected with – besides

---

[23] For an early attempt at conceptualising purity and impurity in India, see an unsigned essay, possibly by Louis Dumont and David F. Pocock, "Pure and Impure", pp. 9–39.

[24] Nahar Singh, *Itihas*, p. 51.

[25] Ganda Singh, *Vithia*, p. 16.

those flowing out of bodily processes – food, dress, speech, social association, and violations of the Sikh code of conduct. While there is rarely a direct reference to danger, we can infer at least three forms of it in contemporary sources: being cut off from God, entailing deprivation of a major source of protection and boons; languishing in the misery of the transmigratory cycle; and sometimes the possibility of turning into a non-human or bhut. These dangers could be eliminated by initiation. An initiated individual stopped occupying a liminal position for he was now part of a chosen collectivity and ritual purity protected him from what his society deemed impure and dangerous.

Unfortunately, ritual purity attained through initiation was not permanent. Even when there had been no direct transgression of the rules of purity, an individual was daily besieged by impurities. To negate their influence, Ram Singh demanded that his followers be unfailing in taking an early morning bath. It is easy to read into this stricture a call for hygiene, but the context – people in an agrarian society with blazing temperatures – shows they were basically being enjoined to do what they would not have wished to avoid in any case: bathe. By stressing a pre-dawn bathing ritual as conducive to a morally clean state, Ram Singh was pressing home the advantage of a general predisposition into a larger religious framework of purity vs impurity. Balak Singh, Ram Singh's mentor, had demanded that his disciples bathe three times a day. Ram Singh is known to have taken this precept seriously. In a rahit-nama issued by him sometime in 1866, to which the Kukas subscribe even today, he demanded: "Rise during the last watch of the night and taking a pot of water [for cleansing] go out into the fields to relieve nature. When you return scour the pot twice, remove the clothes which you were wearing while in the fields, clean your teeth, bathe, and recite [the prescribed portions] of sacred scripture."[26]

---

[26] Reproduced in ibid., *Vithia*, pp. 313–14. The above passage is translated by McLeod, *Textual Sources*, p. 129 (hereafter *Textual Sources*).

Defecation, in this view, pollutes the body but also contiguous objects, so a thorough cleansing of clothes and vessels is a requirement, as is a bath, all to be followed by the recitation of sacred scriptures. This schedule is maintained to this day at the Kuka headquarters in Bhaini. According to S.S. Sanehi,

> a namdahri, or Kuka, living at Sri Bhaini Sahib bids good-bye to his bed at about three in the morning . . . Having been to the toilet, he *purifies his hands seven times* with either sand or ash or earth . . . He cleans his teeth with a branch of a tree used in India for this purpose instead of a tooth brush. Then he takes a bath either with well water or in the holy tank named Ram Sarovar . . . Having taken his bath, the Kuka puts on different clothes, not those he had worn going to the toilet . . .[27]

In order to construct a comprehensive ideology, the purity principle was further extended to encompass diet restrictions, a code of dress, and commandments for social behaviour. Balak Singh had already enjoined his followers not to eat food cooked by those outside the community of disciples and never to drink water from a leather pouch. The latter reflected the community's reverence for the cow and abomination of cow-hide products. Kuka Sikhs were also prohibited from consuming meat and liquor and smoking tobacco. Ram Singh says that "meat and liquor are the diet of *mleccha*. Consuming them pollutes consciousness."[28] Food taboos appear in fact to be the most widely respected rules among Kuka Sikhs in the nineteenth century. Before entering a kitchen to cook they were expected to wash their feet.[29] Food cooked or already part-eaten by others was considered polluted and not to be partaken of among them.[30] According to

---

[27] Sanehi, "Kukas as They Live", pp. 30–1.
[28] Ganda Singh, *Vithia*, p. 288.
[29] Ram Singh's letter no. 32, in Ganda Singh, *Vithia*, p. 277.
[30] Ram Singh's personal instructions in two different letters, nos 46 and 49, in ibid., pp. 305, 310.

a contemporary document, Kuka inmates at a lock-up in the Ferozepore district jail refused to eat jail-cooked food, possibly fearing pollution.[31]

The favoured colour for personal garments and turbans among the Kukas was white. The colour white is in many cultures the world over considered a sign of purity. Kuka Sikhs were also instructed to use a rosary made of white beads.[32] Disciples were expected to uphold injunctions against theft, adultery, ill-speech, female infanticide, and exchanges of large sums of money at the time of marriages. They were to practise seva, perform liberal and charitable acts, and charge no interest in their financial transactions. Visiting brothels was prohibited.[33] Those who disobeyed these commandments were not allowed to participate in congregations of the faithful – the congregation, being deemed holy, the denial to join it amounted to cutting off the accused from a source of holiness.

This discussion raises a question: What was the reason for this level of emphasis on ritual purity in the Kuka ideology? As pointed out, the Kukas shared a concern for purity with the rest of the Sikh panth. While Kuka notions of purity were correlated with the concept of purity and pollution in the caste system, the similarity did not extend much further. Caste for the Kukas was unimportant.[34] They did not employ the purity/pollution opposition to assign impurity to a group of permanent hereditary specialists, thereby enabling the "twice-born" in their society to

---

[31] "A Brief Narrative of the Kuka Sect with Some Account of Ram Singh of Bhaini", in Nahar Singh, *KS*, vol. I, p. 27.

[32] Kahan Singh, *Gursabad Ratanakar Mahan Kos*, p. 1034.

[33] These moral rules are constantly reiterated in Bhai Ram Singh's correspondence and rahit-namas. See Ganda Singh, *Vithia*, pp. 223, 225, 227, 240, 245, 261, 263, 287, 291, 297.

[34] Contemporary official reports repeatedly commented on how members of different castes were freely admitted into the Kuka ranks. For instance, see ibid., p. 29.

be pure because of their birth into a pure caste. In their consanguinity, marriages, commensality, and most importantly in their worldview, Kukas overturned the commonly accepted determinants of the caste system. This should not be taken to imply that they had no rules governing social relationships, but only that their rules at the level of abstraction were not those of the caste hierarchy. To a certain extent, the Kuka expression of pure/impure marks a historical continuity with the Sikh conceptual structure briefly delineated earlier, which also gave a privileged position to the same purity/impurity dyad and its system of meaning – as distinct from the traditional Hindu caste hierarchy.

The colonial inspector general of police for Punjab seems to have got to the heart of the matter. In a report, he commented on how the Kukas "appear anxious merely to revive the Sikh religion in its original state of purity and to eradicate the errors which have from time to time, defiled it."[35] Purity, as Dumont and Pocock argue, is an essential prerequisite for approaching the gods, which "does not mean their [the gods] nature is purity, but that purity is a condition for the contact with them to be beneficial . . ."[36] Purity is simply a crucial requirement for any relationship with the gods. Ritual purity, following the dictates of a strong moral code in everyday life, and cleansing the body represented, in part, the efforts of the faithful to establish a firm nexus with the sacred, build up magico-religious defences, create order out of chaos, and acquire powers that ordinary people lacked.

To recapitulate, Kuka symbolic structure may be represented by the binary opposition of purity/pollution. Underlying it was the belief that through purity one was powerful, almost invincible; in a state of impurity one was weak and susceptible. Those who were pure in the mode of the Kukas were part of the brotherhood, those who endangered purity were certainly adversaries. By the late 1860s, those who transgressed the

---

[35] Inspector General of Police, Punjab, to Secretary to Government, Punjab, 20 January 1868, in Nahar Singh, *KS*, vol. I, p. 64.

[36] Dumont and Pocock, "Pure and Impure", p. 31.

boundaries of purity were to the Kuka Sikhs violating the moral framework of holiness and had to be punished. In other words, upholding holiness called for stern action on the part of the faithful. But who were the adversaries inviting the wrath of the Kukas?

In Defence of Holiness

From 1866 onwards the Kukas, deeply committed to their worldview and with an unshakeable belief that the forces of the cosmos were on their side, spent their energies assailing those they saw as responsible for violating the conceptual principles of holiness. Reports from district police chiefs kept pouring into the provincial headquarters on how Kukas were desecrating, demolishing, and destroying village shrines and other sacred ancestral sites in the countryside. One such report sent by an official from Ferozepore district stated: "some tombs lying between the boundaries of the village of Chuhar Bhainee and Choote Borrshoo were destroyed about the 1st September, 1866 by Wariam Singh, Futteh Singh and Jymal Singh Kookahs. One of the tombs had been erected to the memory of one Sungoor Singh a man held in reverence by the neighbouring villages."[37] The police in Lahore, alarmed, informed their superiors that "on the 24th December, Ruttan Singh, a Brahmin of Shekhwan, reported at the Moreedke Police station that some of the new sect of the Kookas recently established in that village, had destroyed, by digging up with spades, two places sacred to Hunooman and Lutchman, worshipped by the Hindus of the village."[38]

While the colonial authorities in the 1860s were still busy debating what kind of threat the Kuka Sikhs represented to the Raj, four butchers in Amritsar were killed on the night of 5 June 1871. By the time the police caught up with the suspects and the

[37] Contemporary officials used the word tomb loosely, without distinguishing between a grave, shrine, and ancestral site.
[38] From T.H. Thornton, Secretary to Government Punjab, to J.W.S. Wyllie, Officiating Secretary, Government of India, Foreign Department, nos 154–7, 2 February 1867, in Nahar Singh, *KS*, vol. I, p. 34.

investigating detective, Christie, proudly claimed he had solved the crime, butcher families in the town of Raikot were attacked on 1 July and three people killed. To the further embarrassment of the authorities, it turned out that the persons apprehended for the Amritsar case had been hanged and two of them transported for life. On 27 November 1871, two more Kuka Sikhs were hanged on charges of abetting the Raikot murders. Barely two months later, in January 1872, an irregular mass of Kuka Sikhs started on their famous march to Malerkotla, which ended in the tragic disaster outlined above.

These seemingly bizarre episodes have caused much confusion among historians. Contemporary scholarship finds it hard to untangle the mystery of why the Kuka Sikhs should have taken on themselves to protect the cow, particularly in a period when many of their brethren would soon be proclaiming Hindu–Sikh distinctions. Picking up what was visibly a Hindu sacred symbol would hardly have helped an enterprise wanting to establish an independent identity for themselves within the Sikhs. Deciphering targets of civil violence and symbolic protest originating from religious communities is never simple, particularly because unlettered activists do not leave behind textual records containing an account of their motives and actions. For contemporary police and military officials tutored in a colonial epistemology which highlighted crime and insurrection as the major motivations of indigenous populations, comprehending Kuka actions was not too difficult. Using their evocative vocabulary, they categorised Kuka actions as foolish, dangerous, evil, criminal, and premature. Nationalist historians, as pointed out, read in them the imprint of an anti-imperialist consciousness. One historiographical approach questions this interpretation, claiming that the "victims of the Kukas' verbal and physical attacks were nearly all fellow Punjabis, not Englishmen."[39]

---

[39] Major, "Return to Empire", p. 320.

The obsessive concern among historians on whether the targets chosen were anti-British or not is misplaced. This debate diverts attention from more fundamental problems, such as why the Kukas chose to attack and kill butchers, rather than local officials or policemen or moneylenders – the frequent victims of peasant jacqueries in nineteenth-century north India. What were the Kuka Sikhs trying to communicate to their fellow comrades in civil society when they decided to act as defenders of the cow? What was the thinking that lay behind desecrating village sacred spots and demolishing ancestral shrines instead of attacking civil courts, police stations, and railway yards – the more obvious targets of nationalist insurgents? These questions cannot be answered if the locations of Kuka sacrilege and violence are analysed in isolation. This is perhaps one reason why Kuka responses appear to many historians to be incoherent, spontaneous, and ill conceived. To appear meaningful they have to be treated as part of a cultural system, for even madness can have a method and be interpreted as part of an order.[40] In the present case that order was embedded, to use semiotic terminology, in a cultural code of which the core was the purity/pollution antinomy. Once we place the indices of the Kuka actions within the parameters of this code, it becomes easier to recover at least some of their shadowy meanings.

But before doing so, it is imperative firmly to distinguish the two types of protest actions of the Kuka Sikhs, for their referents are different, even if interdependent and occasionally perhaps sponsored by the same activists. In the first instance, the moral indignation of the Kuka Sikhs was directed against ancestral shrines normally located at the edge of the village boundaries and at other sacred sites associated with men who had been deified in their localities. In the second case, the Kuka Sikhs directed their violence against kine-slaughtering butchers and their families. What was the logic behind these two different ventures?

[40] Leach, *Culture and Communication*, p. 39.

It was a common convention among Sikhs in the countryside, as it was among local Hindus and Muslims, to frequently visit khanqahs, pirkhanas, jatheras, mazars, kabars, and samadhs.[41] Visits to these sacred village sites were undertaken to heal illness, beget sons, cure cattle of disease; quite often these visits were propitiatory village rites because such shrines, often located on the boundaries of Punjab villages, were believed to protect against malignant spirits and unseen forms of evil. Annually, at regular seasonal intervals, hallowed ancestors were propitiated by village inhabitants. In the eyes of orthodox Sikhs this amounted to a serious breach of the teachings of the Sikh masters who had consistently stressed the futility of such worship. Sikhism had preached the interiorisation of faith; and now Ram Singh delivered a similar message in his sermons. A perceptive colonial official recorded the fact that "the Kukas have no respect for tombs, temples or shrines, they are also iconoclasts."[42]

The iconoclasm of these doctrines, noticed by the colonial official, was effectively demonstrated to the public when the Kuka Sikhs decided to desecrate and defile village sites. A proverb current among them, it was noted, was translatable as "raze marhi and masani [sacred spots located at village cremation grounds and generally related to the lineage ancestors]".[43] A report lodged by the district administration at Ludhiana clearly illustrates Kuka goals and methods:

> The Deputy Inspector of Police at Dehlon reported that twenty-seven graves had been destroyed at a village named Khuttree Koseh; the parties suspected were four Muzbee

[41] These various sacred memorial sites are defined in the Glossary. For the sake of convenience, I will hereafter simply refer to them as "village sites".

[42] Foreign Department Political, 8 October 1866, in Nahar Singh, *KS*, vol. I, p. 28.

[43] From T.H. Thornton, Secretary to Government Punjab, to J.W.S. Wyllie, Officiating Secretary, Government of India, Foreign Department, no. 154–7, 2 February 1867, in Nahar Singh, *KS*, vol. I, p. 34, my translation.

Kookas (Khazana, Kana, Bussawa Singh and Bahadur Singh). These graves or Murrees are the sites where the cremation of the bodies take place. After burning the body the ashes are collected and a small heap or mound is made, which is plastered over with mud; these may be seen outside every Hindoo village. The graves the four men injured were those of their own friends and relatives. The deed was done in the middle of the day, so that no difficulty was experienced in obtaining evidence and the accused were sent for trial . . .[44]

Three points that the report shares with other such reports must be highlighted. First, Kuka reasoning seems to have been that a powerful way of questioning the sacredness and power of these village sites was to demolish them and show to the rural population that Kuka zealots were unscathed despite the sacrilege. Second, they went about their task in broad daylight, knowing full well their actions would be noticed. The aim of the whole exercise appears to have been to preach through deeds and wean rural folk off worshipping at village sites. In the absence of alternative channels of communication, the desecration of such sites became an effective mode of advertising the Kuka cause. Third, the targets against which the Kuka Sikhs directed their wrath were associated with their own lineage and probably frequented by fellow clan members for worship. These village sites, it should be reiterated, were worshipped at by all village inhabitants – Sikh, Muslim, and Hindu – particularly if supplicants deemed them efficacious in granting boons.

These kinds of actions, demonstrating the profanity of village sites, seem to have peaked by 1867. Thereafter there is almost no

---

[44] From Inspector General of Police, Punjab, to Secretary to Government, Punjab, nos 11–188, 20 January 1868, in Nahar Singh, *KS*, vol. I, pp. 70–1. The use of the term "grave" here conveys a misleading impression. As the report itself indicates, these were not graves but marhis constructed at the cremation grounds.

mention of them in the official record. This then still leaves us the task of explaining the second type of violence directed against the butchers, and the fateful march to the tiny principality of Malerkotla. The meaning of this second action is to be found in the strategies and insensitive policies of the "unholy British Raj". From the Kuka viewpoint, the nature of the Raj was exemplified in its attitude to the holy cow.

For the Kukas, colonial rule had switched the existing cultural codes, producing an ambiguity in the given classificatory system governing purity/pollution, sacred/profane, moral/ immoral, and holy/unholy. The new Christian rulers of Punjab found it hard to comprehend many of the customary categories regulating social behaviour. As representatives of the most advanced nation on earth, confident in their utilitarian ideology, and possessed of unbounded evangelical zeal, they had little patience, leave alone sympathy, with the worldviews of the conquered, believing their traditional religious norms and practices inferior or savage. Having annexed the Lahore state after two stiff wars they had little to fear and were determined to innovate despite the political risks. The "Punjab school of administration", charged with messianic fervour, was determined to present Punjab as a model state for the rest of the Empire, almost as if it had been divinely ordained. Reform, progress, and civilisation were the three key terms in the vocabulary of the men asked to administer the newly conquered frontier province. Christian missionaries, English educators, and British officials were given free rein to experiment with their subjects, spread the new civilising doctrines, and reshape rustic Punjabis. This imperial trinity spared no efforts to purge old customs and impose Victorian ethics, all in the name of God and enlightenment. In the process of changing the face of the land they ruptured the symbolic order underpinning local society, generating cultural conflicts their authority found hard to comprehend or contain.

Unlike earlier empires, political legitimacy in the British was not sought in the normative categories of an indigenous culture but in a racist imperial ideology proclaiming superior moral purpose and an arrogant repudiation of local cultural mores.[45] Men of great piety who had been at the social apex under the Sikh Raj were now dispensable for believing in pagan gods and advocating irrational Oriental beliefs. Those at the bottom, without ritual standing but useful as political collaborators, were given ample privileges and important positions. Departures from accepted political conventions deeply ingrained in a system of local cultural references and a symbolic sacred order are epitomised in the contrasting attitudes of the local population and the English administration on the issue of cow slaughter.

Although the sacredness of the cow is widespread today as a belief common to Hindus and Sikhs, the history of how this came to be and why cow slaughter became taboo is less well known.[46] The cow was frequently alluded to in Vedic texts. By the early Vedic period the animal became a measure of payment; in literary imagery goddesses were compared to cows; the products of the cow were an integral element in Vedic sacrifices; and the cow and the bull came to symbolise maternity, fertility, and virility.[47] During the Gupta age, within the orbit of elitist Brahmanic religion the cow began to be perceived as inviolable,

---

[45] On how the British administration repeatedly tried to dissociate its political authority from local religious culture in the Punjab, although often without success, see Kerr, "British Relationships with the Golden Temple", pp. 139–51; and Gilmartin, "Tribe, Land and Religion", pp. 53–105.

[46] Marvin Harris, an anthropologist, has in numerous writings argued that Indian attitudes towards cattle have to do with ecological adaptation, nutritional efficiency, and bioenergetic productivity. For instance, see Harris, "The Cultural Ecology of India's Sacred Cattle", pp. 51–66; and idem, "India's Sacred Cow", pp. 28–36. This perspective has been bitterly opposed by Diener, Nonini, and Robkin, "The Dialectics of the Sacred Cow", pp. 221–41. These authors argue that the position of the cow can be understood through an analysis of class conflict, power equations, appropriation of surplus, and the rise of Indian empires. Both these approaches remain locked within the polemics of materialism and are uninterested in cow symbolism or its sacredness.

[47] Brown, "The Sanctity of the Cow in Hinduism", pp. 245–55.

and according to one source killing it was a capital offence.[48] A Chola king ordered executions for cow slaughter. By the early-medieval period there is sufficient evidence to show increasing veneration of the cow among the Hindus alongside the practice of cow slaughter among Indian Muslims. To placate Hindu feelings, Akbar prohibited cow slaughter and those who disobeyed the royal edict faced capital punishment.[49]

Cow killing and its prevention became an obvious barometer to gauge state policies on religious matters. Once the Mughal empire disintegrated, its successor states across northern India continued respecting the old tradition of banning the killing of cows. Under Punjab's Sikh rulers cow slaughter was punishable with death and the British authorities, early in their expansionist drive, were not averse to adhering to the prohibition: when signing treaties with princely states like Kutch they agreed to uphold the tradition.[50] According to a Muslim maulvi, 800 Muslims were in Kashmir's prisons in 1882 on charges of cow slaughter.[51] In the Punjab, soon after the First Anglo–Sikh War, when Henry Lawrence was appointed British resident at Lahore, orders were posted outside the Golden Temple prohibiting cattle slaughter in the holy city of the Sikhs. This effort to placate Sikh–Hindu sentiments, however, did not last long.

While this background to India's cattle complex helps us understand, in general terms, attitudes to the cow, to comprehend the nature of the Kuka actions against the butchers it is imperative to specify the position of sacred animals in Punjabi cosmology. People the world over employ a variety of simple and complex symbols to communicate their worldview; this is particularly true when core cultural ideas need to be expressed.

[48] Walker, *The Hindu World*, p. 256.
[49] Smith, *Akbar the Great Mogul*, p. 220, quoted in McLane, *Indian Nationalism*, p. 277.
[50] Crooke, *Religion and Folklore of Northern India*, p. 364.
[51] McLane, *Indian Nationalism*, p. 279.

In nineteenth-century Punjab the cow signified notions of ritual purity and impurity and delineated the sacred terrain as distinct from the profane. Demonstrating the homology between social structure and animal classification, Mary Douglas says: "taxonomy organizes nature so that the categories of animals mirror and reinforce social rules . . ."[52]

It is commonly acknowledged that animal taxonomies are influenced by social structures, reflect social concerns, and help human beings think about the world around them. Through the animal world and the folklore concerning it, people in diverse cultures have constructed symbolic oppositions between pure and impure, good and bad, industrious and lazy, lucky and unlucky, culture and nature.[53] The Karam people in the New Guinea Highlands, for instance, identify the cassowary as their sister's child.[54] In speaking of it during a hunt the Karam use the same language as they do for their cross-cousins and affines. A hunter who successfully kills a cassowary has to undergo the extensive purificatory rites that he would have had he killed a man. The bird, through a complex set of beliefs and maze of kin relationships, mediates here between man and nature.

In classifying animals Punjabis, much as in other cultural traditions, distinguish between wild and domesticated varieties. Those labelled wild belong to the realm of nature, while those classed within the domesticated taxonomy belong to human culture. The wild pig, a dreaded scourge of crops, was viewed with great hostility by peasants and placed beyond the frontiers of human society. The cow belongs to the realm of human culture with an exceptionally high ritual standing among domesticated animals. Its special position in the hierarchy of domesticated

---

[52] Douglas, *Implicit Meanings*, p. 285.

[53] The literature on this subject is vast: see esp. Lévi-Strauss, *The Savage Mind*; Leach, "Anthropological Aspects of Language", pp. 23–63; Bulmer, "Why is the Cassowary Not a Bird?", pp. 5–25.

[54] Bulmer, "Why is the Cassowary Not a Bird?"

animals can be contrasted with its nearest relative, the buffalo.[55] To begin with, the Punjabi language categorically distinguishes between the two through a variety of linguistic terms. Second, the cow as an anthropomorphised figure occupies the position of a deity, while the buffalo is considered both malevolent and inauspicious and commonly called a "black ghost". Third, the cow is a stall animal while the ox is harnessed for farm labour. The buffalo is tethered in the open and its male classed as intractable, therefore not amenable to use in ploughing. A proverb current in nineteenth-century Punjab was translatable as "threshing for a male buffalo, grinding for a man and travelling for a woman, these are all unsuitable."[56] Fourth, a barren she-buffalo is easily pressed into service for ploughing fields whereas the same task is inconceivable for a barren cow, and interestingly there is no Punjabi word for it. Finally, these cultural antinomies posit the cow's milk as highly desirable for a superior intellect while the buffalo's product is deemed suitable only for physical strength.

Punjabis address the cow as "gau mata", i.e. as the mother of man, suggesting human kinship with the sacred animal. An anthropologist carrying out fieldwork in the Punjab often heard the expression, "A man is the calf of the cow".[57] The cow as mother figure in Punjabi thought represents an indigenous ideal of womanhood: virtuous, domesticated, amenable, productive. Constitutive of a maternal image in the culture is the mother who produces children as the cow that produces calves. At times the cow is identified with a virgin: "gau dan" – the gift

---

[55] For the following observations on the ritual importance of the cow, I am indebted to Hershman, "Virgin and Mother", pp. 269–92. Although this work is based on a study carried out in the 1970s, there is no evidence to show the situation was any different in the nineteenth century. Occasionally, I have supplemented Hershman's findings with other contemporary sources.

[56] Purser, *Revised Settlement of the Jullundur District*, p. xxxiii.

[57] Hershman, "Virgin and Mother", p. 281.

of a cow – is undertaken at the same time as "kanya dan" – the gift of a virgin in marriage. Both are garlanded, anointed in red on the forehead, and clothed in red garments on ritual occasions.

The identity between human beings and the cow extends into worship: a cow was hardly perceived as different from a holy figure. In the month of Kattak, men and women went off to worship cows, garlanding their horns with flowers. Each cow was then fed with kneaded flour balls, her feet dusted, and obeisance paid to her with prayers.[58] On the occasion of gau gras – "performed daily in some households and generally on ritual occasions by others" – the first portion of pure untouched food is given to the cow, and at the same time its feet reverently touched.[59] If a woman is pregnant during an eclipse, her clothing and the knotting of her undergarments are loosened to prevent harm to the child by constriction; similarly, any rope tethering a pregnant cow had to be loosened at the time of an eclipse. The placenta of a human body and a calf are both buried in the belief that they are otherwise susceptible to harm. The most striking substitution of human beings by a cow is in the practice of sorcery. In rites of sorcery, killing a human child or a cow produces the same end result: the spirit is captured in the womb of the barren sorceress, enabling her to conceive a child.

For the purpose at hand, the most crucial aspect of the cow is its capacity to act as a channel of purification. While the organic eruptions of human beings – faeces, urine, saliva, and breast milk – are highly impure and polluting, the exudations of a cow are not only pure in themselves but also have the power to purify impurer elements.[60] The cow, in fact, is seen to perform a role akin to Dumont's "specialists in impurity" – the low-caste individuals who, by obliterating all that is unclean and defiled, keep the

---

[58] Rose, *A Glossary of the Tribes and Castes of the Punjab*, vol. I, p. 139.
[59] Hershman, "Virgin and Mother", pp. 283–4.
[60] For an explicit Sikh statement on this, see Giani Gian Singh, *Pustak Khalsa Dharam Patit Pavan Bhag*, p. 20.

high castes in their state of ritual purity.⁶¹ The cow, moreover, is fundamentally superior to the human because of its intrinsic purity, whereas human carriers of impurity remain permanently impure. Empowered thus to invert impurity, the cow mediates the division between the pure and impure. For the Kuka Sikhs, who are much more preoccupied than their fellow Punjabis with the boundaries of the ritually clean and unclean, the importance of the cow can hardly be exaggerated, signalling as she does the most fundamental ideas in the Kuka universe concerning the sacred and the profane, the holy and the unholy.⁶²

For an English administrator brought up in an altogether different cosmogony, the cow was simply an animal to be slaughtered for its meat.⁶³ Once British authority felt secure in the Punjab, it made cow slaughter legal. In Amritsar, the sacred city of the Sikhs, where once the ever-sensitive Henry Lawrence had forbidden cow slaughter, butcher shops were in 1849 given the go-ahead.

Administrative restrictions on the sale of beef within cities were hard to maintain and more often honoured in the breach. Cases of butchers apprehended for selling beef within city limits were

---

⁶¹ Dumont, *Homo Hierarchicus*, pp. 85–7.

⁶² These themes are well illustrated by the treatment meted out among the Sikhs to a person found guilty of killing a cow: he was immediately ostracised and to be admitted back had to undergo prolonged penance. To begin with, he had to visit a major Sikh shrine at Amritsar, Tarn Taran, or Patiala, where he had to bathe and thoroughly cleanse his clothes in the holy tank. Thereafter, he had to sleep on the surface of the earth for eleven days, eat a frugal meal once a day, and repent of his heinous crime. Thereafter he could present himself before the local community and beg their forgiveness. If forgiven, he had to provide food as further penance to community members and holy men. Only upon the completion of these prescribed steps could a Sikh regain his purity and be readmitted to the community. See Giani Gian Singh, *Pustak Khalsa Dharam Patit Pavan Bhag*, pp. 132–3.

⁶³ The oft-reiterated nationalist position that British authorities introduced cow slaughter to divide Hindu and Muslim populations is simplistic. For the nationalist argument, see the works listed in fn. 3 above.

not unknown.[64] A district official in Amritsar candidly admitted that "though there does not appear to have been any systematic violation of rules, it is certain that beef has been brought openly and carelessly into the city to the disgust of the Hindoo community."[65] In the eyes of the civic population, butchers violating rules were too often let off without severe penalties by the colonial authorities. A Sikh zealot, Deva Singh, a disciple of the famous Bhai Bir Singh, shocked everyone when in April 1871 he produced a beef bone before the holy book within the Golden Temple. He claimed he had found the bone within the precincts of the temple. This well-planned publicity stunt visibly angered large sections of the Hindu and Sikh populations in the city, who started a vociferous campaign against the sale of beef in the city and demanded a complete ban on cow slaughter in Amritsar. The circulation of a rumour that the administration was thinking of allowing a butcher's shop in front of the Golden Temple further angered the protesters.[66] During the months of April and May, several minor riots involving Sikh–Hindu groups and Muslims took place in Amritsar. Barely a month later, when the administration appeared to be completely insensitive to public feelings, the Kukas struck against the butchers at Amritsar, killing four. The subsequent violence against the butchers at Raikot and the march on Malerkotla were part of the same cycle of events.

British incomprehension, together with rigid policies, bred moral repulsion among the Kuka Sikhs: the British Raj was clearly a mleccha Raj. The frequent use of the highly loaded word mleccha among the Kukas for the English rulers illuminates Kuka mentalities and their deep-seated contempt for the rulers. Linguistic categories encode collectively held cultural principles

[64] For several instances, see Nahar Singh, *Itihas*, pp. 119–20.
[65] Home Judicial Proceedings, 29 July 1871, (A) 45–61, National Archives of India, New Delhi. Many British officials used the term Hindu comprehensively and included Sikhs within it.
[66] Nahar Singh, *Itihas*, p. 123.

and beliefs. Labelling is a kind of dialogue with social reality, the imposition of taxonomic order fusing diverse human experiences into comprehensible categories. By naming the English as mleccha the Kukas were following the ancient and universal convention of separating "us" from "them". Over the last two millennia, sections of Indian society have employed the term mleccha for barbarians of foreign origin who spoke an alien language, did not perform the prescribed sacred rites, were unaware of what was impure in food and drink, breached all rules of ritual purity, and were beyond the pale of civilisation.[67] Even to be in contact with such barbarians was potentially polluting. Hindu legal treatises prohibited such contact and outlined dire punishment for violations alongside special rites to overcome loss of purity. In the early-medieval period, high-caste orthodox Hindus had deployed the concept of mleccha to designate beef-eating and casteless Muslims who swept across North India; in fact one learned modern commentator specifies that the word mleccha is used by Sikhs for individuals who consume beef, inveigh against the Vedas, and are devoid of noble character.[68] Now the Kukas were applying it to British adversaries who, in less than a generation, had turned their familiar world upside down.

A universe created and ordered by God needed to be defended and decontaminated by men of God before the unholy mlecchas smashed its coherence, classifications, and what appeared to them as eternal. To this end the Kukas created their own symbolic universe: they refused travel by trains (a British innovation) and shunned the newly introduced postal facilities. Devout Kukas exhibited their abhorrence for English textiles by wearing garments

---

[67] Thapar, "The Image of the Barbarian in Early India", pp. 408–36, a comprehensive essay on the evolution of the ideology of mleccha, the nuances and subtle distinctions in its usage, and its cultural implications for Indian history, particularly when the term was used for indigenous populations.

[68] Kahn Singh Nabha, a model of contemporary Sikh learning, notes this in his well-known encyclopaedia of Sikh thought: see Nabha, *Gursabad Ratankaar Mahan Kos*, p. 957.

made of Indian fabrics. They stayed clear of the British judicial system, English schools, and sometimes even government jobs. As members of a millenarian community headed by a prophetic figure, they tended to act promptly against those who violated their symbolic order. The centrality of the cow in this symbolic universe made butchers a prime target; murdering them was perceived as bestowing great religious merit. Ram Singh personally instructed his followers to destroy those who killed cows and is reported to have stated: "If my followers were true to their religion, instead of fighting among themselves they would purify the land from the slaughter of cows, and make some arrangement to stop the work of butchers."[69] His adherents at Amritsar and Raikot who murdered and then marched to Malerkotla were following religion in translating the word of their master into action. Kurrain Singh, when interrogated by British officials on why he marched against Malerkotla, replied: "I did this because God told me to do so."[70] Such statements were nonsensical fanaticism in the eyes of his captors, who dismissed them contemptuously. Nationalist historiography, unsure of how to fit such pronouncements into what it construed as an anti-imperialist struggle, saw it as obfuscating and ignored it, not recognising that it was far from eccentric for a Kuka to declare that there was – to modify *Hamlet* – a divinity that shapes our ends and special providence in the fall of a cow.

The Defenders

Millenarian movements the world over have attracted a disproportionate following from the ranks of the dispossessed, the

---

[69] Memorandum by Lieutenant Colonel G. McAndrew, Deputy Inspector General of Police, Ambalah Circle, 20 November 1871, in Nahar Singh, *KS*, vol. I, p. 152. Ram Singh expressed similar views in a letter reproduced in Ganda Singh, *Vithia*, letter no. 14, p. 245.

[70] "Copy of Correspondence, or Extracts from Correspondence, relating to Kooka Outbreak", *Parliamentary Papers*, vol. 45, 1872, p. 46.

underprivileged, and the poor. This has led to a conviction that economic disaffection and millenarian expectations in certain cultural traditions go hand in hand.[71] To what extent does the Kuka movement fulfil this axiom? It is hard to estimate how far the Kukas were a classical millenarian community pressed by serious socio-economic dislocation. Social expectations are highly variable, subjective, and complex. There is no reliable yardstick to measure unbearable levels of deprivation fuelling violent rebellion. In the first two decades following the British annexation of the Punjab, during which the Kuka movement took shape, central Punjab was economically fairly prosperous by north Indian standards: it was a major reason for the Sikhs of central Punjab staying largely aloof from the 1857 uprising. Dolores Domin, in her extensive examination of the agrarian situation of these years, has shown how in 1855 the Punjab peasantry was the least taxed in British India. In her estimate the per-head incidence of land revenue in the Punjab was Rs 1.34, while in Bombay it was Rs 1.97, in the North Western Provinces Rs 1.65, and in Madras Rs 1.50.[72] This moderate land tax promised higher living standards to Jat-Sikh owner-cultivators. Moreover, British law gave them legal titles to their possessions, making land a highly prized commodity. In the Punjab, the functionaries of the Raj sought "to greatly improve agriculture by providing the means to extensive irrigation systems and internal communication . . . care was taken in the Punjab to avoid the breakdown of the land revenue system as an invariable concomitant to early British land settlements and to promote agriculture by gradually realising productive forces from feudal chains."[73] The theory that once highlighted the deteriorating conditions of the Indian people under colonial rule, and the arguments of nationalist-

---

[71] For example, see Lanterani, *The Religions of the Oppressed;* Hobsbawm, *Primitive Rebels;* Worsley, *The Trumpet Shall Sound.*

[72] Domin, *India in 1857–59*, p. 63.

[73] Ibid., p. 224.

marxist historiography concerning colonial expropriations of peasant property, cannot easily be applied to early-colonial Punjab, especially not to the Sikh peasantry, who, in the central districts of the province, did fairly well for themselves from the commercialisation of agriculture.

Even the Sikh soldiers – a major discontented stratum – who had been demobilised from the armies of the Lahore state on annexation, must have been greatly gratified when recruitment rules were changed in 1857 and they were re-enlisted in large numbers to fight for the British. According to one careful estimate, before the 1857 uprising the Sikh proportion of the Punjab forces was 10 per cent; during the course of the uprising it rose to a staggering 28 per cent.[74] When, after the Revolt, there were apprehensions within official circles about the large number of Sikhs in the army, they were occasionally retrenched from a regiment, only to be re-enlisted soon after to a new force to fight another colonial war. After 1858 over half the Indian segment of the British army came from the Punjab, and among Punjabi recruits Sikhs were proportionately the largest number. Thus, by the 1860s they had once again gained access to a traditional opportunity structure that enabled peasant soldiers to periodically remit funds to rural households. The growth in Punjab's population between 1850 and 1870 – a factor potentially capable of undermining social stability by raising the pressure on land, fragmenting peasant holdings, and increasing rents – was accommodated by the phenomenal expansion in land under cultivation, rising productivity, better marketing facilities due to a rapid expansion in communications, and an increase in the value of agricultural commodities.[75] From 1850 to 1890, land brought under cultivation in twenty major districts of the

[74] Ibid., p. 212.

[75] On the "boom" in Punjab's rural economy in the second half of the nineteenth century, see Kessinger, *Vilyatpur 1848–1968*; and Mishra, "Commercialization, Peasant Differentiation", pp. 3–51.

Punjab, including the area of Kuka influence, expanded by 28 per cent – a dramatic increase, considering the already high ratio of arable land.[76] Admittedly, the gradual transformation in Punjab's agrarian economy benefited proprietary peasants, but through the patron–client network some of the advantages must have seeped into other sectors of the rural population, particularly towards those who had a customary share in agricultural production through the dyadic jajmani system. Indeed, van den Dungen has shown how low castes like the Malis, Labanas, and Kalals improved their position and enlarged their resources under *pax Britannica*. He also notes that there were members of the ritually low Tarkhan caste, traditionally carpenters, who, contrary to their hereditary calling, engaged in agriculture and occasionally even came to own an entire village.[77] As pointed out earlier, many of Bhai Ram Singh's disciples were Tarkhans by caste. Their low ritual status does not necessarily imply they were poor.

It will be useful here to look briefly at some of the agrarian indices for the Ludhiana district, a Kuka stronghold.[78] This was one of the smallest districts of the province, its total area under 644,105 acres. By 1880 an additional 62,506 acres had been brought under cultivation, an increase in cultivation of approximately 10 per cent. On an average this amounted to 2000 acres per year over three decades. Since a standard village in central Punjab was 900 acres, new land brought under cultivation was the equivalent of two villages. In the same period, there was an increase in area under artificial irrigation, new wells were dug all over the province, and communications improved. The construction of a railway line through the district, from the south-east to the north, was a tremendous boon for agricultural marketing, linking Ludhiana not only to the grain markets of

---

[76] Richards, Hagen, and Haynes, "Changing Land Use", pp. 699–732.

[77] van den Dungen, "Change in Status", pp. 55–93.

[78] Details in Davidson, *Report on the Revised Settlement of the District of Ludhiana*; and Walker, *Settlement Report*.

India but to those of England too. Population density in the district rose from 383 per sq. mile in 1855 to 450 in 1881. These steady changes in the region's agrarian economy enabled peasant commodity producers in the district to cope well with the rise in population. During the famine of 1860–1 the rural population was not haunted by the spectre of starvation. In fact, the more substantial peasant households, according to the local administration, greatly profited by selling their grain stockpiles at very high prices. Crops did not fail completely, and the greatest loss sustained by the peasantry was lost cattle. The brunt of the famine was faced by the urban poor, particularly artisans and labourers. Rural labour mostly fared somewhat better because of patron–client relationships. Overall, the conditions cannot have been very bad, for people migrated to the district from the so-called Bangar country, i.e. south-east Punjab, covering the districts of Rohtak and Hissar. According to district officers, the impact of the second famine in 1869–70 was even milder. Although its consequences were again acutely felt by the urban poor, the rural population, particularly in the west, where most of the Sikh peasantry of the district lived, profited from the misfortunes of others and the "advantages to them as a whole far outweighed the evils."[79]

Thus, in the mid 1860s, on the eve of the Kuka march to Malerkotla, there is no substantial evidence indicating any serious economic dislocation suffered by this millenarian community. The rural poor were no poorer than before. Recent economic literature gives us enough reason to believe they had a rising standard of living, at least in the central districts of the Punjab. During 1868–9 when parts of the Punjab, particularly the south-west, faced famine conditions, the administration, full of confidence, noted that no special relief measures were needed for the peasantry in the districts of Ludhiana, Ambala,

---

[79] Walker, *Settlement Report*, p. 124.

Amritsar, and Hoshyarpur. Only in parts of Ferozepore was some special relief instituted.[80] In this sense the Kuka Sikhs were not an underprivileged stratum, and as such do not fit the typology of millenarian movements; their motivations must therefore be located outside the purely economic realm – in the realm of *Homo religiosus*. While this notion may have sounded unusual a decade ago, when the literature dealing with millenarian protest movements repeatedly linked difficult economic circumstances with rites of religious violence, it is not so singular today.

Anand A. Yang, who has studied an 1890s religious riot in a north Indian town with much care – a riot specifically concerned with cow protection and its related sacred space – notes no economic hardships among its participants or leaders. They do not conform to the image of the dispossessed so commonly written about. Rather, they include an entire body of the local Hindu population, "not just Hindus of certain economic and social status."[81] One major difference between the cow-protection movements and riots in the rest of north India on the one hand, and the Kukas on the other, was that while the former were able to bind the rural and urban population to a common platform, at least for a time, the Kukas never achieved this.[82] In its support base the Kuka movement was primarily rural, agrarian, and pluralist. Firmly rooted among the Sikh peasantry of central Punjab, it never succeeded in appealing to the urban sector of the Sikh panth. This is hardly surprising, since the great majority

---

[80] "Memorandum on the Famine in the Panjab, during 1868–69", *Punjab Administration Report: 1868–69*, Lahore, 1869, pp. 1–10.

[81] Yang, "Sacred Symbol and Sacred Space in Rural India", pp. 594. N.Z. Davis, in "The Rites of Violence: Religious Riot in Sixteenth Century France", pp. 51–99, in what is now regarded a classic essay, advances a similar argument about the nature of religious violence.

[82] On urban and rural linkages for the protection of the cow, see Freitag, "Sacred Symbols as Mobilizing Ideology", pp. 597–625. Curiously enough, this fascinating paper, influenced by a diffusionist model, views peasants as passive receptacles of urban ideology, waiting for ideas to fill them.

of the Sikhs lived in rural tracts. By looking at the biographical sketches of 140 Kuka Sikhs I can roughly plot their territorial spread in the Punjab (see Table I).

More than half their numbers came from Malwa, followed by a large segment from the neighbouring Doaba.[83] They also found some representation in the Majha, but their strength certainly lay within the Malwa belt.[84] The pattern of Kuka distribution is fairly understandable; it corresponded to a set of concentric circles: at the centre was Bhaini, the residence of the Kuka leader in Ludhiana, and from this source, where it was most intense, the movement radiated outwards, becoming more diffuse within the outer arcs. This spread coincided approximately with the boundaries of the Sikh faith in the Punjab. A peasant-based movement always finds it hard to overcome its inevitable concomitant – peasant

Table 1: Distribution of Sample Kuka Population in the Punjab

Ludhiana	26	Karnal	1
Ferozepore	11	Jullunder	7
Patiala state	41	Hoshyarpur	7
Malerkotla state	8	Lahore	2
Nabha state	12	Gurdaspur	3
Jind state	4	Sialkot	7
Ambala	4	Amritsar	7

Sources: Inspector General of Police, to Secretary to Government of Punjab, 20 January 1868, Nahar Kuka Sect, in Nahar Singh, *KS*, vol. I, pp. 79–81; Chiefs of the Kuka Sect, in Nahar Singh, *KS*, vol. I, pp. 156–63; Names and Place of Residence for 60 Kukas killed in the march to Malerkotla including the 49 blown away from guns by order of L. Cowan, listed in Nahar Singh, *Itihas*, pp. 203–4; and Proceedings in Case of Sixteen Men tried at Malerkotla on 18 January, in Nahar Singh, *KS*, vol. I, p. 40. Persons common to these lists have been taken into account.

[83] For the Malwa region, see fn. 12. The Doaba region lies between the Sutlej and Beas rivers.

[84] The Majha is the area of central Punjab lying between the Beas and Ravi rivers.

localism – and its associated ecological, ethnic, and cultural differences. The Kuka movement was no exception.

In the countryside the social base of the Kukas was not uniform, but, as we will see, it gradually broadened. In 1867 three deputy superintendents of police from Ludhiana, Amritsar, and Ambala reported that the Kukas had gained adherents among members of ritually low castes like the Tarkhans, Mazhabis, Labanas, and Kalals.[85] Largely on the basis of these reports, the inspector general of police circulated a memorandum confirming the assessment of his subordinates.[86] His perspective has tended to colour most subsequent interpretations of the Kuka following. But the case for this belief does not appear to be as clear-cut as is often made out, even in official sources. T. Gordon Walker, the second settlement officer of the Ludhiana district, who must have had ample first-hand knowledge of the Kuka Sikhs (Bhaini, their base, was in his district), disputed general impressions about the Kuka following: "it is very doubtful whether it can be said that even the majority of Kukas are drawn from the lowest classes, for the sect has made much more progress among the Jat Sikhs than any returns would show."[87] In 1867, during a pilgrimage to Amritsar, Ram Singh was attended by twenty-two leading Kukas, among whom fourteen were Jats and five were like him of Tarkhan background.[88] Roughly similar figures are repeated in a police report compiled four years later. Of the 50 Kukas under examination, 28 were Jats, 7 were Tarkhans, 10 belonged to ten different castes, while the caste of 3 was not specified.[89] The Jats,

---

[85] T.H. Thornton, Secretary to Government Punjab, to J.W.S. Wyllie, Officiating Secretary to Government of India, Foreign Department, nos 154–7, 2 February 1867, in Nahar Singh, *KS*, vol. I, p. 30.

[86] Ibid., p. 37.

[87] Walker, *Settlement Report*, p. 57.

[88] From Inspector General of Police, Punjab, to Secretary to Government, Punjab, 20 January 1868, in Nahar Singh, *KS*, vol. I, pp. 79–81.

[89] "Chiefs of the Kuka Sect", in Nahar Singh, *KS*, vol. I, pp. 156–63. Eight persons were common between this and the report cited above.

the largest numerical group within the Sikh panth, were primarily peasant proprietors famed for their skills in agriculture and their martial prowess: they continued to be the leading constituent among the Kuka Sikhs. But it is hard to be precise about their economic background or the nature of their landholdings. J.W. Macnabb, an officiating commissioner of the Ambala division, provides us with an important clue to the nature of the Kuka movement:

> at the time of the reports mentioned [i.e. earlier official reports] none of the Sardars, except Mangal Singh of Bishanpura in Patiala, was connected with the movement. Now many men of position are joining the sect. For instance, the Sardars of Khamanoh in Patiala, not far from Bhaini; also Gurdut Singh of Naiwalah, in Patiala Sardar Bir Singh of Dialgurh; Sardar Gursaran Singh and his three nephews of Mustafabad; (this Sardar, who is deeply in debt himself, told me he was a Kuka) Hira Singh, Jagirdar of Sadhowara, who went as commandant with 100 men to form the Kuka regiment in Jammu; all other small Jagirdars of Sadhowara; Beda Singh cousin of the Honorary Magistrate of Sohanah, and a connection of the above Dialgarh Sardar; Jaimal Singh and Dalip Singh of the Kalsia state.[90]

> Few of these are really big men, but they are of quite a different class from the carpenters and blacksmiths and low-caste Sikhs who first joined the movement.

Other sources also point in a similar direction. Well-dressed men with respectable social credentials were widely noticed among the Kukas. By the late 1860s the Kukas had a wide support base transcending clear-cut class distinctions. Their actual numbers will perhaps always stay a mystery, for a "Kuka would

[90] Memorandum on Ram Singh and the Kukas by J.W. Macnabb, late Officiating Commissioner, Ambala Division, 4 November 1871, in Nahar Singh, *KS*, vol. I, pp. 144–5.

call himself a Sikh unless he were well known to be a Kuka."[91] In early government reports official estimates fluctuated between 40,000 and 60,000.[92] By the late 1860s one estimate was as high as 150,000 but a more conservative figure stood at 50,000.[93] Fauja Singh, who did extensive research on the Kukas, calculated in the early 1870s that their number was no less than 300,000 or 400,000.[94] Unfortunately, he does not specify the source of his figure; possibly the numbers are based on histories written by Kukas in the twentieth century. But his figures may be accurate since, early in the year 1867, at the Holi festival in Anandpur, Ram Singh gained several hundred disciples in two days, and later in the year, on a visit to Amritsar on the occasion of the Diwali festival, again admitted 2000 new converts to the Kuka fraternity within a few days.[95] At this staggering pace of attracting adherents a Kuka following in excess of 200,000 seems an underestimate. Considering the stringent opposition to the Kukas, it is worth examining the sources of Kuka resolve, their mobilisation strategy, and factors responsible for their feeling of invincibility against the superior forces of the Raj.

A principal reason for the Kuka conviction in their righteousness was Bhai Ram Singh's ability to establish the legitimacy of his cause among his followers. I have already pointed out his place within the Bhai tradition and the close association between Sikh

---

[91] Walker, *Settlement Report*, p. 57.

[92] From T.H. Thornton, Secretary to Government, Punjab, to J.W.S. Wyllie, Officiating Secretary to the Government of India, Foreign Department, nos 154–7, 2 February 1867, in Nahar Singh, *KS*, vol. I, pp. 36–7.

[93] Memorandum by Lieutenant Colonel G. McAndrew, Deputy Inspector General of Police, Ambala, 20 November 1871, in Nahar Singh, *KS*, vol. I, p. 154.

[94] Bajwa, *Kuka Movement*, p. 36.

[95] T.D. Forsyth, Commissioner, Jullundur Division, to T.H. Thornton, Secretary to Government, Punjab, 21 March 1867; and Inspector General of Police, Punjab, to Secretary to Government Punjab, 20 January 1868, in Nahar Singh, *KS*, vol. 1, pp. 51 and 76.

thought and Kuka principles. Let us now look at some additional features of the movement. Like past emperors, the Bhai rode in regal splendour on fine horses and in his frequent sojourns in the countryside was accompanied by an entourage on horse and foot. These accoutrements of royalty will have helped enhance his status and attract fresh disciples.[96] Moreover, the imperial imagery must have evoked among the Sikh peasantry associations with the tenth Sikh Guru, Gobind Singh, who in the Sikh tradition is seen to have followed a similar style. In line with Mughal administrative precedents, Ram Singh carved up the Punjab into territorial zones and appointed deputies in these divisions. Bestowing titles and offices was normally the prerogative of monarchs or sovereign powers, a practice he emulated. In public displays of his authority he accepted homage from leading aristocrats, merchants, and rich peasants. At the same time, he feted and rewarded the poor. To bolster his legitimacy, he followed well-established imperial customs by sending emissaries to the rulers of Kashmir and Nepal, exchanging gifts with them, and seeking their assistance in enlisting armed troops. In the years before he was expelled from the Punjab, Bhai Ram Singh undertook extensive pilgrimages to Sikh holy places at Amritsar, Anandpur, Dera Baba Nanak, and Muktsar. By visiting them on the occasion of heavily attended religious and seasonal cattle fairs, such as those at Baisakhi and Diwali, he made himself highly visible and recruited new disciples amongst the attending peasantry. His large following attests to the success of a mobilising strategy which activated old sacred and market networks. Taking his cue from Sikh sacred places, he named sites at Bhaini after well-known symbolic centres at

---

[96] An envious British official angrily remarked: "he [Ram Singh] visits you attended by half a dozen horsemen; he is followed by scores of men on foot; he comes into your room surrounded by a court like a prince. He and his people are dressed in exquisitely fine clothes": Memorandum by Lieutenant Colonel G. McAndrew, Deputy Inspector General of Police, Ambalah Circle, 20 November 1871, in Nahar Singh, *KS*, vol. I, p. 154.

Amritsar like the Akal Bunga, hoping thereby to replicate the sacredness and high ritual standing of these places.

As part of this quest for legitimacy, Kukas made use of the old Sikh practice of inventing prophecies. They circulated a version of the *Sau Sakhian*, an apocryphal anthology in wide circulation in the nineteenth century. It contained prophetic announcements concerning the forthcoming reign of one Ram Singh, a carpenter – obviously Bhai Ram Singh, leader of the Kuka Sikhs.[97] In relating to the Sikh belief system, the Kukas selectively highlighted the twin concepts of hukam and bhana – the two theological building blocks of Sikh martyrs.[98]

The doctrine of hukam is old and dates back to the time of the first Sikh master, Guru Nanak. He expounded on its meaning in his well-known composition, the *Japji*, the most frequently read text among Sikhs. Hukam may be roughly translated as God's Order; nothing – birth, joy, sorrow, death – can happen outside it. This divine principle creates form, determines the destiny of man, and regulates the universe. Everyone has to submit to it. It is only the ignorant who overlook this principle and thus suffer the unending cycle of birth, life, and death. Those who comprehend God's Order or hukam may also understand the nature of God and in the process attain liberation.[99] The influence of this key principle on the Kuka Sikhs is evident from the following verses in the Guru Granth Sahib: "[of itself, i.e. apart from the Hukam] the soul does not die and it neither sinks nor crosses over. He

---

[97] For an English translation of the *Sau Sakhian* anthology used by the Kukas, see Sardar Attar Singh (of Bhadour), *Sakhee Book*. He believes the circulation of the prophecies was the only reason for the Kuka "disturbances".

[98] For Kuka usage of these concepts, see Bhai Ram Singh's correspondence, reproduced in Ganda Singh, *Vithia*, pp. 212–314, and statements of official witnesses in L.H. Griffin, Secretary to Government, Punjab, to Secretary to Government of India, 20 February 1872, in Nahar Singh, *KS*, vol. II, p. 189.

[99] McLeod, *Guru Nanak and the Sikh Religion*, pp. 199–203. Also see Sahib Singh, *Sri Guru Granth Sahib Darpan*, vol. I, pp. 50–1, for an exposition on the doctrine of hukam.

who has been active [in creation] is still active. In accordance with the Hukam we are born and we die. Ahead and behind the Hukam pervades all."[100] The human soul is thus indestructible. Even birth and death are determined by God, and when Kukas rushed into the principality of Malerkotla many believed their life and actions were being regulated by God or his hukam. Kuka Sikhs, by strictly adhering to the hukam, were simply living in line with Divine Will. In seeking the destruction of the impure, they were following well-established Sikh metaphysical principles and were merely the instruments of God, enacting his Divine play. The Kukas compared the ever-changing human situation to a play, reminiscent of similar metaphors often used by the Sikh Gurus in their writings to suggest the impermanence of the world.

Aiding Kukas in their trajectory of invincibility were well-established collective rituals of solidarity: singing, chanting, and dancing (especially after dark). British informants appear to have misrepresented the nature of these collective rituals. They reported the Kukas as collecting for nightly drills, possibly in preparation for an insurrection. The purpose of these noctural assemblies was in fact to meditate and chant sacred verses. In particular, they were recommended by their leader to recite *Chandi di Var*, an epic composition attributed to Guru Gobind Singh describing the war between the goddess Chandi and demons. In this metaphoric narrative on the struggle between gods and demons, a symbolic transference identifies the Kukas with the former and the mlecchas with unholy demons.

The continuous chanting, music, dance, and trance must have created all kinds of striking images and an ecstatic experience among the participants. As a result of this theatre of sound and sight some people were said to attain the state of mastana, i.e.

---

[100] Gauri 2, *Guru Granth Sahib*, p. 151; W.H. McLeod's translation in ibid., p. 201.

trance. But two other characteristics distinguished a mastana: a greater state of liminality than that of other Kukas, and a transformation into a figure of considerable awe and inspiration for the rest of the brotherhood. It is significant that before the ill-fated march to Malerkotla, on the occasion of the Maghi festival an all-night ritual had been performed. There had been much chanting and dancing during the previous nights, and about a hundred Kukas were declared mastanas. It was many of these men, inspired by and convinced of their powers, who first marched to Malodh and then attacked the butcher quarters at Malerkotla.

With this background to Kuka beliefs, practices, and collective rituals, it is understandable why Bhai Ram Singh, even after being exiled to Burma (and fully aware that his chief disciples had been imprisoned and that the colonial state was in no mood to tolerate his teachings), continued to believe in the righteousness and legitimacy of his cause. This belief in righteousness could only have been deeply shared by those who undertook the march to Malerkotla, for they were not deterred by the knowledge that they were ill equipped to deal with the troops of the Malerkotla principality. Conscious of the strength of their adversaries, they were fortified by a conviction of their moral superiority, the justness of their cause, the efficacy of their beliefs and rituals, and the urge to defend their holy order.

Conclusion

Interpretations of the Kuka movement tend to swing between two extremes: one side dismisses them as an incoherent band – what T. Gordon Walker, the British settlement officer in Ludhiana district described as the "insane proceedings of a small body of fanatics".[101] The other extreme eulogises them for their anti-

---

[101] Walker, *Settlement Report*, p. 36.

imperialist fervour. I have tried here to steer clear of these insufficiently informed judgements and sought to show that there was coherence in both the thinking and actions of the Kuka Sikhs. If their logic was different from ours, it does not mean they were illogical. Within the prevailing belief system their strategies and millenarian visions were plausible. In a society where the sacred was always intervening in human affairs, their deployment of miracles, symbols, prophecies, and rituals was perfectly reasonable and by the standards of their culture capable of yielding results. There was nothing psychopathological in their behaviour, as many colonial officers insisted. Their symbolic and ideological universe was closely related to Sikh cosmology and Indic cultural assumptions. Without their indigenous conceptions of holiness, the Sikh institution of the Bhais, the binary opposition between pure and impure, and the widespread practice among Sikhs of circulating prophecies, it is hard to imagine the emergence and consolidation of the Kuka movement. The Kuka Sikhs did not invent a novel worldview *de novo*; they had a long history behind them which made them oppose the imposition of a new cultural code imported by the "unholy English". This may make them heroes for some and frenzied obscurantists for others; collectively they represented one paradigm of a counter-colonial discourse in nineteenth-century north India.

This analysis of Kuka insurgents and their symbolic universe also suggests some larger conclusions on the nature of empowerment and resistance in colonial India. Over the past several years historians interested in mapping the tropes of indigenous resistance have had recourse to two distinct strategies. The initial push has been towards probing modes of resistance by looking at tribal uprisings, grain riots, peasant rebellions, and other such confrontational popular movements.[102] More recently, influenced

---

[102] For numerous examples of this genre, see Guha, *Subaltern Studies I*, and idem, *Subaltern Studies II*.

by the writings of Foucault, some scholars have begun to argue that if our goal is to recover the history of resistance it is imperative to look at everyday forms of struggle and humbler forms of defiance rather than study spectacular riots and short-lived violent upheavals which are in any case rare in South Asian history.[103] Contrary to these highly polarised positions, I argue that if our objective is the history of dissent and counter-hegemonic ideologies, it is futile to pose the problem by simply dichotomising lived experience into dramatic episodes of confrontation and quotidian modes of defiance. Therefore this reappraisal of Kuka experience in the second half of the nineteenth century points towards the simultaneous existence of insurrection and everyday forms of struggle. In the spring of 1872, when the Kuka crowd undertook a collective march from the village of Bhaini to the Muslim principality of Malerkotla and en route began to turn things upside down, we see in their actions evidence of what would be classified as dramatic assertion and resistance. However, when Kukas in their day-to-day life carved out their own administrative apparatus, refused to travel by British trains, did not enrol their children in Western schools, rejected European clothing, and constructed their own semiotic universe, we can read in their collective behaviour and rituals what James Scott would call everyday forms of resistance.[104] Any project that seeks to write a holistic social history of resistance in South Asia needs to incorporate both the dramatic and the quotidian, without idealising either.

---

[103] For this Foucault-inflected line of inquiry, see O'Hanlon, "Recovering the Subject", pp. 213–15.
[104] See Scott, *Weapons of the Weak*.

2

Empire, Orientalism, and Native Informants
The Scholarly Endeavours of Sir Attar Singh Bhadour

Thought is a labyrinth.
Hugh Kenner

Beneath every history, another history.
Hilary Mantel

EDWARD SAID, IN his influential work *Orientalism*, passionately argued that the West has since ancient times, but particularly over modern imperialism, sought to subjugate the East through a powerful discourse made up of essentialised caricatures, negative images, and insidious categories. Collectively, this discourse under the cover of complex knowledge systems such as philology, travelogue, taxonomy, anthropology, and the study of world religions showed the West as all-prevailing and powerful and the East always ready for submission and subordination. Colonialism was thus not simply a matter of guns, frigates, and superior technology but also involved a complex network of texts, symbolic systems, and scholarly traditions.[1] While a great deal of what Said proposed was initially enthusiastically accepted within the academy, most scholarship has since

---

[1] Said, *Orientalism*.

shown its discomfort with the Saidian paradigm and suggested radical amendments and revisions, if not outright rejection. It is no longer tenable to view the relationship between West and East through simple binaries like powerful metropolitan knowledge and powerless vernacular cultures. The production of colonial knowledge was not simply a matter of what was advanced by knowledge practitioners in the West: indigenous intellectuals and antique traditions of knowledge actively, if not equally, shaped the imperial agenda. Thus, we no longer speak confidently of a hegemonic Western discourse.

Nicholas Dirks has documented how Colin Mackenzie, the first Surveyor General of India, initiated cartographic, ethnographic, and historical work greatly facilitated by his Indian collaborators.[2] Since Mackenzie (1754–1821) knew no Indian languages, he could not have done the monumental work that he did, and across a difficult physical and social terrain, without the assistance of native informants. Key among his indigenous collaborators was a man by the name of Kavelli Venkata Boria. A Brahman by caste, Boria knew four languages (Sanskrit, Tamil, Telugu, and Kanarese) and had an extensive social network across the Deccan. Dirks, being a historian, wants to tell us more about his talent and achievements but is helpless: the colonial archive contains only faint traces of Boria. We would like to know where he was educated; what turned him into a polyglot; what sorts of cultural registers he worked within; what sort of indigenous systems of knowledge he mastered; how he conceived of his collaboration with Mackenzie – was it purely an employment contract or something more? Since the information on these issues is so threadbare, Boria will live perpetually in the shadows. When it comes to Mackenzie, the colonial archive is of course overflowing with data. We have his lavish publications and survey reports; the gigantic ethnographic collection he assembled

---

[2] Dirks, "Colonial Histories and Native Informants", pp. 279–313.

is well preserved in the British Library; his life is the subject of a hallowed biography.³ With such information asymmetry embedded in our archives, the Scottish Enlightenment product Mackenzie looms large as master narrator. The best that Dirks can do is point us towards Boria, complicating the story of the colonial archive.

Dirks has not been alone in this revisionist pursuit. An increasing number of Indologists and historians have argued similarly: Rosane Rocher, C.A. Bayly, and Vasudha Dalmia, for instance, would like us to enlarge our biographies of pandits, maulvis, and munshis – the ensemble that so deeply and consistently contributed to the production of colonial knowledge.⁴ The canon of Orientalist historiography is else too statically stuck with the standard names – James Mill, Mountstuart Elphinstone, John Malcolm, Alexander Dow. An enlarged list would include names like Ali Ibrahim Khan, Bapu Deva Shastri, Radhakanta Tarkabagish, and Sir Attar Singh Bhadour – the last being the subject of this chapter.

But how does one go about matching one's historiographical aspirations with empirical realities? Is it possible for us to transcend the near-silence of the colonial archive? I do not want to sound too optimistic, particularly when it comes to the Punjab, for it was not the site of major colonial institutions like Fort William at Calcutta or the Sanskrit College at Benares. Yet, the tools of historical research promise a considerable yield. I hope to illustrate this possibility of historical recovery by looking at Attar Singh.

Attar Singh first comes to our attention within the imperial archives when he receives a brief mention from the German Indologist Ernest Trumpp – in the introductory essay to Trumpp's

³ Mackenzie, *Colonel Colin Mackenzie*. Also see Howes, *Illustrating India*.
⁴ Rocher, "British Orientalism in the Eighteenth Century", pp. 215–49; Dalmia, "Sanskrit Scholars and Pandits of the Old School", pp. 321–37; and Bayly, "Orientalists, Informants and Critics", pp. 97–127.

infamous translation of the *Guru Granth Sahib*. In narrating the biography of the ninth Guru of the Sikhs, Trumpp approvingly notes: "The Sakhis, which Sirdar Attar Singh, chief of Bhadour, who with an enlightened mind follows up the history and religion of his nation, has lately published, throw a very significant light on the wanderings of Tegh Bahadur . . ."[5] However, soon after this warm proclamation of Attar Singh's achievements, Trumpp resumes his imperious tone and henceforth Attar Singh appears in his text only in a series of footnotes. Some of these footnotes are worth reproducing as they are of considerable help in reconstructing the Attar Singh archive and his role as native informant. The first of Trumpp's footnotes states:

> Their title is: The Travels of Guru Tegh Bahadur and Guru Gobind Singh. Translated from the original Gurmukhi by Sirdar Attar Singh, Chief of Bhadour. January, 1876. Lahore, Indian Public Opinion Press. It would have been very useful if the translator had also added some critical apparatus about the probable time of the composition of these Sakhis. They cannot be very old, as the British territory thereabout is already mentioned.[6]

Despite his critical reservations, Trumpp is deeply intrigued by Attar Singh's scholarship. He again observes, as if talking to himself:

> We must remark here, that in these Sakhis no distinct line is drawn between the wanderings of Guru Teg-bahadur and those of Guru Govind Singh, so that it remains uncertain, where the first end and where the second commence. As I have not the original text at my disposal, I cannot say, if this is owing to some fault of the text or to some oversight of the translator.

[5] Trumpp, *The Adi Granth*, p. lxxxviii.
[6] Ibid.

This great defect seems at any rate not to have struck him, as he makes no remark about it. It is certain that the Sakhis from 51 refer to Guru Govind Singh, the fight at Mukt-sar having taken place under him. In Sakhi 56 it is also stated that the Guru was only thirty-five years old, which could only be said of Govind Singh.[7]

Having made some constructive suggestions concerning Attar Singh's translation, Trumpp again acknowledges his debt to the Sikh intellectual as he begins to record the importance of the rahit and manuals of code of conduct (rahit-namas) for the Sikhs. In a footnote, he again seeks corroboration from Attar Singh's writings:

Two of these Rahit-namas have lately been published in an English translation by Sirdar Attar Singh of Bhadour; but it is a pity that he has not given the Gurmukhi texts also. The translation is very free and gives only the sense generally, not verbally. Fortunately, I brought the original text of the Rahit-nama of Prahlad-rai with me, so that I am enabled, for the sake of accuracy, to quote it, where it may seem necessary. The title of Sirdar Attar Singh's publication is: The Rahit Nama of Pralad Rai, or the excellent conversation of Daswan Padsha, and Nand Lal's Rayhit Nama, or rules for the guidance of the Sikhs in religious matters. Lahore, printed at the Albert Press, 1876.[8]

While the Orientalist archive covering Attar Singh's scholarship can be said to begin with Trumpp, it continues to expand as other European and British authors take note of the Sikhs. In the early 1880s Max Macauliffe wrote a famous essay concerning Banda Bahadur. And almost at the very beginning of his text he says in a footnote:

[7] Ibid., p. lxxxix.
[8] Ibid., p. cxiii.

In the Pant [*sic*] Parkash, [we have] a Sikh work compiled by Ratan Singh to glorify the Sikh religion and clear it of the aspersions cast upon it by one Bute Shah. The work was presented to General Ochterlony. Sirdar Attar Singh, C.I.E., chief of Bhadaur, has favoured me with a MS. Copy. I am principally indebted to it for the following narrative as far as the death of Banda.[9]

Here Macauliffe is acknowledging another aspect of Attar Singh's scholarship and erudition. Among the learned, Attar Singh was famous for his private library. He possessed one of the largest collections of Gurmukhi, Persian, and Sanskrit manuscripts in the Punjab. It is hardly surprising that Macauliffe received a copy of Rattan Singh Bhangu's justly famous history of the Sikhs from Attar Singh. But what sort of other conversations took place between Attar Singh and Macauliffe? Although Macauliffe was to emerge as a major historian of the Sikhs, in the early 1880s his interest in Sikh history and texts was just beginning. In what way was his voice shaped by his long association with Attar Singh? Unfortunately, the existing historical record is of no help here; all we know is that Attar Singh's intellectual influence continued to expand. Increasingly, he becomes indispensable for all scholars who wanted to write anything of value concerning the Sikhs.

We next get to notice Attar Singh's presence in the writings of the Hungarian Orientalist Doctor G.W. Leitner. While Leitner is not a name often encountered in Punjab Studies, he was in many ways critical to the formation of modern Punjabi. As principal of Government College in Lahore, and the first registrar of Panjab University, he pushed hard for the recognition of north Indian vernaculars within the educational curriculum. When many in Lahore refused to have Punjabi language courses taught at the

---

[9] Macauliffe, "The Sikh Religion Under Banda", p. 155.

Oriental College, he turned to his close friend Attar Singh for help. Attar Singh was able to show detractors of Punjabi that the language had an ancient history in the province and possessed a vast literary canon. He demonstrated all this by producing books from his private library and Leitner duly published this extensive list in his report on the state of indigenous education in the Punjab.[10]

Approximately a decade after Leitner's influential work on indigenous education, a reference to Attar Singh's scholarship crops up in Lepel Griffin's first-ever English biography of Maharaja Ranjit Singh. Griffin was closely associated with the British colonial administration in the Punjab and in the early 1890s was asked by W.W. Hunter, on behalf of the prestigious Oxford imprint Clarendon Press, to write a biography of Ranjit Singh. Griffin was eminently suited, having earlier compiled such books as *The Punjab Chiefs* (1865), *The Law of Inheritance to Sikh Chiefships* (1869), and *The Rajas of the Punjab* (1870). It is highly likely that Attar Singh greatly assisted Griffin in the production of his detailed histories of royal lineages in the Punjab. Attar Singh had himself authored in Urdu a genealogical account of royal lineages in the Malwa region of the Punjab entitled *Tawarikh-i-Sidhu Bairaran, Khandan-i-Phul*. There is no certainty of their collaboration because it is more than evident that European Orientalists preferred to stay silent about their native sources of information, and Griffin was in many ways a part of this colonial convention. But in his biography of Ranjit Singh he records a very enlightening footnote: "A valued friend of mine, Sirdar Attar Singh of Bhadour, the head of one of the first Cis-Sutlej families, has translated and published an interesting collection of Sakhis, describing the wanderings and adventures

---

[10] "Appendix IV – List of 389 Books in the Gurmukhi Characters in the Possession of Sirdar Attar Singh of Bhadaur", in Leitner, *History of Indigenous Education in the Panjab*.

of Guru Tegh Bahadur and his son Guru Govind Singh."[11] So, yet again, as in the writings of Trumpp, Macauliffe, and Leitner, Attar Singh makes a brief appearance in a footnote. Griffin clearly deploys Attar Singh's findings in reconstructing the lives of Guru Tegh Bahadur and Guru Gobind Singh. It was uncommonly generous of him to publicly record his intellectual debt.

After Griffin the spoor goes cold. Though the master narrative of the European Orientalists is alive and kicking and in fact pretty much central in contemporary public culture, Attar Singh recedes into the shadows. This is unfortunate for any project seeking to understand how the modern Sikh archive was put together. We urgently need a thick description of Attar Singh's life and scholarly pursuits.

Sir Attar Singh Bhadour

Attar Singh was born to blue blood in 1833. His father, Sardar Kharak Singh, a well-known member of the Sikh landed gentry and a close relative of the Maharaja of Patiala, was head of the house of Bhadour.[12] Kharak Singh was keen that his son receive a first-class education. After an early education entrusted to distinguished private tutors at home, Attar Singh was dispatched to Benares where he trained in classical languages, philosophy, logic, and music. By his early twenties the young aristocrat had mastered five languages: Persian, Sanskrit, Urdu, Punjabi, and English. In many ways, Attar Singh is *the* great north Indian exemplar of what C.A. Bayly calls the "north Indian ecumene".[13]

---

[11] Griffin, *Ranjit Singh*, p. 48.

[12] The life history of Attar Singh is indebted to: Griffin, *Rajas of the Punjab*; Ghose, *The Modern History of the Indian Chiefs, Rajas, Zamindars*, pt II, pp. 471–5; Harbans Singh, *The Encyclopaedia of Sikhism*, pp. 216–18; and Oberoi, *The Construction of Religious Boundaries*, pp. 290–2.

[13] Bayly, *Empire and Information*, p. 368. For the following description of the Indian ecumene, I have particularly drawn from chapter 5 of the book, pp. 180–211.

Besides being a forum for public opinion and debate, this ecumene was a huge network for the circulation of languages – particularly Persian, Sanskrit, and Urdu; pre-colonial knowledge systems – in fields as diverse as rational learning, philosophy, rhetoric, astronomy, legal discourse, and mysticism; and personnel – landed gentry, city merchants, lawyers, judges, doctors and healers. "The guardians of the ecumene," Bayly says,

> represented the views of bazaar people and artisans when urban communities came under pressure. Their connections spread across religious, sectarian, and caste boundaries, though they never dissolved them. A common background in the Indo–Persian and, to a lesser extent Hindu classics, enlightened them. The theme of high-minded friendship animated the poets, scholars, and officials who conversed along these networks and set the tone for them. Though suffused with pride of country, the ecumene remained cosmopolitan, receiving information and ideas from central and west Asia as well as from a dimly defined Hindustan. In this sense, it was closer in spirit to the groupings of philosophers, urban notables and officials in the world of late antiquity – the Christian-Greek ecumene – than it was to Habermas's modern public.[14]

Drawing on the cosmopolitan tenor of the ecumene, Attar Singh, with unusual grace, charm, and wit established a large network of affiliates made up of both native elites and European scholars and administrators. Well-versed in music, philosophy, history, and the arts, he took an active interest in the province's public affairs. We get a glimpse into his passions and interests from a recent biographical sketch:

> A great man, Attar Singh, lived here [the city of Ludhiana] in the 19th century. His life forms an important chapter in

[14] Ibid., p. 182.

Ludhiana's history. He built a big residence for himself. The palace-like complex of buildings had a princely lodge, an audience hall for music and poetry, a prakash-kirtan room, guest-houses, servant quarters, guard rooms, stores, stables, cattle sheds, etc. It had a garden with fountains, lawns and foot-paths. It was called Bhadaur House. The most noteworthy part of this princely residence was its library. It had a rich collection of books. Historians have recorded it and researchers have benefited from it. This library could match Khuda Baksh Library of Patna. The fact that Bhadaur House existed in Ludhiana sounds unreal. The history of this late 19th century building would read like a chapter of a historical novel.[15]

Sardar Attar Singh excelled in historical research and was one of the first Punjabis to become an elected member of the Asiatic Society of Bengal in 1869, and later the Royal Asiatic Society, London.[16] His profound knowledge of the Sikh religion, together with his overall appreciation of Indian culture, his close contacts with many leading Punjabi figures, and his possession of the best-stocked private library in the province made him much sought after among the upper echelons of the provincial bureaucracy. His advice was often sought on religious, social, and political matters. For his part, Attar Singh readily sounded out the administration on potential flashpoints and prepared exhaustive reports on current affairs for submission to high officials. Such earnest loyalty won him several titles and sinecures from the colonial administration. In 1877, on the occasion of the Imperial Assemblage at Delhi under the auspices of Lord Lytton, he was conferred with the title *Mulaz-ul-ulama-o-ul-Fazal*. The title celebrated Attar

---

[15] Cheema, "Sir Attar Singh and His Bhadaur".

[16] The following few paragraphs concerning Attar Singh's biography, unless otherwise indicated, are from Oberoi, *The Construction of Religious Boundaries*, pp. 290–2. Additional information is based on sources listed in fn. 12.

Singh's learning in Persian and Urdu. Another imperial darbar in 1887, this time to mark Queen Victoria's jubilee celebrations, led to him receiving the title *Mahamahopadhyaya*, honouring his learning in Sanskrit and the Indian classics. The next year he was knighted and became Sir Attar Singh Bhadour.

Soon after the Lahore Singh Sabha was founded in 1879, Attar Singh became a member. He acted as a patron to both Gurmukh Singh and Ditt Singh, the two leading lights of the Lahore Sabha, and in fact helped Ditt Singh secure a job at the Oriental College. Jagjit Singh, in his history of the Singh Sabha movement, argues that without the financial assistance of Attar Singh the Khalsa Press, and newspapers started by the Sabha such as the *Khalsa Akhbar*, might not have survived. In order to promote the activities of the Sabha and its ideology, Attar Singh helped start a Singh Sabha at Ludhiana in 1884 and became its first president. His three other prominent positions within contemporary Sikh organisations included presidentship of the Khalsa Diwan Lahore in 1889, vice presidentship of the Khalsa College Establishment Committee, and trusteeship of the College Fund. From the late 1880s he played a key role in the foundation and promotion of the college. Outside Sikh institutions, Attar Singh contributed to the Bengal Philharmonic Society, the Senate of the Punjab University College, and the influential cultural body Anjuman-i-Punjab headquartered at Lahore. His aristocratic lineage led to him being inducted on the board of the Aitchison's Chiefs' College.

Given Attar Singh's literary and scholarly tastes and his interests in public affairs it is not surprising that when in 1872–3 the Kuka civil rebellions were on, he became interested in exploring the reasons for this millenarian insurgency. After consulting the writings of Bhai Ram Singh and an apocryphal text called the *Sau Sakhi* (lit. "A Hundred Stories"), Attar Singh concluded that the Sikhs were basically loyal to the Raj but the circulation of prophesies wrongly attributed to Guru Gobind Singh had prompted them to rebel. As he succinctly put it: "A prophecy worked up, Government disregarding, may be more potent for disturbance than fifty years of authority over them [the Sikhs]."[17] His findings were so well received by the colonial administrators that they encouraged him to publish the results of his research, as well as a translation of the *Sau Sakhi* text, in English. Never one to shirk the offer of scholarship, Attar Singh took on the translation and in late 1873 released a well-researched book entitled *Sakhi Namah; Sakhee Book, or the Descriptions of Gooroo Gobind Singh's Religion and Doctrines* (Benares, Medical Hall Press).

While we may not think much of translation as an activity today, when tens of thousands of people are fluently bilingual in Punjabi and English, Attar Singh was in his day a rarity. Very few people in late-nineteenth-century Punjab could write well in English, the newly introduced colonial language. Moreover, the translation project carried out by Attar Singh called for far greater linguistic skills than ordinary English literacy. Walter Benjamin reminds us that translation is no ordinary task.[18] Translation, he philosophically proposes, is a creative mode of knowledge closely affiliated to scriptures, revelation, and redemption. The freight that a good translator carries is heavy, for in giving an afterlife to literary texts he is obliged to transmit a vector of values: conceptual purity, transcendence, and visions of the extraordinary.[19] Besides these virtues, a translator needs technical skills in linguistics, grammar, language conventions, and archaic usage. What distinguishes a mere translator from a good translator is that the latter possesses a certain magnitude of self-reflexivity, a deep familiarity with community traditions, and, in a frontier province like Punjab, command of several language registers.

---

[17] Sir Attar Singh, "Political Suggestions, Information and Other Services of Sir Attar Singh K.C.I.E., Chief of Bhadaur", Attar Singh Papers, Private Library of Professor Harbans Singh, Punjabi University, Patiala, p. 2.

[18] Benjamin, "The Task of The Translator", pp. 69–82.

[19] Ibid., esp. pp. 72–82.

Attar Singh was an intellectual who possessed in ample measure all of these technical and reflexive skills.

We get a taste of them in his "Translator's Preface". Three passages from this preface demonstrate Attar Singh's intellectual vision and technical prowess. He opens his text with the following statement:

> Oh how wonderful is the creation of God that above all worldly things, religion is the supreme thing. With its corruption, the corruption and degeneration of all things generally happen, for, it is religion that binds thousands in one cord of union. It is the saying of the sage, that religion and secular things are the twins. It is owing to disunion in religion, that rebellion and other disturbances in the country generally happen. The learned foreigners have justly separated religion from legislation. But the real and true management of a country depends upon the strength of religion. Such points of niceties are generally observed by those who are learned and experienced and who are in short, able statesmen to govern a country. Such benign government as this, is an act of kindness of the Almighty, and the management of such a country entirely depends upon human beings.[20]

Attar Singh was fifty years of age when he wrote this passage, and while he is in many ways rather cryptic in what he wants to say, we find in these words a profound understanding of things South Asian. He writes about the importance of religion in the subcontinent and the beginnings of secular modernities under the Raj. It is worth asking here: how does he come to associate himself with the modern category religion? Is this a translation of the Sanskrit "dharma", or is his usage part of a much older Indo-Persian genealogy that through Islam and Persian usage introduced the people of the subcontinent to words like

---

[20] Bhadour, *Sakhee Namah*, p. v.

mazhab, din, and iman.²¹ It is equally possible that he acquired the category religion in its modern usage through his learning of English and exposure to Christian missionaries. The city of Ludhiana, where he lived for much of his life, was a major centre of Presbyterian missionary activities: the first English–Punjabi dictionary was published there and a project to translate the Gospels initiated. Living in Punjab's premier city for translation activity, it is quite possible that his usage of the category religion has modern lineages. But this is all conjecture. However, independently of this history of appropriation, or should we say of translation, Attar Singh also gives contemporary scholarship a major reason to pause. He configures in the passage cited many things conceptual, historical, and sociological to do with religion as a category and secularism as a practice that in our general consensus within the academy supposedly happened much later.

The second passage worth citing speaks eloquently of Attar Singh's linguistic abilities and extraordinary proficiency in deconstructing texts:

> This work [*Sau Sakhi*] was originally written in Hindi prose and poetry. The meanings generally differed from the rules of Grammar and as a matter of course, men of shallow intellect and understanding generally misunderstood those ambiguous meanings and phrases. But such misunderstood words and phrases were considered as words of prophecy, and hence they [the ignorant] always failed to comprehend what the original meanings are. I have tried my best to translate into English those words and phrases with clearness and accuracy. There are words in this book so arranged and placed under the rules of Rhetoric and Syntax that when they are closely read and consulted, they imply that some rebellion will happen soon.

---

²¹ On the evolution of Indo–Persian vocabulary pertaining to matters religious and secular, see the excellent book by Muzaffar Alam, *The Languages of Political Islam*.

It is for this reason that the book is considered strange and uncommon even by the learned sometime. All these will be evident to the reader when they will peruse it.[22]

Clearly, Attar Singh has mastered the skills that we today describe as close textual reading and translation hermeneutics. Using the rules of grammar, rhetoric, and syntax, he is able to warn readers that they ought not affirm the foundational claims of the text. He demonstrates with great élan how the life of the mind can lead to autonomy and critical historical judgement.

And finally, here is Attar Singh on historical reasoning:

After a deep research and careful investigation I observe that the book in question was written in the year 1894 Vicramaditya, corresponding to the Christian era 1834, for there are many events and circumstances [that] happened in and about the above year and some years after it. It contains also the prophecies about some distinguished persons who flourished in the above year. Therein such names are mentioned that if any event happens, the corroboration of event or events comes to pass. This will be proved by several tales that are written in the book.[23]

The *Sau Sakhi* text still confounds scholars on when it may have been written.[24] Attar Singh is the first scholar to want to establish its chronology and he proposes that the apocryphal text was written in 1834. He comes to this conclusion because he feels that certain events and persons described in the text can only be dated to the year 1834, so it could not have been written earlier. Besides chronology, Attar Singh provides an extensive editorial commentary through footnotes. Some of his glosses are worth

---

[22] Bhadour, *Sakhee Namah*, pp. v–vi.
[23] Ibid., p. vii.
[24] For an extensive discussion on when the *Sau Sakhi* text may have been written, see McLeod, *Sikhs of the Khalsa*, pp. 139–48.

reporting for what they say about Attar Singh's way of thinking. I have selected six of his glosses:

(1) *Toork:* Mahammedans
(2) *Sungut:* A body of the true followers of Gooroo Gobind Sing
(3) *Pauhul:* Baptism of the Seikh religion
(4) *Ardasia:* A Servant of Gooroo's shrine
(5) *Maleches:* Nations against Hindooism
(6) *Punth:* The whole body of Seikhs as the word Church denotes whole body of Christians.[25]

From this list, composed at a time when many of these key modern terms were not standardised, we can recover something of Attar Singh's voice, presentation, and philological rigour.

Three years after publishing his first book, in 1876 the energetic Attar Singh released another major work of translation. His scholarly preoccupation with prophetic texts that had possibly contributed to the Kuka uprising had continued and he translated *Malwa Des Ratan di Sakhi Pothi*, a Punjabi manuscript, into English. This seminal text, possibly written by an Udasi mendicant sometime in the early-nineteenth century, documents Guru Tegh Bahadur and Guru Gobind Singh's travels through eastern Punjab, particularly in the Malwa region. Once again, as in his first book, Attar Singh's second provides an introduction, extensive annotations, and editorial comments. In his introductory note Attar Singh outlines his understanding of the text:

> These Sakhis were originally written in a very crude language, intermingled with poetry. Through them we become acquainted with the origin of the Seikh religion, the manner and custom of the Seikhs, and many of their prophecies bearing upon political and ecclesiastical matters. Such prophecies

[25] Ibid. All six terms are citations from Bhadour's, *Sakhee Namah*, pp. 2, 19, 20, 117, 177.

are always found scattered through their historical books, as in the Hadis of the Mahomedans, and are the main sources of errors into which they have often been led.[26]

Clearly, Attar Singh had no confidence in prophecies and was seeking to warn both the colonial authorities and his co-religionists about how prophecies could be misread and mistranslated. However, as a good scholar he is profoundly aware that civil disturbances in the Punjab and historical change in general always flow from multiple sources and causes. This understanding of the complex rhythms of history is apparent when he proposes:

> The ignorance of the people, the tolerance of the government, and the jealousies and suspicions arising out of antagonistic creeds, have often endangered the country. Designing men prompted by the extravagant assurances of prophecy have often lured their countrymen to destruction, and impregnated their minds with an underlying hostility to rulers. Religion itself appears to have lost its hold upon men's minds, for we find many endeavouring to establish new religions, but the old prophecies still retain and maintain their ground, and will yet lead to important changes.[27]

So, while prophecies were important, many passions and hatreds contributed to social upheaval, or to what Attar Singh calls "destruction". Though he again uses the category religion, we still do not get a sense of whether he is translating the term from the Indo–Persian cosmopolis or has appropriated it through his encounter with muscular Christianity and learning of English.

The final two texts that Attar Singh translated are the early rahit-namas of Nand Lal and Prahlad Rai.[28] These are perhaps the

---

[26] Bhadour, *Travels of Guru Tegh Bahadur and Guru Gobind Singh*, quote from the section entitled "Preface".

[27] Ibid., p. ii.

[28] Bhadour, *The Rayhit Nama of Prahlad Rai*.

first translations into English by a Sikh scholar of the important rahit corpus. One wonders what exactly the connections are between Attar Singh's earlier books and his interest in the rahit codifications. The question takes us back to European Orientalism and the production of colonial knowledge. In translating the rahit-namas, Attar Singh is publicly signalling to colonial knowledge brokers the critical importance of the rahit-namas in the self-understanding and religious practices of the Sikhs. We know from the historical record that Attar Singh's intervention proved highly influential. Ernest Trumpp, the German Orientalist who got so much about Sikhism wrong and mistranslated the scriptures, did manage to get one thing right: his understanding and presentation of the Sikh rahit was in many ways solid and well documented in large measure because of Attar Singh's influence and mediations.[29] The Sikh aristocrat wrote in detail to the British government to make sure that the man they had hired to act as official interpreter of Sikhism would include translations of the rahit-namas in his account.[30] Trumpp, as noted, did somewhat grudgingly acknowledge Attar Singh's influence and translation work. Orientalist scholars may out of self-interest have been chary of acknowledging their considerable intellectual debt to native informants, but Attar Singh's scholarly writings offer some of the most solid evidence for the argument that Orientalist knowledge was far from being the product of a solitary European endeavour. Indigenous scholarly traditions, conventions, and conversations, of which Attar Singh is the most conspicuous Punjabi exemplar, were largely unacknowledged and entirely indispensable.

Independent of Trumpp, Attar Singh's translations of the rahit were imbibed by army officials who wrote recruitment manuals for Sikh districts in the Punjab.[31] Given the wide and enduring

[29] Trumpp, in chapter III: "Sketch of the Religion of the Sikhs", idem, *The Adi Granth*, pp. cxii–cxvi.

[30] See T.H. Thornton to C.U. Aitchison, Foreign Department, no. 2696, 14 July 1873.

[31] For instance see Falcon, *Handbook on Sikhs*, pp. 6–10.

impact of Attar Singh's writings, it is imperative that we recognise him as a significant scholar in his own right – as very much the virtuous translator of Walter Benjamin's reflections. We see Attar Singh's intellectual autonomy in the way he presented his findings, his subtle variance from colonial discourse on matters of religion and secularism, and his leadership positions across a wide spectrum of public institutions. It was for good reason that T.H. Thornton, one of the most senior colonial officials in the Punjab, described Attar Singh as "the most learned of the Sikh aristocracy."[32]

Conclusions

This case study of Sir Attar Singh Bhadour's scholarly endeavours lends itself to some larger conclusions. First, it allows us to query what Tony Ballantyne so aptly describes as "the systematisation of Sikhism".[33] This systematisation, as we have come to understand it, at least within the Orientalist discourse, begins with James Browne's well-known tract, "An History of the Origin and Progress of the Sicks" (1788).[34] But while we widely acknowledge Browne's contributions to our knowledge concerning Sikhism, we rarely pause to reflect on how much of what he learned about the Sikhs was based on what he appropriated from his two key native informants – Budh Singh Arora and Ajaib Singh Suraj.[35] In fact, the largest portion of Browne's tract, entitled "History of the Origin and Progress of the Sicks", was based on Budh Singh and Ajaib Singh's Persian manuscript entitled *Risala Dar Ahwal-i-Nanak Shah Darwesh*. It is remarkable that Browne only

---

[32] See T.H. Thornton, cited in Attar Singh, *Travels of Guru Tegh Bahadur and Guru Gobind Singh,* p. ii.

[33] Ballantyne, *Between Colonialism and Diaspora*, p. 34.

[34] James Browne's essay on the Sikhs appeared as part of his larger work, *India Tracts*, pp. i–xii, and 1–30. Browne's essay on the Sikhs can also be accessed in Ganda Singh, *Early European Accounts of the Sikhs.*

[35] A historian who is an exception to this is the late Fauja Singh. See his excellent essay, "Early European Writers", pp. 1–20.

wrote fifteen pages of his tract, the other twenty-seven pages were simply an abridged translation of the Budh Singh and Ajaib Singh manuscript. Browne never fully acknowledges his informants; all he tells us is that while he was in Delhi in 1783 he "met with two Hindoos of considerable knowledge, who were natives of Lahore, where they had resided the greater part of their lives, and who had in their possession, accounts of the rise and progress of the Sicks, written in Nuggary (or common Hindoo) character, I persuaded them to let me have a translation of one of them in the Persian language, abridgeing it as much as they could, without injuring the essential purpose of information."[36] It is only because of the pioneering work of Ganda Singh that we now know that these so-called "two Hindoos" – the key informants, or rather Browne's co-writers – were actually two Sikhs, Budh Singh and Ajaib Singh.[37]

Contrary to Said's reductive understanding of how knowledge constructions took shape in the East, Attar Singh's career shows us that non-metropolitan scholars had plenty of agency and intellectual agility. And the knowledge base of Budh Singh and Ajaib Singh reinforces the evidence for native intellectuals and informants being central in the chain of European knowledge gathering.

Much like Brown, John Malcolm, another employee of the East India Company, acknowledges his intellectual debt to a native informant. In the introduction to his well-known work on the Sikhs, Malcolm enlightens us about the nature of his knowledge-gathering enterprise. With exceptional candour he writes:

> When with the British army in the Penjab, in 1805, I endeavoured to collect materials that would throw light upon the history, manners, and religion of the Sikhs. Though this

[36] Browne, *India Tracts,* pp. iii–iv.
[37] Ganda Singh, *Early European Accounts of the Sikhs*, pp. 1–8.

subject had been treated by several English writers, none of them had possessed opportunities to obtain more than very general information regarding this extraordinary race; and their narratives therefore, though meriting regard, have served more to excite than to gratify curiosity. In addition to the information I collected while the army continued within the territories of the Sikhs, and the personal observations I was to make during that period, upon the customs and manners of that nation, I succeeded with difficulty in obtaining a copy of the Adi Granth, and some of the historical tracts, the most essential parts of which, *when I returned to Calcutta, were explained to me by a Sikh priest of the Nirmala order, whom I found equally intelligent and communicative, and who spoke of the religion and ceremonies of his sect with less restraint than any of his brethren whom I had met with in Penjab.*[38]

This collaboration with a native should compel us to read Malcolm in a very different light. And we need to know much more about his Nirmala instructor. In what language did the two converse? Did Malcolm's Nirmala instructor provide him with translations? Unfortunately, for the moment we know much more about John Malcolm than the Nirmala scholar, and it is only when we have accumulated thick descriptions of native intellectual traditions that we will be able to write a cogent account of modern Sikh Studies.

The asymmetry of the imperial intellectual grid continues to haunt us as we probe the colonial archives. Although the acerbic Trumpp pauses to pay homage to his native informant, true to character he does so with far less gratitude and enthusiasm than Malcolm. The huge debts he must have incurred are only worthy of a single sentence: "One Nirmala Sadhu of the Amritsar establishment, Atma Singh, was for a considerable time my instructor."[39]

---

[38] Malcolm, *Sketch of the Sikhs*, pp. 1–2. Emphasis added.
[39] Trumpp, *The Adi Granth*, p. cxiii.

And, as with much else, it is only with Max Macauliffe that we get a massive outpouring of affection and acknowledgement of native paradigms of learning. His humility within his context is a form of civility exceptional enough to seem endearing:

> For literary assistance I must acknowledge my indebtedness to Sardar Kahan Singh of Nabha, one of the greatest scholars and most distinguished authors among the Sikhs, who by the order of the Raja of Nabha accompanied me to Europe to assist in the publication of this work and in reading the proofs thereof; to Diwan Lila Ram Watan Mal, a subordinate judge in Sind; to the late Bhai Shankar Dayal of Faizabad; to Bhai Hazara Singh and Bhai Sardul Singh of Amritsar, to the late Bhai Dit Singh of Lahore, to the late Bhai Bhagwan Singh of Patiala, and to many other Sikh scholars for the intelligent assistance they have rendered me.[40]

Macauliffe's six-volume magnum opus acquires I believe a greater receptiveness in the eyes of modern readers on account of the generosity, respect, and warmth of his acknowledgement to people he perceives as fellow scholars. Overall, however, the imperial order makes it impossible to render fully transparent the production of colonial knowledge. We cannot, for instance, know which parts of Macauliffe's volumes rely on Bhai Kahan Singh's encyclopaedic knowledge and which are more the exclusive product of Macauliffe's intellect. In the preface to his six-volume work on the Sikhs he notes: "It is believed that a work of this nature cannot be accomplished again."[41] To what is Macauliffe alluding? One possible interpretation is that, having spent considerable years among Sikhs in the Punjab, Macauliffe was prescient about colonial modernity eventually completely destroying traditional

---

[40] Macauliffe, *The Sikh Religion*, pp. xxix–xxx.
[41] Ibid., p. xxxii.

articulations of knowledge and understanding.[42] Future projects of knowledge gathering, particularly those on the monumental scale that Macauliffe himself had undertaken, would become impossible because the sorts of traditional intellectuals who had nurtured and sustained his scholarship would have perished. An entire way of being, a complete knowledge system, was headed for total dissolution, to be replaced by the furies of colonial modernity.

This consideration of Macauliffe brings me to a second conclusion, adumbrated earlier, namely that Said, while often brilliant and incisive, was misguided in conceiving of imperial knowledge as the exclusive product of metropolitan scholarship. The reductiveness of the assumption that all knowledge about the East had flowed from the West was, even prima facie, obvious enough not to have required so many years of painstaking correction and rebuttal. His mistaken belief led Said to focus on European figures such as Ernest Renan, Edward Lane, and Hamilton Gibb, with no search for men like Kavelli Venkata Boria, Bapu Deva Shastri, Ali Ibrahim Khan, and Attar Singh. The critiques of Said for his numerous factual errors and the partisan nature of his work (for instance, his support of Palestinian nationalism) would be better directed to the testing of his truth claims purely on theoretical grounds.[43] Tested thus, his hypothesis on the making of the imperial archive would reveal an obvious black hole: his ignorance of a massive repertoire of Bhais, Gyanis, Munshis, Pandits, and Maulvis, the traditional bearers of indigenous knowledge systems who enabled and expanded colonial knowledge.

[42] For pre-colonial knowledge systems, see Nandy, *The Intimate Enemy*; and *Modern Asian Studies* (special issue), "Knowledge in Circulation in Early India", esp. the articles by Rosalind O'Hanlon and Nile Green.

[43] For an extensive list of factual errors in Said's *Orientalism* and a critique of his political affiliations, see Irwin, *For Lust of Knowing*, pp. 277–309. The most incisive theoretical critique of Said is Ahmad, *In Theory*, pp. 159–220. Also see Clifford, *The Predicament of Culture*, pp. 255–76.

It would be appropriate to end by reverting to Attar Singh, who belonged to Bayly's "north Indian ecumene". Based on what we have by way of Attar Singh's biography, we need to see him as a core member of this cosmopolitan ecumene. The son of an aristocrat who from an early age excels in languages and receives extensive training in the domains of philosophy, logic, poetics, aesthetics, and music, and turns into a leading litterateur and raconteur, Attar Singh could in fact be seen as Crown Prince of the ecumene. And yet by early 1870 we see him parting ways with the ecumene. Why this change of direction in the last quarter of the nineteenth century? Why did he abandon his natural habitat, the cosmopolitan ecumene in which he seems to have revelled and been valued? Our preliminary answers to these questions would include a list made up of such thing as the policies of the colonial state, the census operations, the workings of the Arya Samaj and other socio-religious organisations, evangelical Christianity, print capitalism, vernacular nationalism, and the cultural homogeneity so central to the project of modernity.

And yet there is, in the end, still something deeply dissatisfying about this list. How could an ecumene that was the product of several centuries dissolve so easily? Perhaps a more confident answer to this and similar questions can only emerge once we have fully mapped not only colonial but also pre-colonial modes of knowledge.

3

Religious Protest

From Gurdwara Rikabganj to the Viceregal Palace

"WANTED 100 MARTYRS to save Gurdwaras" – an unusual appeal under this heading was part of Sardul Singh Caveeshar's passionate letter printed on 2 September 1920 in the columns of an up-and-coming newspaper of Punjab, *The Akali*.[1] Sardul Singh sought a hundred martyrs who would be willing to sacrifice their lives to reconstruct, in defiance of the British authorities, a portion of Gurdwara Rikabganj's outer wall in Delhi. The wall had been dismantled in 1913 by engineers of the Public Works Department in their vigorous efforts to beautify the landscape in the vicinity of the viceregal palace, and to enable them to construct a road through the estate of the gurdwara. The demolition of the sacred enclosure

---

[1] Sardul Singh Caveeshar (1886–1963), to whom there will be frequent references in this chapter, started his career as a journalist and was appointed an editor of *The Sikh Review* in 1913. In 1918, on being expelled from Delhi, he shifted to Lahore, where he started *The New Herald*. He was elected secretary of the All India Sikh League in 1920, secretary of the Punjab Congress in the same year, and president of the Sikh League in 1921. He actively participated in the Non-Cooperation movement and early Akali party campaigns. The reference to *The Akali* newspaper is based on Chief Commissioner's Office Home Proceedings (hereafter CCOHP), file 134, May 1920, 38–39 B, Delhi Administration Archives (hereafter DAA).

led to a prolonged agitation in the Punjab, largely among the Sikhs, and has come to be known as "the Gurdwara Rikabganj agitation or affair".[2]

Though accounts written by contemporaries of the Akali movement, and later by some historians, have succinctly referred to the Rikabganj movement as an indicator of the growing resentment against British rule, on the whole it has either been ignored or studied as a minor event deserving only a brief description.[3] The general neglect of the Rikabganj movement in historical works is understandable because the first two decades of the twentieth century witnessed various crucial developments in the Punjab, such as the agrarian unrest of 1907, the Ghadar movement, the Rowlatt Satyagraha, and the Jallianwala Bagh tragedy, all of which had a considerable role in India's freedom struggle. Historians have tended to concentrate on these events, by comparison with which the Rikabganj movement has seemed of less import. Consequently, till the late 1960s, with the exception of a brief article by Sardul Singh Caveeshar, which is more of a participant's memoir written in the tradition of nationalist historiography, there was no detailed historical analysis of the genesis, development, and significance of the movement. However, once the focus of historical research shifted to the study of regional movements in colonial India, the Rikabganj movement

---

[2] Due to the varied connotations of the terms "agitation" and "affair", which are generally used while describing the Rikabganj incident, I have preferred to use the term "movement", which may be described as "the attempt of a group to effect change in the face of resistance." D.F. Aberle, *The Peyote Religion among the Navaho*, cited in Gough, "Indian Peasant Uprisings", p. 2.

[3] For a contemporary noting the Rikabganj movement, see Sahani, *Struggle for Reform in Sikh Shrines*, pp. 58–9. Brief mentions of the Rikabganj movement are available in several works. Notable among such works are the following: Ganda Singh, *A Brief Account of the Sikh People*, p. 64; Harbans Singh, *The Heritage of the Sikhs*, pp. 149–50; Khushwant Singh, *A History of the Sikhs*, vol. 2, pp. 196–7. For a work that completely ignores the movement, see Joshi, "Circumstances Leading to the Rise of the Akali Movement".

was sought to be historically analysed and its significance for the political developments in the Punjab came to be discussed.

Sohan Singh Josh, a prominent communist leader of the Punjab, refers in his study of the Akali movement to the last year of the Rikabganj movement, 1920, when he was personally involved in it. Unfortunately he does not provide for the Rikabganj movement the analytical insights he does for the Akali movement. Besides, he touches merely on one year of the agitation. And, like Sardul Singh Caveeshar, his account of the movement's culmination is written from the perspective of a participant.[4] Josh's account of the Rikabganj movement is basically a description of events related to himself, not a historical assessment.

Subsequently, Sangat Singh's book on the freedom movement in Delhi devoted a chapter to the Rikabganj movement.[5] Sangat Singh partly compensated for the inadequacies in the accounts of Caveeshar and Josh by basing his work on primary sources — mainly the files in the office of the chief commissioner of Delhi — which he refers to as the Rikabganj Papers. His chronological account of the Rikabganj movement is basically sound, but he offers hardly any analysis, his framework of discussion being overly dependent on and coloured by the files of W.M. Hailey, who was at the time chief commissioner of Delhi. From these files Sangat Singh uses three documents extensively: (i) correspondence between Raja Sir Daljit Singh of the Kapurthala royal family and Mr de Montmorency, private assistant to the chief commissioner; (ii) a report in *The Tribune* of 19 April 1914 on the Sikh Educational Conference at Jullundur; and (iii) a pamphlet issued by Harchand Singh, a prominent participant in the movement.

These contemporary sources, especially official files, have to be used with a certain amount of caution to prove a hypothesis

---

[4] Josh, *Akali Morchian da Itihas*, p. 26.
[5] Sangat Singh, *Freedom Movement in Delhi*, pp. 198–215.

or record the occurrence of an incident or report on official policy discussions, but they are no substitute for a dispassionate understanding of the past. Even where Sangat Singh transcends his sources, he is carried away by the importance of the Rikabganj movement. He characterises it as a "revolutionary movement" conducted on "revolutionary lines".[6] It was in fact a limited movement on a limited issue which came to an end in 1920. It neither had a revolutionary ideology nor were its participants motivated by an ambitious programme.

Mohinder Singh, in his well-known work on the Akali movement in the 1920s, has a brief description of the Rikabganj movement which he cites as an illustration of the impotence of the Chief Khalsa Diwan – the most influential Sikh organisation of the day – to deal with the British government.[7] Though Mohinder Singh's monograph begins in 1920, when the Rikabganj movement reached its climax, he makes no attempt to study it or assess its historical importance – in spite of the fact that this movement and its key leaders had a considerable role in the rise of the Akali movement and its programme, organisation, and strategy. For him the agitation serves a better purpose as illustration of the manoeuvres of the Chief Khalsa Diwan, rather than as a significant development in the Punjab situation over this period.

S.C. Mittal, in his work on the national movement in the Punjab, has discussed the Rikabganj movement as a background to gurdwara reform, but this by itself does not explain much, and is especially lacking on its linkages and leadership.[8]

The major weakness of these approaches is that they concentrate on the external functioning of the Rikabganj movement and do not analyse its internal functioning – which would help in answering such questions as: What was the social character of

[6] Ibid., pp. 209–10.
[7] Mohinder Singh, *The Akali Movement*, pp. 16 and 93–4.
[8] Mittal, *Freedom Movement in the Punjab*, pp. 150–1.

the movement? From which social group(s) did its leadership emerge? Why did the movement collapse from late 1914 to 1918?

Most scholars working in the field of Punjab Studies refuse to see that every religious reaction – just as every political one – far from being the total reaction of a whole society, is always the reaction of a specific group or a coalition of groups, and that even as it fulfils certain functions of defence, it also and necessarily constitutes an internal settlement of accounts. The Rikabganj movement was no exception. On account of the analytical inadequacies, conventional assumptions, and factual errors – especially chronological – in the existing literature, I will here study the origin and development of the movement and the various stages of British policy towards it. In conclusion I will discuss the implications of the Rikabganj movement for future developments in the Punjab, the movement's social character, and the nature of its leadership.

The Demolition of the Gurdwara Rikabganj Wall and the Agitation in the Punjab

Gurdwara Rikabganj, situated in the heart of New Delhi behind Parliament House, was in 1912 a small structure in what was then known as Raisina village. According to Sikh religious tradition, the shrine was built in memory of Guru Tegh Bahadur, the ninth Sikh Guru, whose headless body was cremated in November 1675 at the spot where the gurdwara now stands. The Sikh religious tradition traces the construction of the building to the last years of Guru Gobind Singh, who it is believed verified the exact spot where his father was cremated and subsequently had a small gurdwara built there.[9] Since then the gurdwara has stood like a barometer of Sikh power, being demolished when

[9] For the history of the gurdwara and the various phases of its construction, see Trilochan Singh, *Historical Sikh Shrines in Delhi*, pp. 31–3; and Mehar Singh, *Sikh Shrines in India*.

the Sikhs were at their weakest (1710), then reconstructed once again in 1783 when they were dominant in the Punjab; at present it is a palatial marble complex which hardly reminds anyone of its vicissitudes.

In December 1911 the British government decided to shift the capital from Calcutta to Delhi. A Capital Committee was set up to recommend the best physical location within Delhi where the new government house and offices could be located. The committee, in consultation with the viceroy, Lord Hardinge, decided that the new imperial complex should be built south of the old city in the village of Raisina.[10] The spot chosen was adjacent to Gurdwara Rikabganj.

For a devout Sikh, a gurdwara is the most holy of all sites, but to Lutyens, the chief architect of New Delhi, and other authorities charged with the mission of constructing the new capital, Gurdwara Rikabganj with its ancient building, a large barren estate, and an uneven boundary wall must have appeared a structure ill suited to the new neighbourhood of a viceregal palace.[11] Lutyens wanted Gurdwara Rikabganj demolished to accommodate his architectural plans for his imperial palace, but the local authorities were unwilling to take such a drastic step.[12]

The chief commissioner of Delhi, W.M. Hailey, after consulting the chief engineer, formulated a plan to pull down the hexagonical stone wall enclosing the gurdwara, replace it with a quadrangular iron railing, and convert the inner area of the shrine into a garden.[13] To acquire the land, which was part of the

---

[10] Hardinge, *My Indian Years 1910–16*, p. 72.

[11] Chief Commissioner, Delhi, to Lieutenant Governor, Punjab: "It would be undesirable to have this large walled enclosure close to the Government House." D.O. letter no. 2950, 30 April 1914, CCOHP, file 81(1), February 1914, 46–56/DAA.

[12] Chief Commissioner's note, 9 May 1912, CCOHP, file 81(4), February 1914, 70/B, DAA.

[13] Chief Commissioner, Delhi, to Chief Engineer, Delhi, D.O. letter

gurdwara estate, a sum of Rs 39,133 was deposited in the name of a charitable trust controlled by the mahant of the gurdwara.[14] In May 1913 the wall enclosing Gurdwara Rikabganj – 78 feet on the north and 322 feet on the east – was demolished to make way for a straight road to pass through the north-east corner of the gurdwara and thence to the viceregal palace.[15] Trees that fell within the alignment of the road were also cut.

Initially, the government action went unnoticed because of Delhi's sparse Sikh population and the gurdwara being located outside the city, but soon the news spread to Punjab and sparked vehement opposition against the government's action.[16] A spate of telegrams, petitions, and memoranda against the sacrilege were addressed to the viceroy, the lieutenant governor of Punjab, the commander-in-chief of the army, and the chief commissioner of Delhi.[17] Sikhs in Burma, China, Hong Kong, and the United States sent telegrams asking for the reconstruction of the dismantled wall.[18] Meanwhile, Sikh devotees from Punjab started arriving in Delhi to gauge the lie of the land for themselves. On 27 January 1914 Harchand Singh, a member of the landed gentry from Lyallpur district, visited the gurdwara. On his return to Punjab he published a pamphlet which gave an eyewitness account of the gurdwara and its demolished wall. He concluded

---

no. 9345, 23 December 1913, CCOHP, file 81(1), February 1914, 46–56/B, DAA.

[14] An enquiry from I.M. Crump, Political Agent, Phulkian State, regarding the compensation money, CCOHP, file 86, May 1919, 110–13/B, DAA.

[15] Many scholars who have written on the Rikabganj movement have given the wrong year for the demolition of the Rikabganj wall. According to Khushwant Singh, *A History of the Sikhs*, vol. 2, it is 1912, and according to K.C. Gulati, *Akalis Past and Present*, it is 1914. A portion of the Rikabganj wall was demolished in May 1913. See a note by Mr de Montmorency, Private Assistant to the Chief Commissioner, Delhi, file 94, 1913, DAA.

[16] *Khalsa Advocate*, 26 July 1913.

[17] CCOHP, file 81(7), May 1914, 76/B, DAA.

[18] Ibid., vol. II.

the pamphlet by noting: "the officers are informed that the Sikh public totally disapproves of a railing being put up instead of the rampart and that by so doing the religious sentiments of the Sikhs shall be wounded."[19] In February a series of diwans were held at Lyallpur, Lahore, Shimla, Amritsar, Ludhiana, Jullundur, Tarn Taran, Rawalpindi, Patiala, Montgomery, and various other places protesting the action and asking the government to rebuild the demolished wall at its own expense. These protest meetings brought home to the administration the gravity of the situation. Urgent steps were needed before the Kanpur riots could be repeated in multi-confessional Punjab.

British Policy and the Gurdwara Rikabganj Movement

Colonial policy towards the Rikabganj movement can be analysed by focusing on three distinct phases: initially, an attempt to mislead the people; subsequently, the exploitation of divisions existing among the Sikhs by alienating those who demanded reconstruction of the wall; and finally, when even this imperial ploy failed, working out a compromise in face of the mounting opposition.

The first response of the British administration to the numerous protest letters and telegrams was to say that Gurdwara Rikabganj and the enclosure wall would not be touched. Hailey instructed his private assistant, de Montmorency, to reply all whose letters and telegrams demanded reconstruction of the dismantled wall by saying, "All that has been taken up is a garden attached to the Gurdwara and the wall of the garden is being taken down as it is intended to make the Gurdwara the centre of a much larger garden."[20] In other words, the government

---

[19] CCOHP, file 81(5), February 1914, 71/B, DAA.
[20] W.M. Hailey's note, 22 December 1913, CCOHP, file 81(7), February 1914, 76/B, DAA.

stand was that the wall which was demolished was not a part of the main gurdwara but merely that of a garden, and by this demolition of the irregular wall and the development of a garden the shrine would find itself positioned in the centre of a square park. Only one Sikh association immediately accepted this argument.[21] Others vacillated; most opposed it vociferously, arguing that the walls, the bricks used in its construction, and the garden were all an integral part of the gurdwara and could not be isolated from it.[22] Even after substantial opposition against the government plans, Hailey wrote to H.T. Keeling, chief engineer of Delhi, in December 1913: "there is, I think going to be some agitation on the subject of the demolition of outer wall at Rikabganj Gurdwara . . . I think we should begin work on these roads at once."[23]

When it became obvious to the British officials that their stratagem of misguiding the public had not gone down well, they sought help from their local collaborators. Hailey asked Raja Sir Daljit Singh to mobilise support for government policy. Daljit Singh promptly contacted the leaders of the Chief Khalsa Diwan, the most influential Sikh organisation at the time,[24] which was dominated by the Sikh aristocracy. As a moderate body, with its own class interests usually in view, it showed ample willingness to accept the government proposal for the replacement of the Rikabganj wall by an iron railing and make adjustments in the boundary of the gurdwara precincts. Sir Sunder Singh Majithia,

---

[21] Anup Singh, Secretary, Guru Nanak Singh Sabha, Bhadarwa, to the Personal Assistant, Chief Commissioner, Delhi, 14 January 1914, CCOHP, file 81(7), February 1914, 76/B, vol. 1, DAA.

[22] Ibid. See, for example, Secretary, Bhujangi Singh Sabha, Lyallpur, to Chief Commissioner, Delhi, 21 January 1914.

[23] Chief Commissioner, Delhi, to Chief Engineer, Delhi, DO letter no. 9345, 23 December 1913, CCOHP, file 81(1) February 1914, 46–56/B, DAA.

[24] Ibid., Daljit Singh to de Montmorency, 15 April 1914.

secretary of the Chief Khalsa Diwan, used all his resources to gather support for the government.[25] He issued a pamphlet explaining the history of Gurdwara Rikabganj, the changes proposed by the government, and the policy of the Chief Khalsa Diwan.[26] When Harchand Singh tried to raise the issue of the Rikabganj wall at a Sikh educational conference in Jullundur in April 1914, the leaders of the Chief Khalsa Diwan forced him to leave the conference on the grounds that "his words spoken before such a gathering who are unable to discriminate between right and wrong can create very bad effect."[27] The "very bad effect" would have been that the pro-government activities of the Chief Khalsa Diwan would have been made public in a conference attended by the Sikh masses from all over Punjab.[28]

When the Sikh public learnt that representatives of the Chief Khalsa Diwan had agreed with British officials in principle that the Rikabganj wall might be replaced by an iron railing, it denounced the move of the Diwan as a "stab in the back of the community". Once again, letters and telegrams from all over Punjab started pouring into the chief commissioner's office asking him not to view the Chief Khalsa Diwan as a representative body of the Sikhs.[29] The opposition being quite vocal, the leaders of the Chief Khalsa Diwan decided they needed to be cautious in their support to the government. To give its decisions the appearance of a general consensus, the Chief Khalsa Diwan, under government influence, convened a meeting in the Town Hall at Amritsar on 3 May 1914. This meeting was attended by about

---

[25] Sunder Singh Majithia was secretary of the Chief Khalsa Diwan from its inception in 1902 to 1921, and president of the Khalsa College Committee from 1920 onwards. He was a wealthy aristocrat who owned sugar mills.

[26] Majithia, *Gurdwara Rikabganj*, pp. 1–3.

[27] Daljit Singh to de Montmorency, 15 April 1914, CCOHP, file 81(1) February 1914, 46–56/B, DAA.

[28] *Tribune*, 19 April 1914.

[29] CCOHP, file 81(7), May 1914, 76/B, vol. III, DAA.

250 hand-picked people who were sure to support the government. Six resolutions were passed, one of which was:

> The government should restore the acquired land and if for exigencies of state, government considered a change necessary, then keeping the area of the land equal to what it was originally, its rectangular shape may in the opinion of this committee be accepted, by which the newly granted plot of land may abut the two roads on two sides and the Gurdwara may occupy a central place. Changes should be carried out by the Khalsa Committee of the Gurdwara and the expenses are to be borne by the government.[30]

This equivocal stand of the Chief Khalsa Diwan further antagonised those who were opposed to its policies. An organisation which had been representing the Sikhs for over twelve years was seen as having betrayed Sikh interests at a critical juncture. Protest meetings against the Diwan's resolutions were held in Lahore, Patti, Ropar, Gojra, Khanna, and Bhasaur. The growing opposition found a powerful financial supporter in Maharaja Ripudaman Singh of Nabha. It was not the first time that he had come out in support of his community.[31] He now proposed financing a trip to England by the eminent Sikh leader Master Tara Singh to present the case of the Rikabganj wall to the British parliament and the country more generally.[32] A monthly magazine, *Sikh Review*, was launched from Delhi in March 1914 under the patronage of Bhai Arjan Singh Bagrian, a religious mentor of the Sikh maharajas and close friend of the maharaja of Nabha. Sardul Singh Caveeshar was appointed its editor.[33]

---

[30] Deputy Commissioner, Amritsar, to Chief Commissioner, Delhi, 19 April 1914, CCOHP, file 81(1), February 1914, 46–56/B, DAA.

[31] *Khalsa Advocate*, 16 May 1914.

[32] Daljit Singh to de Montmorency, 28 May 1914, CCOHP, file 81(1), February 1914, 46–56/B, DAA.

[33] For the origins of the *Sikh Review*, its aims and policy, see "The Publishers Notice", *Sikh Review*, 1, no. 1, March 1914.

With the situation fast developing into a crisis, the Punjab government decided on a firmer policy to deal with the Rikabganj movement. The security deposit of the *Khalsa Akhbar*, a weekly newspaper financed by Harchand Singh, was confiscated in July 1914.[34] Harchand Singh was threatened with prosecution. Just when the movement was beginning to gain support in rural areas, the First World War began, which considerably weakened the agitation and forced its more radical activists, such as Bhai Randhir Singh, to forge links with members of the Ghadar party. Sardul Singh Caveeshar, a key participant in the movement, records: "With the beginning of the first world war, the law against meetings was strictly enforced. Those who were most sore did not consider it appropriate to press their demands and they felt that the Sikhs who had contacts with the government, and who were helping in the war effort, would manage to have a peaceful solution to the problem."[35] Good harvests from 1911 to 1917 kept the peasantry contented.

The third plank of the British policy towards the Rikabganj movement was laid after the First War. From the time of the 1857 uprising the Sikhs had, as was well recognised, provided the majority of recruits to the British Indian army. During the First World War, Sikh recruits in the army had risen from 35,000 at the beginning of 1915 to more than 100,000 by the end of the hostilities.[36] Sikh soldiers fought in Africa, Turkey, and Europe. The Sikhs felt they were the backbone of the British war effort

---

[34] Home Department (Political A), Government of India Proceedings, August 1914, nos 65–6, National Archives of India (hereafter NAI).

[35] Caveeshar, "Gurdwara Rikabganj da Jhamela", p. 209. According to a government intelligence report: "The Rikabganj agitation has been stopped for the present as it seems to be generally recognised that the best policy at the present moment is to refrain from embarrassing the government." Home Department (Political B), Government of India Proceedings, December 1914, nos 216–17, NAI.

[36] Leigh, *The Punjab and War*, p. 44.

in India, and should for their heroic contributions be honoured with the status of "most favoured community".

These expectations were not fulfilled. The wounds of the Budge Budge firing following the return of the *Komagata Maru* from Canada in late September 1914, the Ghadar uprising hot on the heels of that episode, and enforced recruitment under the indentured labour system were still fresh.[37] Arguments offered to justify British rule were wearing thin. Under the Government of India Act of 1919, the Sikhs did not get the 33 per cent representation they had expected.

The issue of the Rikabganj wall in 1919, which had agitated the Sikhs for the past six years, had thus not yet been settled. This provided a ready-made channel for the expression of social discontent and for challenging those seen as responsible for it. Master Mota Singh, Harchand Singh, and Teja Singh Samundri, all of whom had initially been prominent leaders, now formed the Central Sikh League in December 1919, under nationalist inspiration, to act as a political body of the Sikhs and oppose the policies of the Chief Khalsa Diwan. Under the auspices of the Central Sikh League, Sardul Singh Caveeshar convened a meeting to discuss the problem of the reconstruction of the Rikabganj wall. At this very well attended meeting, held in the Bradlaugh Hall, Lahore, it was decided that a Shahidi Jatha (party of martyrs) consisting of a hundred volunteers should proceed to Delhi to reconstruct the demolished wall of the holy shrine. If the government attempted to prevent the accomplishment of this "noble task", the Jatha volunteers should lay down their lives.[38]

According to a decision reached at the meeting, Sardul Singh inserted a call in *The Akali*, a newspaper of Lahore, for the hundred men who would be willing to sacrifice their lives to

---

[37] For background history, see Johnston, *The Voyage of the Komagatamaru*, and Wagner, *Amritsar 1919*.
[38] Caveeshar, "Rikabganj da Jhamela", p. 213.

reconstruct the Rikabganj wall. In the same communication addressed to all Sikhs he wrote:

> If any irreligious officer stops you from serving your religious place, you should not turn from the service of the Guru even though your body is cut to pieces . . . if anyone, whether black or white, through his foolishness, strikes his bayonet on our chests, we shall lay bare our chests to him and say, "strike us, do strike us." But, for the sake of God, before dying, let us place one brick towards the rebuilding of the demolished temple of our beloved one.[39]

The plan was that when the required number of people had responded to the appeal, an action committee would be formed and a notice period of two months served on the chief commissioner, Delhi, asking him to reconstruct the Rikabganj wall, failing which the Shahidi Jatha would proceed to Delhi and take upon itself the responsibility for reconstructing the dismantled wall.

Sardul Singh's appeal in *The Akali* so swayed the hearts of the Sikhs that within fifteen days seven hundred volunteers, some of them Muslims and Hindus, joined the Shahidi Jatha.[40] Some even sent in their volunteering letters written in blood.[41] *The Akali*, in its issue of 17 September 1920, wrote: "The Guru's devoted disciples have sent in their names, proving that the wave of sacrifice is surging high in the Sikh community and the Sikhs are prepared to undergo all sufferings for their honour."[42] The stage was set for an open confrontation with the Raj.

Meanwhile, the British administrators had decided to find an "honourable solution" to reconstruct the Rikabganj wall. In

---

[39] Cited in CCOHP, file 134, May 1920, 38–9/B, DAA.
[40] Caveeshar, "Rikabganj da Jhamela", p. 213.
[41] Josh, *Akali Morchian da Itihas*, p. 26.
[42] Cited in CCOHP, file 134, May 1920, 38–9/B, DAA.

March 1920 a meeting was arranged between the local authorities and a committee of the Khalsa Diwan, Delhi, to resolve the issue. It was agreed in this meeting that a new wall enclosing the gurdwara would be built on a pattern approved by the chief engineer. No further additions were to be made to the gurdwara, nor were new buildings to be erected without permission of the Imperial Delhi Committee. The gurdwara and its estate were to be placed under the management of the Khalsa Diwan, Delhi.[43] As a face-saving measure, the British authorities entirely ignored the notice issued by Sardul Singh Caveeshar. They sought to uphold the view that the Chief Khalsa Diwan was still the true representative body of the Sikhs: the administration were not ready to parley with or acknowledge the new Sikh leadership, for such recognition would have upset the older equilibrium of collaboration and resulted in loss of respect for the Raj. Consequently, those who were most vocal about the Rikabganj issue were not informed of the government's policy and decisions. The view was that any government contact with the new body would give them authority to stake their claims to leadership of the "Sikh community". However, intelligence reports on the success of Sardul Singh's call prompted the government to issue a press communique "to clear public misapprehensions." It declared:

> A wall six feet high is being built outside the limits of the older wall, which will largely increase the compound of the Gurdwara. To this step the local Khalsa Diwan have agreed and it has been arranged that the Diwan should provide the labour to build the wall, while government will give the material free. Objections were raised to the building of the outer wall on two grounds. Firstly, that it was intended to be built on the top of the old wall and secondly, on the ground that having built new outer wall, government proposed forcibly to destroy the old inner wall. Both of these allegations have

[43] Ibid.

no vestige of truth in them whatsoever. This administration is in close touch with the local Khalsa Diwan in the matter. The Secretary has been supplied with plans of the site for all Sikh newspapers and advised to get a representative deputation from Chief Khalsa Diwan, Amritsar to visit the spot and study the plan. If the Khalsa Diwan wish to rebuild the inner wall, they are perfectly at liberty to do so.[44]

Thus, much before Sardul Singh and the Shahidi Jatha arrived in Delhi, the plan for the construction of the Rikabganj wall had been given wide publicity. When the wall was constructed, the government had its photograph published in newspapers to satisfy people. Though British officials were, by their timely action, able to stall the Rikabganj movement, it was only a lull before the storm. The Akalis were soon to storm the bastions which the Raj so earnestly sought to protect.

The Social Character of the Rikabganj Movement

The Rikabganj movement brought about a radical change in the social consciousness and leadership of the Sikhs. Though an open confrontation between the government and those who demanded the reconstruction of the Rikabganj wall was averted by the timely action of the authorities, the dramatic way in which Sardul Singh sought to fight it out with the British generated a great deal of enthusiasm among the people. "An issue which the resolutions, deputations and memorandums of the last seven to eight years could not solve," writes Sohan Singh Josh – one of those who had responded to Sardul Singh's appeal for volunteers – "was now settled within days, when it was decided to make sacrifices . . . This was a great victory."[45]

---

[44] Ibid.
[45] Josh, *Akali Morchian da Itihas*, p. 51.

The Rikabganj movement was, at one level, part of the growing resurgence among the Sikhs and their quest for a *Weltanschauung*. At another level it was a manifestation of unresolved contradictions within the Raj. Starting with the Singh Sabha movement in the last quarter of the nineteenth century, the Sikhs, reeling under the challenge of Christian missionaries, militant Arya Samjists, census quantifications, municipal elections, and the race for jobs and patronage rapidly moved towards a community identification in which gurdwaras were to be symbolic of their cultural and religious identity. Sikhism was to be rid of all Brahmanical accretions so that it could recover its original teachings and practices. Mahants who had converted the gurdwaras into their personal fiefs and installed Hindu idols within their precincts had to be thrown out along with the images. A rising middle class was now confident of managing its own affairs and was in no mood to accept archaic priestly groups seen as representatives of a bygone age. British administrators had since the time of annexation used the Sikh religion, its "heroic tradition", and gurdwaras as instruments for establishing imperial hegemony over the Sikhs.[46] British solutions for the nineteenth century were not destined to work eternally. The opening of the twentieth century was also the beginning of "Punjab in ferment". Agrarian unrest, rising post-war inflation, and demobilised soldiers coupled with the frustrations of the commercial castes created new challenges for British rule. The new duels were to be fought at all levels: economic, political, and religious.

Every religious movement fulfils social and political functions as well, and expresses certain social interests. In colonial societies, where the state had unlimited powers of suppression, religious movements became potent instruments of social protest. Sardul Singh Caveeshar's plan for an unarmed Shahidi Jatha, which

---

[46] See D. Petri, "Secret CID Memorandum on Some Recent Development in Sikh Politics", rpntd in *Panjab Past and Present*, vol. 4, 1970.

would "lay bare chests ... and request 'strike us, do strike us'", had a certain rationale behind it, as did the subsequent passive resistance of the Akalis. Any violent demonstration or armed uprising could be ruthlessly suppressed by the colonial state, but passive resistance would be a challenge to its hegemony – to the very basis of its authority. The Rikabganj movement fulfilled such a role.

The movement had a considerable impact in moulding future developments in the Punjab – especially in the rise, programme, and tactics of the Akali movement. During the Rikabganj movement Mangal Singh, editor of *The Akali*, wrote in a letter to the chief commissioner, Delhi: "On our part we make bold to emphatically remind the government that the Sikhs would no longer tolerate any kind of interference whatsoever in the religious temples on the part of the government."[47] This was to be one of the major demands of the Akali movement. All those who actively participated in the Rikabganj movement went on to become prominent leaders in the Akali movement. To the future struggle of the Akalis, the Rikabganj movement bequeathed a concrete legacy – *The Akali* – a newspaper which was initially started during the Rikabganj movement but which was to be for the Akalis, in the words of Sohan Singh Josh, a prominent participant in the Akali movement, "not a newspaper but a new leader ... the flag carrier of anti-imperialist freedom struggle."[48] Its first issue listed a four-point programme to (i) liberate gurdwaras from the control of the mahants, (ii) bring the Khalsa College under the control of the Sikh community, (iii) rebuild the demolished wall of Gurdwara Rikabganj, and (iv) inspire Sikhs to actively participate in the freedom struggle.[49]

---

[47] Mangal Singh to Chief Commissioner, Delhi, 19 July 1920, CCOHP, file 134, May 1920, 38–9/B, DAA.

[48] Josh, *Akali Morchian da Itihas*, p. 27.

[49] From Dard, *Merian Kuchh Itihasak Yadan*, p. 153. Hira Singh Dard served as an editor of *The Akali*.

Though the Rikabganj movement had a considerable role in articulating the religious and political sentiments of certain sections of the Sikhs, and in making a tangible dent in the prestige of the British, Sangat Singh's characterisation of it as a "revolutionary movement" conducted on "revolutionary lines" is questionable.[50] Micro studies have an inbuilt tendency to compartmentalise the fluidity and continuity of human experience. This, at times, especially when the researcher is unaware of his historical model, creates a fragmented picture of the past. For their own convenience, researchers create boundaries, chronological codes, and conventions which never existed; and so what surfaces in their work is an over-magnified imprint which has no focus on the totality of social developments. If the Rikabganj movement was a revolution, how would Sangat Singh characterise the freedom struggle – the key theme of his work? The Rikabganj movement was in fact a limited movement focused on a set of limited issues. It did not mobilise the people of Punjab in large numbers. Except for a few Hindus and Muslims who supported it, the movement remained confined to a small number of Sikhs. And understandably so, since the issue involved a Sikh shrine – making it difficult for Hindus and Muslims to be too deeply concerned. Even among the Sikhs, not all social classes were caught up in the agitation.

The leadership of and the participation in the Rikabganj movement were confined to landlords and an embryonic middle class. Harchand Singh, a prominent leader of the Rikabganj movement, was an influential landlord. "It was commonly said in Lyallpur that his land was a gold mine," writes Niranjan Singh. After noting Harchand Singh's wealth, he adds:

> He lived in great style . . . Any one who came to Lyallpur for work, and had to stay there for a few days, could do so at Harchand Singh's palatial house. The guests would get a bed,

[50] Sangat Singh, *Freedom Movement in Delhi*, pp. 209–10.

meals and milk or lassi in the morning. The house was very spacious and had always a lively atmosphere. In the afternoon there was a game of chess. In the evening many residents of the town used to visit Harchand Singh's house for physical training. Later at night there was singing as a couple of mirasis (musicians) were always staying at Harchand Singh's house.[51]

Harchand Singh made a large investment in starting a weekly Urdu newspaper whose major demand was the reconstruction of the Rikabganj wall. Another notable activist in the movement was Teja Singh Samundri, headman of the village Samundri. He too owned substantial lands in Lyallpur. Other prominent leaders of the movement included Master Tara Singh, Sardul Singh Caveeshar, Professor Niranjan Singh, Master Sunder Singh, Randhir Singh, Mota Singh, and Sunder Singh Lyallpuri. All these men belonged to the burgeoning middle class. They were monopolisers of the cultural capital generated by colonial modernity.

It is this narrow social base of the movement and its lack of any concrete ideological programme which explains its failure to make any headway during the war years, 1914 to 1918. The Rikabganj movement lacked mass support. From 1915 to 1918 there is hardly any reference to it in either contemporary newspapers or official records. It had virtually come to an end by 1919, except for the persistent efforts of a few individuals to keep it alive. In late 1919 and early 1920, when it again picked up momentum, it was confined to the same narrow social stratum.

The narrow social base of the movement, its dormancy from 1915 to 1918, its concentration on a single issue – all these factors make it impossible to subscribe to Sangat Singh's characterisation of the Rikabganj movement as revolutionary. And yet the movement left many long-term legacies. The historic gurdwara structure was fully protected and the principal architect,

---

[51] Niranjan Singh, *Jiwan Vikas*, pp. 38–9.

Lutyens, did not have his way. Many of those who occupied the front ranks of leadership went on to help found the famous Akali movement. In 1924 one of these leaders, Sunder Singh Lyallpuri, founded the *Hindustan Times*, a major daily newspaper in India to this day. Although he later lost control of the paper, the media skills that he acquired led to the flourishing of print capitalism in the Punjab.

In retrospect, given the passage of a hundred years, it looks now like the Gurdwara Rikabganj movement was more a Gurdwara Rikabganj moment. It was a precursor of bigger things, a harbinger. In the domain of the colonial state there emerged the realisation that even when you possess limitless power, discretion can be the better part of valour. Beyond the colonial state, the Rikabganj movement foreshadowed what Henry Maine famously described as the transition from *status* to *contract*. For Maine, status represents tradition, particularly aristocratic landed interests; and contract heralds modernity, dilution of hierarchy, individualism, and the new professions.[52] This sociological insight of Maine is concretised in the Rikabganj movement. The aristocratic landed interests that dominated Sikh affairs prior to the Rikabganj movement now began to be replaced by men from new professions: lawyers, teachers, journalists, and doctors.[53] These new men would in the decades to come seek to redefine Punjab through agitational politics, insurrectionary ideologies, and legislative jostling. However, the category distinction between status and contract was never going to be a simple bifurcation in Punjab. Often, the two categories would overlap and fuse. The eclipse of the *ancien regime* in the province would prove to be temporary.

---

[53] Maine, *Ancient Law*.

[53] A fascinating tabulation of the new men is available in Joginder Singh, "The Sikh Gentry".

4

The Ghadar Movement and Its Anarchist Genealogy

> A Revolutionary is a dedicated man. He has no personal interests, no dealings, feelings, attachments or property, not even a name. Everything in him is solely directed towards one exclusive concern, one thought, one sole passion – revolution.
>
> **Sergi Nechayev,** *Catechism of a Revolutionary*

> If you talk, talk of Ghadar, if you dream, dream of Ghadar; if you eat, eat for the sake of Ghadar.
>
> *Hindustan Ghadar*

Early in the winter of 1913, the inaugural issue of a weekly periodical published in San Francisco carried the following advertisement:

Wanted: Brave soldiers to stir up revolution in India
Pay: Death
Prize: Martyrdom
Pension: Liberty
Field of Battle: India[1]

This extraordinary notice, written without the help of either an expensive marketing consultant or a professional copy-editor, might rank as one of the most successful pieces of political

---

[1] *Hindustan Ghadar*, 1 November 1913.

propaganda ever produced by amateur revolutionaries. In less than a year of its circulation, this call for political recruits yielded a crop of thousands of militant activists, all eager to launch an armed revolution in colonial India. While geographically the bulk of these new revolutionaries lived on the Pacific Coast of the United States and Canada, many other diasporic Indians from as far afield as Panama, Manila, Tokyo, Shanghai, Canton, Bangkok, Rangoon, Singapore, Penang, Borneo, Kabul, Istanbul, and Berlin became enthusiastic collaborators. Collectively they all identified with an incipient organisation that came to be known as the Ghadar party. The Urdu word *ghadar* has a range of meanings, but commonly denotes a rebellion. Although the movement emerged in tandem with the Hindi Association of the Pacific Coast, it took its popular name Ghadar from the vernacular newspaper launched in co-ordination with an association called Hindustan Ghadar.[2]

The Ghadar movement, in part, expressed the community experience of early Indian immigrants to the west coast who began arriving into the region in the early 1900s. While initially the construction of transcontinental railroads and a boom in the lumber industry allowed these immigrants to gradually establish themselves in cities like Vancouver, Seattle, and Portland, this early good fortune came to an abrupt halt. By 1907, as the economy went into recession, these early settlers faced widespread racial discrimination and political exclusion. While we do not have a comprehensive archive covering the early phase of the South Asian diaspora, we do have fairly detailed empirical

---

[2] We are very fortunate to have an activist of the Ghadar movement provide us with an insider's account of party activities in Lal, "Detailed Account of the Ghadar Movement", pp. 19–56. An overview of the early institutional history of the Ghadar movement is available in Harish K. Puri's pioneering monograph, *Ghadar Movement*, pp. 54–67. The following two are also useful for background: Khushwant Singh and Satindra Singh, *Ghadar 1915*; and Deol, *The Role of the Ghadar Party*.

knowledge – based on the writings of Norman Buchignani, Hugh Johnston, Karen Leonard, and Archana Verma – of what was going on within the immigrant communities.[3] For instance, in 1907 the Canadian government stipulated that all immigrants arriving from Asia would only be permitted in if they had $200; and in May 1910, to make entry even more difficult, the government created through an order in council what came to be known as the Continuous Journey Provision. This new law was intended to make it impossible for people from the subcontinent to come into Canada because, henceforth, only immigrants who had journeyed directly from their place of origin to Canadian ports would be allowed in. And everyone knew very well that there were no direct shipping lines between India and Canada.[4] At one stage the Canadian authorities even plotted to expel all Indians from Canada.

To resist these alarming developments, a few among the pioneers began to experiment with a variety of forums and publishing ventures. However, their early struggles were considerably hindered by the fact that the bulk of the immigrants had almost no formal education, and many could not communicate in English. Gradually, early efforts to find a political voice crystallised when Lala Hardayal (1884–1938), widely acknowledged for his charisma and educational distinction, agreed to provide a helping hand to the young party. Since Hardayal is so central to the ideology and to many of the strategic choices made by all involved in the Ghadar party, it will be useful to list a few of his biographical details.

Hardayal belonged to a high-caste Hindu family that had lived in the capital city of Delhi for many generations.[5] His father

---

[3] See Buchignani and Indra, *Continuous Journey*; Johnston, *The Voyage of the Komagata Maru*; Leonard, *Making Ethnic Choices*; and Verma, *The Making of Little Punjab*.

[4] Jagpal, *Becoming Canadians*.

[5] For the following biographical note I have relied on Emily C. Brown's magnificent biography, *Hardayal*.

worked for the Raj as a reader in the District Court. As a child, Hardayal was sent to a mission school and then graduated from St Stephen's College. Upon winning a government stipend he moved to the city of Lahore, where he first earned an MA in English and quickly followed it with another MA in History, this time breaking the university's record for the highest marks. With these impressive credentials Hardayal had at the age of twenty-one no difficulty in securing a state scholarship to study at St John's College, Oxford. While in England from 1905 to 1907, something fundamentally shifted within Hardayal. Externally, he gave up his Western attire and began wearing a dhoti and kurta, undaunted by the winter climate. He slept on the floor, refused food cooked by English people, and turned into a strict vegetarian. A few months before his academic programme at Oxford was over, he resigned his scholarship and took up the cause of pushing Indian nationalism into uncharted territory. Dissatisfied with the prospects of moderate nationalism – which he thought of as inherently ineffective and below his cultural dignity inasmuch as it sought only to petition and persuade the colonial rulers – Hardayal cast his lot with an emerging network of militants associated with the India House in London.[6] This network included many of the leading ideologues of what can best be described as a turbo-charged hybrid nationalism made up of an uneasy amalgam of Hindu nationalism, anarchism, syndicalism, and socialism. The most prominent protagonists of this hybrid ideology were Shyamji Krishanvarma (1857–1930), V.D. Sarvarkar (1883–1966), Madame Bhikaji Rustom Cama (1861–1936), and V. Chattopadhyaya (1880–1937). All of them, keen students of emerging trends in radical European political thought, were persuaded that the way forward called for a vigorous propaganda blitz against colonial rule, which in

---

[6] While for long the India House network was rather obscure, recent scholarly work has begun to shed more light on this radical hub. See Fischer-Tine, *Shyamji Krishanvarma*.

turn would fuel quick strategic strikes against British interests in the subcontinent, thus leading to national liberation. The key idea was to abandon the liberal framework of moderate Indian nationalism that believed in procedural rules and incremental progress, and instead try armed resistance. This line of direct action greatly appealed to Hardayal and, as a gesture of solidarity for this new thinking, he wrote an essay entitled "A Sketch of a Complete Political Movement for the Emancipation of India (1907)".[7] Perhaps no one in England at the time could have realised that in less than six years the intellectual architecture of this essay would inform a concrete armed struggle for the liberation of India.

In February 1909 Hardayal, who had never held a paid job in his life, was compelled by financial hardship to leave London for Paris where he was able to reside almost free with expatriate friends. He loved living in Paris and within a short period of time enlarged his initial circle of associates by making contact with Russian revolutionaries and Egyptian nationalists.[8] But, given his strange sartorial habits, Hardayal's health began to suffer. He was advised to live in a warmer climate, and it was this search for temperate surroundings that led him first to Algiers, then to Martinique, and finally in April 1911 to California, where he was to reside the next few years. In less than a year of his arrival on the west coast, Hardayal was hired as a lecturer in Indian philosophy at Stanford. But when the university president received news that he was advocating free love on campus and calling for dissolving private property, religion, marriage, and government, he was asked to resign. Hardayal quickly acceded to the request

---

[7] This essay was written in the same year as the International Anarchist Congress that gathered in Amsterdam in 1907. A copy of the entire essay is available in Dharamvira, *Lala Har Dayal*, pp. 335–42.

[8] For Russians in Paris, see Srivastava, *Five Stormy Years*, pp. 74–5. And for Hardayal's links with Egyptian nationalists, Barooah, *Chatto*, pp. 27–8, and Khan, *Egyptian-Indian Nationalist Collaboration*.

and informed his friends, "I am too erratic and explosive to be institutionalized."⁹

Freed from institutional constraints and enthused by news of a new wave of militancy in India, Hardayal now directed all his energy and attention to mobilising various segments (farmers, workers, and students) of expatriates on the west coast for the liberation of India.¹⁰ His general optimism, simplicity, and poetic temperament contributed to his spectacular success. Within a few months he was able to attract sufficient moral and material support to launch four critical initiatives: first, in October 1913, in collaboration with Sohan Singh Bhakna and Pandit Kanshi Ram, the Ghadar (or Revolutionary) of India was founded; second, he and his associates purchased a printing press; third, they launched vernacular newspapers in Urdu and Punjabi; and fourth, they purchased a house on 436 Hill Street in San Francisco that was to house the publishing venture and serve as a meeting place. This new abode was given the name Yugantar Ashram (Advent of a New Age Ashram). As news of the fledgling party spread across the west coast, it attracted many student volunteers, particularly from Berkeley. Within months, as the hand-fed press churned out weekly papers, anthologies of revolutionary poetry, and chronicles of Indian heroic figures and past armed struggles – such as of the great rebellion of 1857 – the organisation began to expand at the astonishing rate of three to four hundred new recruits a week.¹¹ Prominent among the

---

⁹ Letter from Hardayal to Van Wyck Brooks, 24 November 1914, cited in Brown, *Hardayal*, pp. 112–13.

¹⁰ During this time he also came under the influence of the Industrial Workers of the World. Background in Cole, Struthers, and Zimmer, *Wobblies of the World*.

¹¹ We get this estimate from a published account of Guy Aldred, an English radical and anarchist. Aldred was a close friend of Hardayal from his days in England and the two regularly corresponded. See Aldred, "Stop this Infamy", *Herald of Revolt*, IV, p. 47, cited in Brown, *Hardayal*, p. 144.

new recruits was a large body of Sikh factory workers, farmers, agricultural labourers, and students. The close association of the Sikh diaspora with the Ghadar movement was to remain one of its defining characteristics.

Why the Sikhs? Right from the beginning, the seduction of Ghadar anarchism included – to use Charles Taylor's felicitous phrase – "social imaginaries" made up of hospitality to strangers, mutuality, autonomy, heroic sacrifices, the dignity of labour, extreme disdain for the establishment, and a deep desire for political freedom. These social imaginaries, deeply embedded in anarchist thought, corresponded neatly with the life-worlds of Sikhs, a key constituency of the Ghadar movement.[12]

Within six months the membership list of the party grew to over six thousand. The Ghadar leadership was unprepared for this phenomenal expansion. It was one thing to dream of a revolution in India but quite another to bend history to human will. How were they, in some concrete sense, to start an uprising in the subcontinent while living on the Pacific Coast of North America? Fortunately for the Ghadar leadership, the breaking out of war between Germany and Britain on 4 August 1914 provided an immediate opening to strike against the empire. Hardayal proposed that, with Britain distracted by the war effort in Europe, it was the perfect time to start a revolution in India. This line favouring imminent action was strengthened when German agents in America offered to help the Ghadarites with tactical advice, money, and arms. In October 1914 the German Foreign Office in Berlin instructed its embassy in America to buy a large cache of arms for onward shipment to revolutionaries in India.[13]

This number does not seem to be exaggerated since by mid-1914 several thousand Ghadarites did leave the United States for India.

[12] For Sikh connections to the Ghadar movement, see Grewal, Puri, and Banga, *The Ghadar Movement*.

[13] For the German influence over Ghadar, see Mukherjee, *Taraknath Das*, p. 71. Also useful is Barooah, *Chatto*.

Three German banks were nominated to remit funds and act as hubs for communication between the German authorities and their Indian operators.

Prominent Ghadar leaders – Maulvi Mohammad Barkatullah, Bhagwan Singh, and Ram Chandra Peshawri – toured the west coast holding large meetings in mill towns and diasporic enclaves. They repeatedly informed audiences that they had enlisted the support of a large number of Indian troops, that an arsenal had been assembled, and that as soon as a sufficient number of Ghadar party members were back in India a general uprising would begin.

Fully trusting these assurances, the first batch of revolutionaries left Vancouver on 22 August 1914 by a regular steamship service operated by Canadian Pacific, a large shipping company. A few days later a second group sailed from Victoria. On 29 August Jawala Singh, a major financier of the party and popularly known as the potato king of California, left with sixty-two men on board a ship, the *Korea*.[14] In Canton, Jawala Singh was joined by another ninety sympathisers. Over the next three months these departures kept gaining momentum and by the end of November three thousand men are said to have left for India.

The colonial state, alerted by an extensive intelligence network in Canada, the United States, and Hong Kong, took the threat posed by the Ghadarites very seriously. Passenger manifests from all the leading shipping companies plying in the Pacific region were thoroughly combed. Lists of those deemed dangerous were handed out to various port authorities. As the unsuspecting Ghadarites reached Calcutta, many were immediately arrested: the prominent leader Jawala Singh and his band of men who left Hong Kong in mid October were all arrested as soon as their ship, the *Tosa Maru*, docked in Calcutta. From police records we know that, between 1914 and 1917, out of a total of 8000

---

[14] My chronology of these sailings is based on Jensen, *Passage from India*, p. 190, and Khushwant Singh, *A History of the Sikhs*, vol. 2, pp. 181–2.

returning immigrants, approximately 1700 were interned.[15] Despite these strict police measures, many revolutionaries slipped through undetected, in particular almost all those who returned through Sri Lanka and some of the southern ports.

As the Ghadarites who had evaded arrest gathered in Punjab, they became aware that, contrary to what they had been told in California, the country was not on the verge of a revolution.[16] With the start of the war, many Punjabis were in fact enthusiastically supporting British recruitment efforts. In the countryside, village councils agreed to report on anyone suspected of sympathising with the radicals. Deprived of leadership and with no ready access to arms, party activists started contacting local radical organisations. Within a short period, with the help of Berkeley-returned Vishnu Ganesh Pingley, a new nexus was established with militants in Bengal.

By early January 1915 the well-known Rash Behari Bose – who occupied a top perch within radical circles because he had masterminded the assassination attempt on the British viceroy, Lord Hardinge, in 1912 – was inducted into the leadership of the Ghadar movement. This new collaborative exercise emboldened the Ghadarites to revert to their earlier strategy of starting a general uprising. When Ghadar emissaries received strong assurances from army units in Lahore, Ferozepore, Meerut, Agra, Benares, and Lucknow that they were ready to defect, Bose fixed the night of 21 February 1915 for the start of a general revolt. All fresh recruits were instructed on how to cut telegraph lines and destroy railway lines. Once again, British intelligence agents had successfully planted spies right into the party headquarters in Lahore and all the Ghadar plans were known well in advance in the colonial establishment. So, just before the fateful night, all

---

[15] Ibid., pp. 363–4.

[16] For the following empirical information I have drawn on two key sources: Ker, *Political Trouble in India*, pp. 363–71, and Khushwant Singh, *The Sikhs*, vol. II, pp. 183–5.

the disaffected army regiments were either moved or disarmed. Any help that the Ghadarites may have expected from outside army circles was minimal. The revolution was over even before it began.

Although Bose evaded the police, almost all the other leaders and several hundred activists were arrested. Armed with the Defence of India Act (1915), the colonial state set up special tribunals to try the Ghadarites. These special courts were convened in Lahore, Benares, Mandalay, and Singapore. Although the Ghadar movement was virtually crushed in the Punjab, many party loyalists continued with their revolutionary activities in such diverse locations as the United States, Germany, Afghanistan, Malaysia, Indonesia, and Japan.

An Alternative Genealogy

What is puzzling at the outset about the Ghadar movement is that it comes out of the shadows and rapidly takes over the consciousness of an entire diasporic community. What was so compelling in its message that it could uproot an entire project of migration and settlement and turn it upside down? Why would thousands of migrants from many different regions of India, though predominantly Sikhs from the Punjab, suddenly become interested in waging an armed struggle against British colonialism? We do not have much within the existing historiography to answer these questions. One compelling and plausible answer is provided by the political scientist Harish Puri, who suggests that the diasporic militants so strongly imbibed the egalitarian values of American culture that they were inspired to transpose this social framework to colonial India.[17] There is also the argument of Maia Ramnath who, in a revisionist piece, informs us

---

[17] See Puri, "Ghadar Movement", pp. 120–41. A somewhat similar argument is to be found in Naidis, "Propaganda of the Ghadar Party", pp. 251–60. But subsequently Harish Puri appears to have revised his understanding of

that the Ghadar political formation was actually made up of two overlapping movements, one rooted in Bengali radicalism and the other in Punjabi diasporic concerns.[18] But in concluding her essay she acknowledges a certain unity between the two movements:

> Ghadar crystallised at a moment of zenith for political and cultural radicalism in the United States. At the same time, the North American immigrant workforce was beginning to link its grievances of labor exploitation compounded by racial discrimination to its position within a global political-economic structure. Within these contradictions, the Ghadarites parlayed the experience of peripatetic intellectuals and immigrant laborers in early twentieth-century California into a revolutionary anticolonial movement.[19]

The arguments put forward by Puri and Ramnath deserve careful attention for anyone interested in understanding the dramatic rise and expansion of the Ghadar movement. But as we search for possible answers to our questions concerning causation and motivation, I would like to argue that the issues we are raising are better addressed if we switch the Ghadar movement from the cultural register of Indian nationalism, within which it is commonly understood, to the revolutionary theories and practices of global anarchism.

The reason the Ghadar party appears to be coming out of nowhere is that to decipher it we are using every possible trajectory and category coming to us *from within the Raj*, and therefore it repeatedly slips our grasp. The Ghadarites, unlike the Indian National Congress, had no discourse of liberal political spaces, municipal politics, electoral reform, or an unjust British empire.

---

the Ghadar movement. See Puri, "The Influence of the Ghadar Movement on Bhagat Singh's Thought", pp. 70–84.

[18] Ramnath, "Two Revolutions", pp. 7–30.
[19] Ibid., p. 28.

The following Ghadar poem signals their distrust of the status quo:

> If our leaders had fought for our self-respect
> We would not have lost our country and honour
> The kind of Bannerji, Bipin Chandra Pal, Gandhi
> And Madanmohan Malviya should not
> Have licked the boots of the British
> Deputations and resolutions are a waste of time
> These leaders of the Congress who have a soft corner
> For the British have become our leaders
> Because you were asleep and not conscious
> Freedom is not obtained by begging
> By appeals political power is not won
> Do not petition like cowards
> Get hold of the sword and they will run
> What have all the petitions done?
> Brutal British have plundered our land.[20]

Ghadar activists viewed liberty and political freedom as natural rights, as "givens" not requiring negotiation with a colonial regime. Nor did the Ghadarites share the theological underpinnings of Maharashtrian and Bengali schools of terror. They simply refused to be caught up with issues of religious chauvinism, metaphysics, yoga, and secret pacts to serve the mother goddess (whether Durga or Kali). They did not invoke the life of Krishna or the text of the Bhagavad Gita for inspiration and political action.[21] Among the foundational texts for the Ghadar ideologues

---

[20] http://india_resource.tripod.com/ghadar.html. Retrieved on 12 July 2006.

[21] Due to this widely shared secular imagination of the Ghadar movement, I disagree with Ramnath's view in "Two Revolutions", where she proposes splitting the movement and speaks of a Bengali and Punjabi dichotomy. The most fascinating aspect of Ghadar is that, besides Punjabi and Bengali participants, it included a dedicated Maharashtrian cadre. And the reason all

we should count Pierre-Joseph Proudhon's commentary on the revolutionary process entitled *The General Idea of the Revolution in the Nineteenth Century* (1851), Mikhail Bakunin's *God and the State* (1871), and Piotr Kropotkin's classic *Memoirs of a Revolutionist* (1899).

Hardayal, given his life experiences and extensive reading of Proudhon, Bakunin, and Kropotkin, could free himself from the cultural hegemony of the Raj and the trajectories of nationalism made possible within the colonial universe. He was not tutored by Indian nationalists like Dadabhai Naoroji, G.K. Gokhale, and B.G. Tilak, but instructed by the Russian anarchists and possibly the Italian futurists. While still a student at Oxford, he had gone and met the Russian anarchist Kropotkin, who then lived in exile in London. One of Hardayal's closest friends was the British radical Guy Aldred who wrote an influential biography of Bakunin and published many collections of Bakunin's writings.[22] During his early days in the Bay Area in San Francisco Hardayal founded the Radical Club, and, although we do not have many reports on its activities, one report of a meeting held on 12 October 1912 is highly illuminating. The topic of discussion that evening was "Heroes who have killed rulers and dynamited buildings". In 1912 Hardayal proposed the founding of the "Fraternity of the Red Flag" and published a short manifesto in its support. A section of the manifesto was devoted to "Institutional Revolution". Some of its principles are worth considering:

1. The abolition of private property in land and capital through industrial organisation and the General Strike.

---

these regional and varied religious identities did not count for much within the Ghadar social space was because of its predominantly secular orientation and a shared ideological platform.

[22] For a detailed background to Guy Aldred's connections to Hardayal and his associates, see the richly detailed account by Ole Birk Laursen, "Anarchist Anti-Imperialism", pp. 286–303.

2. The establishment of free fraternal co-operation, and the ultimate abolition of the coercive organisation of Government.
3. The promotion of science and sociology, and the abolition of religion and metaphysics.
4. The establishment of Universal Brotherhood, and the abolition of patriotism and race-feeling.
5. The establishment of the complete economic, intellectual and sexual freedom of women, and the abolition of prostitution, marriage, and other institutions based on the enslavement of women.[23]

Many of the key doctrines of nineteenth-century anarchist thought are vividly expressed in these principles. From the time of Proudhon, anarchists had considered private property a form of theft and traced almost all social ills to the institution of private property and the right of inheritance. Other themes listed in this manifesto, such as the abolition of government, internationalism, a universal revolution, and the freedom of women were all taken directly from anarchist political theory. To give these ideas concrete shape Hardayal, at one point, set up a Bakunin Institute in Oakland. In naming the institution after Bakunin, he seems to have been publicly acknowledging his philosophical debt to one of the most influential anarchists of the nineteenth century, who, very much like Hardayal, was never an armchair revolutionary.

Bakunin saw people everywhere ready for revolution – thus his doctrine of spontaneous revolution – but they required to be armed and trained. A similar incendiary line of action was an integral part of the Ghadar agenda from its inception. There was never any policy debate among the Ghadarites over the use of militancy; the party was from the start committed to an

---

[23] Brown, *Hardayal*, p. 115.

armed struggle. Even before the foundation of the Ghadar party, Hardayal had been singing the praises of what he termed the "bomb and pistol policy". The deployment of terror was in his view a virtuous political instrument for it helped avenge colonial oppression. It turned stasis into action, transformed powerlessness into power, and redeemed people from the shame of having been enslaved; violence concentrated the moral will of a people, frightened the government into making concessions, and awoke the slumbering masses.

This fascination with bomb throwing and its poetic celebration became an obsessive part of Hardayal's six-step programme: it had begun with the pen and culminated in the bomb.[24] The ability of Indian nationalists to use a bomb was for Hardayal a significant moment of catharsis. In his logic it cleansed all the previous sins of his compatriots for having collaborated with the colonial regime. Liberty, Hardayal proposed, could only be had with targeted bombs.

These ideas of Hardayal were further developed by another major ideologue of the Ghadar movement, Gyani Bhagwan Singh, who in 1915 wrote a book entitled *War and Freedom*, published by the Ghadar Press in San Francisco.[25] The basic thesis of the book was that no country had ever won political freedom without waging a revolutionary war. The author illustrated this proposition by looking at armed resistance in Ireland, Russia, and China. His intervention clarified for the Ghadarites the difference between individual acts of terror and mass-based movements.

In reading the Ghadar archives it is easy to become distracted by its talk of guns, bombs, and armed struggle. While this chatter was not rhetorical, it should not be overlooked that Ghadar was also simultaneously a war of ideas. The first item acquired by the

---

[24] The other four steps in between the pen and the bomb were the tongue, the sword, the gun, and the general strike.

[25] Bhagwan Singh, *Jang Aur Azadi*.

party was a printing press, and within the year it was publishing periodicals in three languages: Urdu, Punjabi, and Gujarati. In the summer of 1914 the Ghadarites published their first collection of poetry entitled *Ghadar di Goonj* (Echo of Revolt). This anthology was simultaneously released in Urdu and Punjabi and the first print run was an impressive 12,000 copies. When the police raided Ghadar party headquarters in San Francisco on 4 June 1918 they found an entire room, about 6 ft x 5 ft, fully stacked with publications, numbering between 150,000 and 200,000.[26] As we know, all the major leaders of the Ghadar movement published books, pamphlets, and newspaper articles. Hardayal taught at Stanford and Barkatullah had a long stint at Tokyo University. Many Ghadar activists were students at the University of California, Berkeley. Hardayal had admonished Indian students to give up the study of theology and metaphysics and instead acquire knowledge of sociology.[27] In his model curriculum there was no place for Sanskrit. Study of the sacred language was to be replaced by French, Spanish, and Italian.

Perhaps it is these cosmopolitan yearnings that account for the modern social space carved out by the Ghadarites. Here it is important to make the point that although we often tend to associate cosmopolitanism with metropolitan societies and modern cultural networks, a certain sort of cosmopolitanism exists outside urbane environments. This alternative cosmopolitanism, prior to the age of high modernism, has been ably theorised by Akhil Gupta: "Not only did a range of people transact and translate across different languages, but also they knew how to conduct themselves in different cultural settings with people of different religious beliefs, while respecting the disparate religious, social and cultural practices of their neighbours. This was a form of cosmopolitanism that did not assume that equality and even

[26] D.C.I.'s report of 28 September 1918, Home Political A, Proceedings, October 2018, nos 191–4, cited in Puri, *Ghadar Movement*, p. 96.
[27] Hardayal, "India and the World Movement", pp. 185–8.

intimacy in social relations assumed or required commensurability."[28] This alternative cosmopolitanism is best exemplified within the Ghadar movement by the life of Sohan Singh Bhakna (1870–1968), the man who was in many ways instrumental in the foundation of the Ghadar party.

Sohan Singh was the only child of a rich farmer living in close proximity to Amritsar.[29] When his father died, Singh inherited at a young age a considerable amount of land – close to sixty-five acres. Despite such a substantial landholding his formal education was restricted to what was available in the village school – a total of five years of instruction that provided him with a working knowledge of Urdu, Persian, and Punjabi. In his own account, while he often transgressed as a young man, an accidental meeting with a spiritual mentor, Baba Kesar Singh, was deeply transforming. Three things impressed Sohan Singh about his new teacher. First, the Baba was actively opposed to all religious distinctions. His following was made up Sikhs, Hindu, and Muslims. Second, the Baba actively railed against caste distinctions and ridiculed the idea of untouchability. Third, he did not believe in elaborate religious rituals. In short, the Baba opened the doors to a vast reservoir of pre-colonial cosmopolitanism for Sohan Singh. The first public declaration of a greatly transformed Sohan Singh was when he started an annual multicultural and multi-religious festival in his village, appropriately named after him: Bhakna Hola. This spring festival, among other activities, included a large kitchen-like facility dispensing free food to all those attending. It is quite possible that Sohan Singh lost the bulk of his inherited fortune defraying the expenses for this annual festival and free kitchen. Financially ruined, he decided at the age of

[28] Gupta, "Globalization and Difference", p. 18.
[29] My account of Sohan Singh's life is based on his memoir, *Jiwan Sangram*, and a biography, *Baba Sohan Singh Bhakna*, written by an admirer, Sohan Singh Josh. For his time in the United States, see Gould, *Sikhs, Swamis, Students and Spies*.

thirty-nine to migrate to the United States. Arriving in Seattle in 1909, he started his new life as a daily-wage labourer there. The broad outlines of his early life reveal a man deeply rooted in the eclectic milieu of the Punjab: this would come in handy when he decided in 1913 to lead a movement made up of men drawn from various parts of the subcontinent, and of distinct confessional identities and castes.

The Ghadar party, right from its beginnings, was suspicious of any sort of parochial identity, in particular those based on caste, religion, ethnicity, or region: the party membership and leadership both drew from a plurality of castes, regions, and religions. What was most striking about the Ghadarites was that, unlike many contemporaneous militant organisations, they were actively hostile to religion. In remembering Hardayal, a close affiliate had this to say: "He never worshipped; never said a prayer; the words, 'Ram', 'Ram', never entered his mind or passed his lips. He never read the *Vedas*. He never bothered with the *Gita* . . . He always spoke in terms of historical references and naturalistic arguments: no mysticism, no yoga, no Brahman, no metaphysics. Tilak would talk about God, but Hardayal would never say anything like that – never."[30]

Although Hardayal's atheistic leanings may not have been widely shared, the party did succeed in privatising matters of faith. This distancing from confessional politics is widely evident in Ghadar poetry. One poem proclaims:

No Pandits or Mullahs do we need,
No prayers or litanies we need recite,
These will only scuttle our boat.
Draw the sword, it's time to fight.[31]

---

[30] Brown, *Hardayal*, pp. 41 and 53.
[31] "Ghadar di Goonj, San Francisco, 1913", cited in Khushwant Singh and Satinder Singh, *Ghadar, 1915*, p. 20.

Such hostility to religious leadership, sacred texts, and worship has been rare in the history of modern India.[32] If one combines this critique of religious identities with the hostility that the Ghadarites expressed towards local affinities, we are faced with a powerful project of modernism. It was this inversion of primordialism (under the banner of universalism) and vigorous celebration of hybrid ideologies that led me to think of Ghadarites in terms of cosmopolitan space, but it would be a mistake to believe that all this cosmopolitanism was embedded solely in the project of modernity.

This narrative of Ghadar history opens up the possibility for certain reconsiderations of Indian nationalism. First, I suggest that the role of the Indian diaspora is under-theorised in our readings of Indian nationalism. It has now become a truism in the historiography of modern India that Indian nationalism was a composite movement, but in saying this historians are primarily pointing out that Indian nationalism drew various regions and social classes together within the political space of the subcontinent. However, this thesis of a composite movement does not include one particular fragment, namely the Indian diaspora. And this brings me to a second reason for reconsidering Indian nationalism. While at a very general level the Ghadar movement confirms Partha Chatterjee's influential reading of Indian nationalism, at a more specific level it manifests something rather different.[33] Chatterjee's argument is that Indian nationalism's architecture included a sharp dichotomy whereby interior, spiritual, and cultural space was seen as continuing to belong to Indians, and that what had been surrendered to the British was really only the outer, material, and political domain. The part of this proposition that Ghadar confirms is the striving of this diasporic movement towards a communitarian orientation – i.e.

---

[32] For parallels between Hardayal and Ramasamy Naicker "Periyar" (1879–1973), see Jeyaraman, *Periyar*.

[33] Chatterjee, *The Nation and Its Fragments*.

a celebration of the Hegelian community instead of Lockean (or English) notions of contractual society. But in another sense the Ghadar charter and activists refuse to be roped into that large argument about nationalism because in them the inner and the outer – at the level of both rhetoric and everyday life – remained unpartitioned. Chatterjee's understanding is possibly based rather strongly on his interpretation of Bengal, and the largely forgotten fragment of Ghadar from the Pacific North West may be an interesting way into aspects of nationalism that jut out of the paradigm.

Moving Beyond Ghadar: A Certain Timeline of Indigenous Anarchism and an Intellectual Critique of Gandhian Nationalism

The British colonial state was confident that by interning and convening special tribunals (Lahore Conspiracy Case Proceedings, 1915–17) it had successfully crushed the incipient Ghadar movement. The confidence of state officials was bolstered when, based on extensive British lobbying, the American government convened the German–Hindu Conspiracy Trial in 1917 in San Francisco and started prosecuting Ghadar radicals in the United States. Those who follow state transcripts swiftly note that the rolling Lahore Tribunals led to the trials of 291 Ghadar radicals. The outcome of these trials has been tabulated: "Of the 291 sent up for trial, 42 were sentenced to death and hanged, 114 were transported for life, 93 were imprisoned to varying terms and 42 were acquitted."[34] In the United States, when the trials concluded, the list of the indicted included 105 names, of which 36 were Indians and the rest predominantly German foreign-service officials and American arms dealers. But the ideological thrust of the Ghadar crucible was too powerful and seductive to simply

---

[34] Choudhary, *Growth of Nationalism in India*, p. 220.

vanish under draconian state measures.³⁵ History, as we have recognised, rarely progresses in unencumbered straight lines: the dynamic unfolding of time carries within its crevices whispers, echoes, traces, and shadows from the past. This past may have been local once, but by the late-nineteenth century this localised past had in many locations, and under the impetus of European empires and imperialism, turned global, providing new milieus and novel geographical spaces for translating anarchist discourse.

In what follows I therefore explore how the global past of anarchism influenced the radical nationalism of the legendary Bhagat Singh (1907–31); how he successfully managed through his independent intellectual grit to position Indian anarchism in radically new directions; and how with him anarchism infiltrated nationalism more consequentially than the Ghadar party ideologues could ever have imagined. It is critical to recover this independence and autonomy of Bhagat Singh and his associates, for what they went on to offer was firmly anchored in the Indian political experience and had no reference to the struggles of the South Asian diaspora.

Some of the relevant biographical details on Bhagat Singh's background are necessary at the outset.³⁶ Unlike Gandhi or Nehru, both children of extreme elite privilege, Bhagat Singh came from a rural background. Born in the village of Banga in western Punjab, he went to a local school early on, and after finishing his primary grades was enrolled at a DAV (Dayanand Anglo-Vedic) school in the colonial metropolis of Lahore, which was both the political capital of the frontier province of Punjab and its educational and cultural hub. It was as a student in the

---

[35] For the Ghadar movement's passage into marxism, communism, and socialism, see Sharma, *Radical Politics in Colonial Punjab*; and Jan, "A Study in the Formation of Communist Thought".

[36] For my biographical reconstruction of Bhagat Singh's life I have relied on Deol, *Shaheed Bhagat Singh*; Waraich, *Bhagat Singh*; and Nayar, *Without Fear*.

metropolis that Bhagat Singh discovered a rich universe of books, libraries, publishing houses, literature, and theatre.

On leaving the DAV school in 1921, Bhagat Singh was admitted to the National College, a new institution set up under the inspiration of the Punjabi nationalist Lala Lajpat Rai. Given his highly politicised background, it does not come as a surprise that Bhagat Singh became closely involved with two incipient organisations: the Hindustan Republican Association and the Naujawan Bharat Sabha. Both these bodies had emerged from disenchantment with elite nationalism, particularly Gandhi's insistence on non-violence. Following the Jallianwala Bagh massacre of April 1919, the Mahatma had initiated his first mass campaign under the banner of the Non-Cooperation movement (1920–2). The Indian public expected a great deal from this mass campaign; some even thought that independence was finally round the corner, but all hopes were quickly dashed when the Mahatma suspended the campaign on the grounds of the movement becoming violent – a crowd had attacked a police station in Chauri-Chaura and twenty-two police personnel had been killed.[37] Gandhi was paralysed by the fear of such violence spreading. His sudden suspension of a popular upsurge incensed many Indian political leaders – youth activists, in particular, were sorely disappointed. Some of this disenchantment is obvious in the policy documents of the Naujawan Sabha, the radical student organisation with which Bhagat Singh had closely aligned himself. The Sabha's *Manifesto* forcefully critiques elite nationalism:

> Our country is passing through chaos. There is a mutual distrust and despair prevailing everywhere. The great leaders have lost faith in the cause and most of them no more enjoy the confidence of the masses . . . We want people who may be prepared to fight without hope, without fear and without

[37] The most detailed account of this episode is Amin, *Event, Metaphor, Memory*.

hesitation, and who may be willing to die unhonoured, unwept and unsung. Without that spirit we will not be able to fight the great two-fold battle that lies before us – two-fold because of the internal foe, on the one hand, and a foreign enemy, on the other . . . Without going into details, we can safely assert that to achieve our object, thousands of our most brilliant young men, like the Russian youth, will have to pass their precious lives in [their] village and make people understand what the Indian revolution would really mean. They must be made to realise that the revolution which is to come will mean more than change of Masters. It will above all, mean the birth of new order of things, a new State.[38]

Who is the "internal foe" of which this modern document speaks in such strident terms? For the radical youth of north India the "internal foe" were elites who either directly collaborated with the Raj or composed memoranda supplicating colonial officials. In either case, the objective of such Indians was self-centred and class-centred: it was to gain concessions for themselves and for those like them that they hobnobbed with the viceroy and his bureaucracy. This effort at squeezing incremental political advantage was a species of pusillanimity, a blot on Indian honour: although Gandhi is not formally identified in the *Manifesto*, there is scarcely room for doubt that when reference is made to the failures of "great leaders" the finger is being pointed at the Mahatma in the context of his decision after Chauri-Chaura. Bhagat Singh and his comrades were being vehement in their critique of every concession nationalists made to the British, and of every variety of moderate nationalism.

[38] "Manifesto of Naujawan Bharat Sabha, Punjab", in Verma, *Bhagat Singh on the Path of Liberation*, pp. 200–4. According to the editor, Shiv Verma, an associate of Bhagat Singh, the *Manifesto* was written by Bhagwati Charan Vohra and released on 6 April 1928. However, a close reading of the text shows a clear involvement of Bhagat Singh in the writing of the *Manifesto*.

Within a year of the release of the *Manifesto*, Bhagat Singh and his colleague B.K. Dutt checked into the visitor's gallery of the Central Assembly in Delhi and dropped smoke bombs on its floor. The intention was not to hurt the assembled, but, as the heading of the handbill that accompanied the dropping of the bombs proclaimed, "to make the deaf hear".[39] In other words this was signature anarchism – "propaganda by the deed". The emotional heat that went into the bomb-throwing exercise becomes explicit in the political language of the handbill:

> It takes a loud voice to make the deaf hear. With these immortal words uttered on a similar occasion by Vaillant, a French anarchist martyr, do we strongly justify this action of ours. Without repeating the humiliating history of the past ten years of the working of the reforms [the Montagu-Chelmsford Reforms] and without mentioning the insults hurled at the Indian nation through this House – the so-called Indian parliament – we want to point out that, while the people are expecting some crumbs of reforms from the Simon commission, and are ever quarrelling over the distribution of expected bones, the Government is thrusting upon us repressive measures like the Public Safety and the Trade Disputes Bill, with the Press Sedition Bill reserved for the next session. The indiscriminate arrest of labour leaders clearly indicates whither the wind blows . . . we want to emphasise the lesson often repeated by history, that it is easy to kill individuals but you cannot kill ideas. Great empires crumbled while ideas survived. Bourbons and Czars fell, while the revolution marched ahead triumphantly . . . *Inqulab Zindabad*, Long Live the Revolution.[40]

[39] See Verma, *Bhagat Singh on the Path of Liberation*, pp. 79–80.
[40] This extract of the one-page-long handbill is based on "To Make the Deaf Hear", reproduced in Verma, *Bhagat Singh on the Path of Liberation*, pp. 79–80.

Given that Bhagat Singh's bomb-throwing episode was inspired by the French anarchist Auguste Vaillant (1861–1894), who had done the same thing in Paris, in the French Chamber of Deputies in 1893, it seems pertinent to pose some questions: How did Bhagat Singh in faraway provincial Punjab hear about the anarchist Vaillant? What exactly is the French connection? Where does Vaillant fit into Bhagat Singh's intellectual endeavour to develop an independent indigenous perspective on anarchism free of Ghadar concerns and interpretations?

Two caveats are in order before exploring these issues and the story of Bhagat Singh, Vaillant, and global anarchism.[41] First, it is critical to point out that, unlike Hardayal and many other Ghadar activists interested in launching a revolution, Bhagat Singh's anarchism was fully home-grown. As against the diasporic activists, Bhagat Singh had never been to London, Paris, or San Francisco. However, he had found alternative avenues to anarchist thought. We know that Bhagat Singh had access to the writings of Bakunin and Kropotkin, but in what order he read

---

[41] The issue of Bhagat Singh's anarchism was first addressed by his colleague Shiv Verma, ibid., p. 37. This was followed by Grewal, *Bhagat Singh*, pp. 41–55. A pioneering scholar of Ghadar history, Harish Puri, has turned to examining the impact of Ghadar on Bhagat Singh. See his excellent essay, "The Influence of Ghadar Movement on Bhagat Singh's Thought", pp. 356–66. However, Verma, Grewal, and Puri are largely interested in Bhagat Singh's abjuring of terrorism and his transition from anarchism to socialism. My point of departure, in contrast to the existing scholarship, is that Bhagat Singh eventually developed his own mature understanding of anarchism independently and very differently from that of Ghadar. So he should not be seen simply as an echo chamber of Ghadar or a continuity from Ghadar. His brand of home-grown anarchism in Lahore needs to be examined in light of how he assimilated Bakunin, Kropotkin, and Goldman very much on his own initiative and as an independent critical thinker. He was entirely capable of reading at a very fast pace a vast number of books on history and abstract political philosophy, to then discuss his formulations with colleagues like Azad and Vohra; and then they would put these beliefs into political practice on lines that differed radically from the Ghadar paradigm.

these aristocratic Russians in exile, and by which of their many texts he was most influenced, we have no idea. The very fact that he could read the Russians is altogether astonishing because the colonial state maintained a very active programme of surveillance, vigilantly banning radical texts. But Bhagat Singh was very passionate about books and had in Lahore cultivated contacts with booksellers who specialised in proscribed literature. Given the active censorship programme, and the fact that Bhagat Singh was basically on the run from the age of nineteen and was hanged soon after turning twenty-three, he could not have developed a systematic understanding of anarchism. And yet, because of his intellectual brilliance, acumen, and perspicacity, what he assimilated is very impressive and very new in the Indian context.

In the summer months of 1928, Bhagat Singh wrote a three-part series on anarchism in the newspaper *Kirti*. In the opening essay he says:

> Today we are hearing too much about Communism and Socialism but the highest ideal among them is considered to be Anarchism . . . People are very afraid of the term Anarchist. When somebody comes out with a bomb or pistol to achieve one's own freedom, the ruling class or their stooges immediately start crying Anarchist! Anarchist! Anarchist! . . . The Anarchist is thought to be a very dangerous person, who does not have an iota of sympathy in his heart and is bloodthirsty: who gets pleasure out of devastation and destruction. The word "Anarchist" has been so defamed that revolutionaries in India have been termed Anarchists to create hatred against them.[42]

Besides defending anarchist ideas, Bhagat Singh's popular series included biographical portraits of Proudhon, Bakunin,

---

[42] This translation from Hindi into English and quote is from Habib, *Inquilab*. All three essays of Bhagat Singh, constituting the series, are available in this collection.

Kropotkin, Berkman, and the Chicago Haymarket activists. This evolutionary sketch of anarchist thought and practice is unprecedented in the Indian context. And, interestingly, Bhagat Singh's understanding of it does not derive from the Ghadar party. Other than the writings of Hardayal, I have neither seen nor heard of a Ghadar publication directly dealing with the history of anarchist thought; and it is quite possible that Bhagat Singh had no access to Hardayal's writings.

Sohan Singh, a close associate of Bhagat Singh, records in his memoirs a visit to the home of one of Bhagat Singh's closest friends: "We were friends, and one day Bhagat Singh took me to a meeting place of theirs in Lahore. The house, well decorated and neatly kept with pictures of Kropotkin and Bakunin hanging on the walls, was occupied by Bhagwati Charan Vohra and his wife."[43] Clearly, there were others in Lahore who, besides Bhagat Singh, had an abiding interest in anarchist political thought. What sorts of conversations and debates they conducted about anarchism is rather hard to gauge, but the very fact that a house in Lahore had portraits of Kropotkin and Bakunin speaks of the fascination anarchist philosophers held for Indian youth in the 1920s. It is worth noting that there is also a brief entry on anarchism in Bhagat Singh's famous prison notebooks.[44]

The second caveat to list is based on recent historiography assessing Bhagat Singh's role in national politics. One historian, Neeti Nair, after examining extensive archival records and reviewing north Indian newspapers over long spans of time, concludes that in the late 1920s Bhagat Singh was in the horizons of the Indian public as popular as Mahatma Gandhi.[45] For a stripling of an anarchist thinker and activist like Bhagat Singh to rival the Mahatma, who had been active in Indian politics since

---

[43] Josh, *My Tryst With Secularism*, p. 135.
[44] See Malvinder Singh, *Bhagat Singh's Jail Note-Book*, p. 33.
[45] Nair, "Bhagat Singh as 'Satyagrahi'", p. 677.

1915, is if true something of a revelation. A somewhat similar proposition is put forward by the British visual anthropologist Christopher Pinney.[46] Based on his hunch that bazaar posters in South Asia encode an entire historical process, he suggests that we are staring at a massive disconnect between the official elite historiography of Indian nationalism and the ubiquitous presence of Bhagat Singh in visual representations. While Bhagat Singh is often missing in the official narration, at the popular level he had a colossal following – this being attested to by vast archives of chromolithographs that commemorate Bhagat Singh's actions and political vision. At times, it would seem – if such archives are relied on in lieu of the elite nationalist master narrative – popular sentiment in favour of Bhagat Singh overshadows that of the Mahatma.[47] What Nair and Pinney are telling us is that Bhagat Singh's popularity needs to be significantly recontextualised; it will not do to elide his political charisma and role in modern Indian politics. Indirectly, this seems to me to suggest that anarchist thought in India should not be confined to footnotes. It may be that it was in fact far more influential than we have been led to believe because of the overwhelming dominance of nationalist historiography.

Having registered the caveats, let us turn to the making of Bhagat Singh's anarchism independent of the influence and legacy of the Ghadar party. We know from various book lists

---

[46] See Pinney, *Photos of the Gods*.

[47] This reconstruction of Pinney's argument is based on his, *Photos of the Gods*, pp. 117–24. Summing up his argument he says: "This is a remarkable and fundamental fact about the nature of visual history presented here that bears reiterating: textual histories of the freedom struggle in India focus overwhelmingly on 'official' practitioners such as Nehru and Gandhi; visual histories celebrate 'unofficial' practitioners such as Bhagat Singh" (p. 203). The Nair–Pinney findings have been corroborated and enriched by Kama Maclean's outstanding, *A Revolutionary History of Interwar India*. My understanding of Bhagat Singh's role in national politics in the 1920s is indebted to Nair, Pinney, and Maclean.

that he was familiar with the writings of Proudhon, Bakunin, Kropotkin, Victor Serge, and William Owen.[48] We are alerted to his thirst for political and cultural knowledge when he records:

> An incessant desire to study filled my heart. 'Study more and more' said I to myself so that I may be able to face the arguments of my opponents . . . And I began to study in a serious manner. My previous beliefs and convictions underwent a radical change. The romance of militancy dominated our predecessors; now serious ideas ousted this way of thinking . . . As there was no election activity going on, I got ample opportunity to study various ideas propounded by various writers. I studied Bakunin, the anarchist leader. I read a few books of Marx, the father of Communism. I also read Lenin and Trotsky and many other writers who successfully carried out revolutions in their countries. All of them were atheists. The ideas contained in Bakunin's *God and State* seem inconclusive.[49]

Clearly, what seems imperative is first to discover how Bhagat Singh got to know about a relatively unknown French anarchist like Vaillant.[50] The existing literature on Bhagat Singh has not shown much interest in this question, perhaps because it sees him only as an extension of Ghadar anarchist thought. This needs to be textured and examined more minutely. New and intriguing possibilities about Bhagat Singh's independent understanding of anarchism have emerged and require more thorough exploration. Inspired by Edward Said's famous theoretical proposition concerning the importance of contrapuntal readings of texts, J. Daniel Elam has articulated how Bhagat Singh may in 1931

---

[48] For various booklists very ably collated, see Malvinder Singh, *Bhagat Singh's Jail Note-Book*, appendix III, pp. 340–61. To cross-check, it is useful to consult the list in Waraich, *Bhagat Singh*, pp. 97–9.

[49] Bhagat Singh, "Why I Am An Athiest", p. 119.

[50] For a better understanding of Vaillant and his fellow Parisian anarchists in the 1880s and 1890s, see Merriman, *The Dynamite Club*, esp. pp. 10–23 and 69–97.

in his Lahore cell have received and read the writings of the Russian anarchist Emma Goldman.[51] While speculating on how Bhagat Singh acquired Goldman's writings, either through his revolutionary uncle Ajit Singh or perhaps even Hardayal, Elam is primarily interested in how Goldman and Bhagat Singh can be read in tandem: not just as autonomous authors inhabiting different geographical spaces, but as fellow readers.

While it is indeed worthwhile to establish this critical coexistence, it is equally imperative to provide a deeper and more concise genealogy of how the Vaillant–Goldman connection materialised in Bhagat Singh's reflexive world. Such an exercise demonstrates for us that Bhagat Singh was aware of both Vaillant and Goldman at least as early as 1927, several years before he was imprisoned in Lahore. And this timeline shows most importantly that anarchist thought and history were not merely forms of passive reading in prison for Bhagat Singh, but that they provided him early in his life concrete historical exemplars and theoretical justifications, and deeply influenced many of his key political actions – particularly his bomb throwing in the Central Legislative Assembly in Delhi in 1929. It is worth recalling that the handbills Bhagat Singh circulated at the Delhi Assembly cited slogans by Vaillant.

Bhagat Singh's interest in acquiring and reading books, as we have started to appreciate, was legendary. Ajoy Ghosh tells us in his memoirs that Bhagat Singh "was crazy about books".[52] In

---

[51] Elam, "The 'Arch Priestess of Anarchy'", pp. 140–54. My points of difference with Elam's excellent essay are: (i) we must not only focus on the Goldman–Bhagat Singh connection but complicate historiography by proposing at the very minimum a trinity that includes Goldman, Bhagat Singh, and Vaillant. For it is Vaillant that leads Singh to publicly act and throw a smoke bomb; (ii) we must go beyond the reading habits of Bhagat Singh in prison to see how in his pre-incarceration days anarchist texts directly and urgently influenced his political choices and actions; (iii) establish a new genealogy that locates the availability and circulation of these texts within metropolitan Lahore and not in distant California.

[52] Ghosh's memoirs concerning Bhagat Singh, as quoted in Gupta, *Bhagat Singh and His Times*, p. 201.

his student days at Lahore, Bhagat Singh became a close friend of the young librarian there, Raja Ram Shastri, who worked at the Dwarka Das Library, which was affiliated to the National College, Bhagat Singh's alma mater. Based on an oral history project of the Nehru Memorial Museum and Library in New Delhi, we now have available the transcripts of several interviews with Raja Ram Shastri. In one such interview he helps us reconstruct the Vaillant story:

> Bhagat Singh was highly disturbed by communal discords and riots. He wondered about this phenomenon since God is perceived to be a uniting force. Perhaps fed up with this he turned to the study of philosophers like Bakunin and studied his book, *God and the State*. Among the galaxy of books he read, one Paul Vaillant needs particular mention. In this book, there was an article titled "Psychology of Violence" by a French anarchist revolutionary, containing his statement which he made before the court during his trial. When asked as to why had he thrown bomb in the assembly? . . . Why did he not adopt some other way of protest? Vaillant's reply was, "I led workers' demonstrations, held meetings, made speeches. All this made no difference to the Government. I was observing that French society was sitting on the mouth of a volcano which was about to explode. Realising that to shake this deaf society out of sleep, a bang was needed. I caused an explosion in the assembly. I have no regrets over my act." The article was quite lengthy, which had been completely reproduced in that book. I had read it myself. I strongly recommended it to him. I issued the book to him. When he came back after having read it he, while embracing me warmly, said: "Dear, you have given me an extremely valuable piece of reading." Also, he patted me on my back. He read it so many times that I lost count.[53]

[53] For this transcript and the English translation quoted here I am deeply

Although this interview was recorded when Shastri was in his seventies, his memory seems impeccable. The essay he draws our attention to, "The Psychology of Political Violence", is a lecture that Emma Goldman delivered in 1909: it was later incorporated in her widely read collection entitled *Anarchism and Other Essays* (1910). Bhagat Singh seems to have memorised verbatim the Goldman lecture-essay, and for our purpose what needs to be highlighted is the fact that Goldman's defence of anarchism also included the entire speech that Vaillant delivered in a Parisian court before he was guillotined. We do not know if Bhagat Singh read only the "Psychology of Political Violence" lecture-essay, or all twelve essays in the Goldman anthology.[54] Based on his *Kirti* essays on anarchism, it seems to me that he had read the entire volume. Also, in his reminiscences Shastri speaks repeatedly of "the book", implying Bhagat Singh was aware of the entire Goldman text.

What I have proposed here is only a preliminary account, a rudimentary sketch of Bhagat Singh's intellectual engagement with anarchism, and how its framework helped him order his political universe. As suggested earlier, given Bhagat Singh's tortured life, he could not have developed a systematic understanding of the intricacies of anarchist doctrine. For instance, was it by choice that he disagreed with anarchism on such issues as the role of the party in guiding the masses and the future role of the state? Or was this something he merely happened not to articulate because of being mostly on the run as a young radical hiding from the colonial police? What we can say with considerable confidence is that his anarchism had matured beyond that of the Ghadar ideologues and that this maturity in thought, despite his youth,

---

indebted to Waraich, *Bhagat Singh,* p. 64. Waraich has consulted both Hindi and Punabi translations of Raja Ram Shastri's oral interview transcript. His Punjabi transcript is based on *Amar Shahidan Dian Yadan.*

[54] See Goldman, "Psychology of Political Violence", pp. 85–114.

helped him deliver a devastating critique of elite nationalism, Gandhi, and the Congress party. It has always been a hallmark of anarchist thought to view the hierarchical nature of the party apparatus with great suspicion. In his writings Bhagat Singh was able to offer a sophisticated critique of elite nationalism which was not just couched in the emotive language of the Ghadar past, but as digested and absorbed knowledge of things like antecedents, historical parallels, strategy, tactics, and long-term historical trajectories.[55] Only a few months before he was hanged he observed this of Gandhi: "As Mahatmaji is great, he is above criticism, as he has risen above, all that he says in the field of politics, religion, ethics is right. You agree or not, it is binding upon you to take it as truth. This is not constructive thinking. We do not take a step forward; we go back many steps."[56]

Conclusions

In its social composition, intellectual imagination, and the interventions it proposed, the Ghadar party had little in common with other militant organisations in India. The Ghadar project of a secular and non-denominational armed struggle, boldly looking towards the future rather than being held hostage by the past, made it an exception within the confessional and atavistic milieu of Indian militancy. By upholding universalistic and egalitarian values the Ghadarites were proposing something that the segmented countryside in India was unwilling to entertain. They came to be seen as alien troublemakers. The Ghadar movement was permanently marked by its genesis in exile, and, despite its endeavours in the direction of cultural translation, could never present itself as an indigenous movement. The mixing, matching, and mingling suggested by the Ghadarites represented too much

---

[55] See Bhagat Singh's famous letter, "To Young Political Workers", dated 2 February 1931, in Verma, *Bhagat Singh on the Path of Liberation*, pp. 107–15.

[56] Bhagat Singh, " Why I Am An Atheist", p. 122.

of a rupture from the familiar and the quotidian. An episode narrated by a Ghadarite named Tuly Singh Johal gives us a glimpse into the sort of new social transcripts the movement was seeking to inscribe. As Johal returned to India from California he was, like many other rebels, caught by the colonial police and interned in his native village Jandiala for a total of eight years. In the village, he recalled, a Brahman policeman asked him to salute him – the policeman – daily. The curt reply the Brahman received was: "If you want me to salute you, you can do it to me first."[57]

Freed of its nativistic moorings, the Ghadar turns into an interesting case – a transnational social movement. The leaders of the Ghadar movement were in close contact with the highest echelons of three different governments – Japanese, Chinese, and German – and its energies were simultaneously apparent in at least ten different countries. Moreover, even as it fought for national liberation, such liberation was only one of its several yearnings: it also sought social, economic, and cultural transformation. Perhaps this is what renders the Ghadar movement something of an anomaly in contemporary historiography, for it cannot be easily assimilated into any of the existing grand narratives, whether those of the nation-state or of militancy within the British Empire. For North American historians the Ghadarites had something to do with colonial India. Within India, for many of their contemporaries and subsequently for the scholarship on them, they had something to do with those who had left the shores of the motherland. We might term this the movement's hermeneutic slipperiness: from the perspective of the two dominant narratives of the past, the Ghadar movement has always seemed difficult to read and decipher.[58] But

---

[57] This episode is based on Jensen, *Passage From India*, p. 193.
[58] A work on Indian militancy that totally misses the significance of the Ghadar movement is Heehs, *The Bomb in Bengal*. Similarly, Metcalf's highly detailed *Imperial Connections* only devotes a few sketchy lines to the Ghadar movement.

if we are seeking to understand its dynamic as a spontaneous revolutionary upsurge, anarchist political theory provides us with rich resources to comprehend it as a movement that once mesmerised the South Asian diaspora, succeeded in fostering critical new departures, and touched an unexpected chord in the young Bhagat Singh and his associates in Lahore. As Bhagat Singh and his associates – such as Bhagwati Charan Vohra – matured in cosmopolitan Lahore, they wrote a brand new indigenous chapter in the history of Indian anarchism that, in its intellectual heft, desire for revolutionary change, and political practices moved away in many critical ways from the initial musings of Ghadar activists on the west coast of North America. Based on their independent study of the past and anarchist thought they, unlike the Ghadar leadership, concluded that the masses were not yet ready for revolution. All that could be done for the moment, as Bhagat Singh proposed, was "to study" in order to refute elite nationalism and offer new examples of courage and commitment that would likely jolt the Indian masses. The Ghadar idea of a spontaneous revolution had been abandoned.

This alternative narrative of Ghadar history, I would argue, opens up the possibility of certain reconsiderations of Indian nationalism. There seems little room for doubt that the role of the Indian diaspora has been under-theorised and perhaps underestimated in our readings of Indian nationalism, including in the influential understanding of it by Partha Chatterjee.[59]

---

[59] Chatterjee, *The Nation and Its Fragments*.

5

The Inner Life of Bhagat Singh and the Making of a Maximal Self

THE INDIAN NATIONALIST leader Bhagat Singh was hanged at the Central Jail in Lahore on 23 March 1931. Not far from the jail courtyard lived the famous poet and Muslim philosopher Muhammad Iqbal. While Bhagat Singh and his political associates were under trial as part of the Lahore Conspiracy Case, the poet was absorbed in completing his most celebrated work, *Javid-Nama* (Book of Eternity). In this long poem, written in Persian, the key protagonist – an interplanetary traveller called Zinda Rud – asks at one point: "Who am I?"[1] Fortunately, Zinda Rud manages to secure the thirteenth-century mystic poet Rumi as his guide in seeking answers to his existential questions regarding self-identity and personhood. Together, Zinda Rud (surely a pseudonym for Iqbal) and Rumi roam across the cosmos visiting distant planets like Mercury and Mars, and the far corners of the earth, securing answers to human anxieties. They even manage a meeting with Nietzsche in Germany. Ironically, although Iqbal was a keen advocate of conventional religious traditions he ended up posing the most troubling of modern questions in his epic poem: What constitutes a human being?

[1] Iqbal, *Javid-Nama*, verse 3609, p. 139.

The expansive nature of colonial modernity in South Asia meant, as one historian of ideas reminds us, that sooner or later those who thought of themselves as political leaders or intellectuals had to engage with the troubling questions of self-identity and the crafting of modern selves.[2] The reason this project of self-fashioning was fraught with anxiety was that individuals could no longer rely on the certitudes of tradition. While they might once have looked for guidance towards great religious traditions, classical philosophy, familial units, caste groupings, and regional affiliations, these traditional communitarian options were rapidly shrinking.[3] Colonial education and the rise of new professions in areas such as medicine, journalism, law, and banking not only opened up alternative avenues of social mobility but also modern cognitive systems and social practices. Knowledge systems that were once highly stable and promised the delivery of eternal truths now faced epistemological ruptures and philosophical crisis. The new paradigms of thought that were gaining hegemony in the subcontinent were a complex series of knowledge claims and verification protocols potentially open to quick and radical revision. Subscribing to any one of these very provisionally stable hypotheses, not only in such disciplines as physics or chemistry but also in the way colonial society was being constantly restructured, was a risky proposition, both at the individual and collective level. No wonder that for many in South Asia, as elsewhere in the world, some form of nativism or return to primordial truth claims seemed attractive for promising a kind of "anchoring".[4] Why give up the promise of eternal truth for the poor substitute of provisional knowledge?

[2] Kaviraj, *The Invention of Private Life*.

[3] Here I am closely following the analytical distinctions and categories proposed in Giddens, *Modernity and Self-Identity*, pp. 7–8. Giddens is particularly illuminating on the theme of risks both at the micro and macro level and epistemological departures from traditional modes of knowledge.

[4] Ibid., p. 8.

Returning once again to Iqbal, we see the poet summing up with great brevity the central dilemma for all colonial subjects encountering the intense project of modernity: "Noble Sir, do you know what it is, to be?"[5]

With this foregrounded, I now want to turn to Iqbal's younger contemporary and fellow resident of Lahore, Bhagat Singh. Unlike many leading nationalist leaders – for instance, Gandhi, Nehru, and Lajpat Rai – Bhagat Singh has not left us a voluminous autobiography that sheds light on how he went about the precarious task of crafting his self in colonial India. Yet, much like Lajpat Rai, Gandhi, and Nehru, Bhagat Singh poses in his own way the challenging existential question: Who am I? If Bhagat Singh had not been so cruelly hanged at the age of twenty-three, it is highly probable that he too would have provided a thick description of his life, given how fond he was of ruminating and writing.

All the same, despite the brevity of his life, Bhagat Singh left an extensive corpus of published work covering many aspects of his moral and political engagements. Are these writings sufficient to recover the inner life of Bhagat Singh? To a great extent, the answer has to be "yes", although what we possess in terms of first-person narration is largely fragmentary. However, despite their lack as direct pointers, these fragmentary materials can be supplemented by reviewing the sorts of books Bhagat Singh read, what interested him in poetry, and what he so diligently inscribed in his prison notebooks. In attending to these themes I try to chart how, starting with a "minimal self" – a key feature of global modernity – Bhagat Singh goes on to constitute what I think of as a maximal self. And this was in many ways an audacious transition: it indicates why explorations of Bhagat Singh's inner self via his lived experience continue to fascinate so many in South Asia even today.

[5] Iqbal, *Javid-Nama*, verse 3545, p. 138.

Before we start looking at Bhagat Singh's lived experience, let us pause and explore a few definitional issues. To begin with: What constitutes a "minimal self"? This category of personhood has drawn considerable attention in a variety of fields, ranging from psychology to consciousness studies. Philosophers and sociologists have also weighed in to define the varieties of personhood available to modern men and women. Drawing on these disciplinary resources, I define "minimal self" as a person enmeshed in quotidian life, always looking out for safe harbours, uninterested in existential questions or personal autonomy, and largely satisfied with hegemonic narratives and ongoing social and cultural arrangements.[6] The maximal self is the polar opposite. Normatively, an individual can be said to occupy the zone of a maximal self if she is highly reflexive, seeks personal autonomy, and grapples with meta-questions such as – How is the good life to be attained? What constitutes the greater good? How does one express empathy towards fellow human beings? What norms of social justice can be practised? How can the past and present be reinscribed? And the inner compulsion to answer such questions is often so pressing for individuals in search of this maximal selfhood that they may even risk their lives in the quest to ferret out the answers that feel right to them. It is important, additionally, to say that both minimal and maximal selves as categories of personhood and subjective experience are largely, though not exclusively, only possible in modern societies. Occasionally, we may indeed find in pre-modern societies biographical instances of lives similar to modern ones. But such instances are rare and confined largely to a small niche made up of intellectuals, artists, and poets – the sorts of people that we would today describe as belonging to the creative classes.

[6] For my understanding of the minimal self and its historic permutations I am greatly indebted to Taylor, *Sources of the Self*; Lasch, *The Minimal Self*; and Siderits, Thompson, and Zahavi, *Self, No Self*. Also see Glasgow, *The Minimal Self*.

We get an intimate portrait of Bhagat Singh's inner life and his epic pursuit of a meaningful life through his prison ruminations. He was incarcerated in Lahore prison from April 1929 to March 1931. As a political prisoner he maintained a hectic daily schedule of reading, writing essays, composing letters, consoling fellow political activists, and conferring with his lawyers and admirers. Emotionally and intellectually provoked by a fellow prisoner in the Lahore jail to provide a statement concerning his beliefs, Bhagat Singh wrote a long tract that offers useful insights into his modes of thinking and inner struggles. He starts by telling us about his upbringing:

> It is true that I was a favourite with some college teachers, but others did not like me. I was never a hard working or studious boy. I never got an opportunity to be proud. I was very careful in my behaviour and somewhat pessimistic about my future career . . . I was brought up under the care and protection of my father. He was a staunch Arya Samaji . . . After my elementary education, I was sent to D.A.V. College, Lahore. I lived in a boarding house for one year. Besides prayers early in the morning and at dusk time, I sat for hours and chanted religious mantras. At that time, I was a staunch believer. Then I lived with my father. He was a tolerant man in his religious views. It was due to his teaching that I devoted my life for the cause of liberating my country . . . His God was an all-pervading entity. He advised me to offer prayers every day. In this way I was brought up. In the Non-Cooperation days, I got admission to the National College.[7]

We do not find evidence of much inner turmoil in this. But following this account of his upbringing and early education, there is a pithy sentence: "Then I joined the Revolutionary Party."[8]

---

[7] Bhagat Singh, "Why I Am An Atheist", pp. 117–18.
[8] Ibid., p. 118.

And now things within him begin to shift, transform, and cause inner friction. Henceforth, all that Bhagat Singh was going to accept in terms of his inner convictions and political frameworks had to pass through the prism of reason. The revolutionary party, which he does not name, was the newly founded Hindustan Republican Association (HRA). For any proposition to be accepted as truthful in matters of politics, economics, or culture, Bhagat Singh wants an open and rational debate. "Any person who claims to be a realist," he says,

> has to challenge the truth of old beliefs. If faith cannot withstand the onslaught of reason, it collapses. After that his task should be to do the groundwork for new philosophy. This is the negative side. After that comes in the positive work in which some material of the olden times can be used to construct the pillar of new philosophy. As far as I am concerned, I admit that I lack sufficient study in the field. I had a great desire to study the Oriental philosophy, but I did not get an opportunity or sufficient time to do so. But so far as I reject the old-time beliefs, it is not a matter of countering belief with belief, rather I challenge the efficacy of old beliefs with *sound arguments*.[9]

We can discern here Bhagat Singh transforming himself into the archetypical "argumentative Indian".[10] He is willing to take the risk of jettisoning the old for the new. He is unafraid of the future and feels confident that the youth of his generation can, by relying on rational thought, generate a new set of values that will mesh well with the project of modernity. But he does realise that this transition from the old to the new is not going to be easy. Fully conscious of the psychological and cultural pitfalls, he

---

[9] Ibid., p. 123. Emphasis added.
[10] A phrase popularised by the title of Amartya Sen's book, *The Argumentative Indian*.

observes: "You go against popular feelings [when] you criticise a hero, a great man who is generally believed to be above criticism. What happens? No one will answer your arguments in a rational way; rather you will be considered vainglorious. The reason for such a position of being frozen in time is mental insipidity. Merciless criticism and independent thinking are two necessary traits of revolutionary thinking."[11] In his pursuit of "merciless criticism" and "independent thinking" Bhagat Singh provides us with a cryptic manifesto of modernity. For outside the project of modernity there was no major compulsion, particularly in tradition-bound societies, to voice relentless criticism and think beyond normative truths.

The first major thinker to grapple with the problematic of modernity was Hegel. Historically, he located modernity in the early-eighteenth century and saw it as a culmination of the Reformation, the Enlightenment, and the French Revolution. The Reformation established the autonomy of the subject; the Enlightenment freed man from the terror of nature; and the French Revolution gave people rights and morality that were derived not from divinity but civil society. Philosophically, too, modernity for Hegel marked a radical departure from earlier epochs in not having to seek legitimacy from past authority and in establishing its own modes of validity. Based on his historical and philosophical deliberations, he proposed four features as characterising modernity: (1) individualism: each person is entitled to his own subjective freedom; (2) the right to criticism: nothing need be taken for granted; (3) autonomy of action: an individual is responsible for his own actions; and (4) philosophy of reflection: the subject can know himself without having to rely on explanations grounded in tradition.[12] All these four Hegelian principles, ranging from subjective autonomy to the generation

---

[11] Ibid., p. 121.

[12] My reading of Hegel's reflections on modernity in this passage is based on Habermas, *The Philosophical Discourse of Modernity*, pp. 1–74.

of critical ideas, are strikingly apparent in Bhagat Singh's thought and political ideology.

The Books He Read

A similar engagement with the project of modernity can be discerned in the books that Bhagat Singh read. A story told is that on the day he was to be hanged in the Lahore Central Jail he requested his lawyer to bring him a book by Lenin. We do not know if the lawyer managed to, or whether if he did Bhagat Singh was spared enough time by his stern jailers to read the book. Perhaps the story is apocryphal, but regardless of its veracity it is a powerful reminder of how deeply Bhagat Singh was immersed in the world of ideas and books. Though hanged just a couple of months after he had turned twenty-three, he had devoured a corpus that many educated readers do not manage over their entire lives. He had read novels, political treatises, history, jurisprudence, biology, colonial ethnographies, poetry, plays, and philosophy.[13]

What accounts for this voracious reading? Why was Bhagat Singh so possessed with the idea that, more than anything else, he must always surround himself with a library? His eclectic reading tastes took him from the classical tradition to high modernity. In poetry he read both Mirza Ghalib and William Wordsworth. When it came to political treatises he immersed himself in both Rousseau and Marx. His range in fiction was much greater: Dostoevsky, Gorky, Dickens, Jack London, and Upton Sinclair. The opening page of Bhagat Singh's famous prison notebooks is inscribed with two epigraphs: one from Shakespeare, the other from Ghalib.[14] How does one decode his reading habits?

---

[13] For an excellent survey of intellectual life in Lahore and how this influenced Bhagat Singh, see Moffat, *India's Revolutionary Inheritance*, pp. 30–59.

[14] Several editions of the prison notebooks are available. I have followed the latest: Waraich and Jain, eds, *Bhagat Singh Jail Notebook*. This can be supplemented by Lal, *The Bhagat Singh Reader*.

Some clues can be found by comparing him to Nehru, another great politician-reader of the period. Between 21 May 1922 and 29 January 1923, in one historian's tally, Nehru read fifty-five books.[15] This translates to at least a book a week. And a Bhagat Singh biographer says of his subject: ". . . he read nearly 50 books during his schooling (1913–21), about 200 from his college days to the day of his arrest in 1921, and approximately 300 during his imprisonment of 716 days from April 8, 1929, to March 23, 1931."[16] Much as we ask of Bhagat Singh – what was driving him to read so voraciously? – we may ask of Nehru. It is never easy to fathom all of Nehru's complexities, but when it comes to his reading it seems clear enough that he was often concerned with truths to be gleaned from India's past that might guide the nation's future. We get a clear sense of his abiding concern with the civilisational past from many passages in his writings and speeches. Here is one prominent example of his synthetic mode of thinking:

> What is my inheritance? To what am I an heir? To all that humanity has achieved during tens of thousands of years, to all that it has thought and felt and suffered and taken pleasure in, to its cries of triumph and its bitter agony of defeat, to that astonishing adventure of man which began so long ago and yet continues and beckons to us. To all of this and more, in common with all men. But there is a special heritage for those of us of India, not an exclusive one, for none are exclusive and all are common to the race of man, but more especially applicable to us, something that is in our flesh and blood and bones, that has gone to make us what we are and what we are likely to be. It is the thought of this particular heritage and of its application to the present that has long filled my mind, and it is about this that I should like to write . . . I cannot do justice to it, but in attempting it I might be able to do some

[15] Hasan, "Nehru: The Writer, the Historian".
[16] Juneja, "Bhagat Singh Used to Literally Devour Books".

justice to myself by clearing my own mind and preparing it for the next stages of thought and action.[17]

This was written in 1944, while Nehru was imprisoned in the Ahmadnagar fort. Try as he might, and despite his avowed internationalism and interest in world history, Nehru could never unshackle himself from India's past, even when he found himself nettled by parts of it. He was usually saved from disillusionment by his self-confidence and unbridled optimism, which seem to have reassured him that the uglier aspects of the past could always be sanitised and repurposed for the greater good.

Bhagat Singh carried no such brief for the past. He took India's civilisational distinctiveness as a given fact. The burdens of the past required no excavation. The traumas and glories of the previous five thousand years did not call for exercises in myth-making. And this principled insistence on refusing to deploy the past, either symbolically or rhetorically, was not because Bhagat Singh was essentially a man of action – my argument is that to see him so is to diminish and caricature his personhood. The core of his character, the inescapable fact about him which contradicts the caricaturing myth of Bhagat Singh as the local Samson or Hercules, is that he was intellectually inclined and deeply reflective, a man who spent long hours scouring and reading books with uncommon passion. And what he learned was often retained either through spectacular feats of memory or by taking extensive notes. Like all avant-garde artists, Bhagat Singh was an iconoclast in a hurry wanting to break old moulds, burn putrid canvases, and remake the world. As a result, the central question that possessed him was: In what image should the world be remade? To answer this question – as Walter Benjamin might have put it – Bhagat Singh unpacked his library.

What his reading list derived from his library does not tell us is the persistent hardship – in terms of logistics and intellectual

---

[17] Nehru, *The Discovery of India*, p. 25.

mapping – that Bhagat Singh had to negotiate to get to those books. He faced at least three challenges in his pursuit of an unscripted future. First, the sorts of books Bhagat Singh wanted to read were in many instances proscribed by the colonial censors. Fortunately, he found obliging booksellers in metropolitan Lahore who were happy to smuggle texts that the colonial administration, always paternalistic and insecure, deemed too seditious for local consumption.[18] Second, English was not his first language. Unlike Nehru, who was home-schooled by European tutors and went on to Harrow and earned a Tripos from Cambridge and a law degree in London, Bhagat Singh had to make do with a patchy provincial education. He was not, however, one to be deterred by the odds stacked against him. What he lacked in formal education he made up in ingenuity and perseverance. To decipher unknown English words in the books he read he always carried a pocket dictionary. Third, it is much easier for a public intellectual to articulate a worldview if through an elite or comprehensive early education he has already imbibed the established canons of ideas and outlooks: Nehru for example is constantly able to tap the past. And Nehru is far from alone in finding comfort and involvement in classical traditions. Public intellectuals and political activists the world over demonstrate similar intellectual trajectories. In the world of thought it is very hard to start from ground zero: the intellectual genealogy of Marx shows how much he owed to Hegel, Marx's idea of the existence of historical laws being based on Hegelian phenomenology and historicity; Kant's acclaim as *the* Enlightenment thinker is indebted to Hume's philosophical formulations concerning

---

[18] On how Bhagat Singh, despite colonial censorship and police-administered lists of proscribed books, managed to access Emma Goldman's writings, see Elam's excellent "The 'Arch Priestess'", pp. 140–54. We get a slightly different account in Shastri, Oral Interview Transcripts. Shastri, as mentioned in the previous chapter, was a librarian at the Dwarka Das Library affiliated to the National College, Lahore, and a good friend to Bhagat Singh.

empiricism and the role of emotions; Freud's cauldron of discontents is inconceivable without Nietzsche's philosophical hammer; Gramsci, with whom Bhagat Singh has often been compared, wrote extensively in his prison notebooks on the nature of the modern state, cultural hegemony, and wars of attrition, but could often and effortlessly turn back for inspiration and affirmation to Machiavelli.[19] And finally Lenin, closest to Bhagat Singh's time, refined his understanding of dialectics and the unfolding of history via close readings of Hegel's *Science of Logic* and *Philosophy of History*.[20] In this respect Bhagat Singh is anomalous. He could not, for his hyper-modernist South Asia political project, draw on any such deep cultural genealogies or intellectual affiliations. His idea of a revolutionary future for India had to start with himself, more or less from scratch. Unlike well-educated Indian liberals such as Gokhale, Gandhi, and Nehru, Bhagat Singh had no philosophical predecessors to count upon.[21] He had to find them for himself, knowing only that in order to forge an intellectual path for himself and a possible political future for an India free of the British he needed to immerse himself in the writings of Rousseau, Marx, Engels, Dostoevsky, Lenin, and Trotsky.[22]

[19] On how Machiavelli becomes a key resource for Gramsci, see the Modern Prince section, particularly "Brief Notes on Machiavelli Politics" and "Machiavelli and Marx" in Hoare and Smith, eds, *Selections from the Prison Notebooks*, pp. 125–35.

[20] Two of Lenin's well-known tracts, *Imperialism* and the subsequent *State and Revolution,* rely heavily on Hegelian dialectics. For Lenin's "Hegel Notebooks (1914–15)", sometimes also called "Philosophical Notebooks", see Anderson, *Lenin, Hegel and Western Marxism*. Bhagat Singh certainly seems to have read extracts if not the entire work, *Imperialism* (1916). See Waraich and Jain, *Bhagat Singh Jail Notebook*, p. 119. And it has often been speculated that the book by Lenin that Bhagat Singh wanted to read just before he was hanged was *State and Revolution* (1917).

[21] For the long chain of liberal thinkers in India, see Bayly, *Recovering Liberties*.

[22] The easiest way to get a glimpse of Bhagat Singh's prodigious readings is to consult his prison notebooks. See Waraich and Jain, *Jail Notebook*.

And as he reflected on the epistemic universe of these intellectual greats we experience first-hand in Bhagat Singh's writings a palpable excitement at his discovery of what lay beyond India: a world of new ideas and novel metaphors, a modern political vocabulary and possible structures of alternative thought that provided a vision of post-colonial India. We get a taste of what he was savouring:

> Having discussed the present situation, let us proceed to discuss the future programme and the line of action we ought to adopt. As I have already stated, for any revolutionary party a definite programme is very essential. For, you must know that revolution means action. It means a change brought about deliberately by organised and systematic work, as opposed to sudden and unorganised or spontaneous change or breakdown. And for the formulation of a programme one must necessarily study: 1. The goal; 2. The premises from where to start, i.e. the existing conditions; 3. The course of action, the means and methods.[23]

Bhagat Singh's long hours of reading and surmounting challenges eventually produced a new narrative for India. What had once been an unscripted future turned into a viable political and ethical project. In the process of self-fashioning he paid systematic attention to such grand themes as honour, heroism, suffering, fate, mutual obligations, "moral luck", justice, redistributive mechanisms, and the nature of our collective beliefs and illusions. To provide evidence of thought on such a variety by the age of twenty-three is remarkable, but what is truly admirable is that through his writings he sought to converse on equal terms with Marx, Bakunin, Lenin, and Trotsky. Nehru has countless institutional and literary accomplishments to his credit, including a profound understanding of India's past and an uncanny ability to

---

[23] Bhagat Singh, "To Young Political Workers (1931)", pt 3.

read Gandhi's mind, but he does not have the distinction of sparring with the theoretical founders of a revolutionary modernity. In his intellectual originality, ethical orientations, and ultimate sacrifice Bhagat Singh remains singular – and in this respect he is of far greater significance than the heroic bomb thrower who as a man of action opposed colonialism to the end. The benefit of interpreting his reading habits is that by this hermeneutic effort we begin to see how he provided a supplementary narrative for what has since Tagore been described as the idea of India.

But though we do get a fair idea of Bhagat Singh's inner life by reviewing and annotating the modernist texts he read, for a more nuanced appreciation of his personality it is also essential to supplement his wide-ranging engagement with philosophy, history, and political economy with his love of poetry. Bhagat Singh was a great admirer of two Urdu poets: Ghalib (1797–1869) and Iqbal (1877–1938). Biographically oriented scholars have recovered from family collections several loose leaves that list the shers (verses; Urdu couplets) that Bhagat Singh inscribed from published anthologies of Ghalib and Iqbal. Perhaps these loose leaves belonged originally to his prison notebooks. In fact the latest edition of his prison notebooks includes, in two appendices, the poems that Bhagat Singh – in his striking handwriting – had copied out.[24] The total number of shers he inscribed is sixty-two, and, though several remain unattributed, we know that twenty-five of them are from Ghalib and twelve from Iqbal. Since we know so little about Bhagat Singh's non-political life in general and of his inner life even less, it may aid analysis to reproduce some of these poems in their entirety.

In the interim the question arises: Why Ghalib? Why Iqbal? To which there is perhaps a simple answer. Both were modernist poets deeply concerned with the fate of individuals in an uncaring world. It is not surprising for Bhagat Singh to have

---

[24] Waraich and Jain, *Jail Notebook*, pp. 337–9.

been attracted to their poetry, for, much like his favourite poets, he was a keen observer of individual lives. Beyond these broad modernist affiliations, Ghalib and Iqbal were in many ways different sorts of poets.

Iqbal had a very essentialist conception of human nature. He believed in such old-fashioned things as foundational values, community solidarities, and the human need for spiritual and political salvation. Ghalib had no such high hopes. Never mind collective utopias, he was even unsure if we ought to chase individual utopias. Iqbal focused as a poet on the public good and was much more hopeful than his predecessor Ghalib.

Ghalib's driving passion was the private good. If a journalist had conducted a face-to-face interview with Iqbal and asked him what exactly he sought to accomplish through his verse, his answer would have been on these lines: "I am sorry there is so much suffering in the world. But this suffering can be eliminated if we believe in the divine spark and organise collectively, say as Muslims." Ghalib's response would have been rather different: "I am sorry there is so much suffering in the world. Sorry . . . but there's not much hope for this suffering to end. Get used to it. Tragedy is very much a part of life. Still, let me hold your hand . . . for your troubled fate troubles me."

Good poetry has always posed difficult existential questions: What is the purpose of life? How is one to cope with the inevitability of death? And, of course, questions pertaining to the pleasures and pains of quotidian life, human encounters, love, piety, virtue. The writing and reading of poetry, Bhagat Singh himself may have asserted, share a common horizon: both are intense endeavours towards solving central human dilemmas. This seems a plausible assertion to make on his behalf because in reading Ghalib and Iqbal we observe Bhagat Singh's heart and mind preoccupied with the many puzzles of human existence. We know from history that many great political leaders were engrossed by music – Lenin's fascination with Beethoven's "Appassionata" is well known – and, more often, read poetry: some even commissioned the writing of poetry: the Roman emperor Augustus commissioned Virgil's *Aeneid*. By consuming verse they both grappled with perennial questions about the eternal verities and arrived at new metaphors and alternative cultural vocabularies. The reading of imaginative texts has, besides, allowed political leaders to deal with ethical quandaries and the frequent disappointments of their private and public lives: Mahatma Gandhi was fond of reciting Iqbal's "*Saare Jahan se Achha*" (Better than the Whole World) and Nehru was enamoured of Robert Frost's "Stopping by Woods on a Snowy Evening".

These preliminary thoughts on the multiple functions of poetry are a way in to one of Bhagat Singh's favourite Ghalib ghazals, entitled: *"Ye Na Thi Hamari Kismet"* (This Wasn't Meant to Be My Fate):

> This was not to be my Kismet, that all should end in lovers meeting
> Even had I gone on living, I should still be waiting, waiting
>
> Did your promise save my life? Yes! – for I knew you would not keep it
> Would I have not died of joy if I had thought you would fulfil it?
>
> Am I still to call it friendship when my friends start preaching at me?
> Someone should have brought me comfort, someone should have shared my sorrows
>
> From the flint blood would come flooding – such a flow that none could staunch it
> Had what you see as my sorrow been the fire that hides within it
>
> Grief wastes our life away, and yet – how shall we flee the heart within us?

Had we not known the grief of love, we would have known the grief of living

With what style you handle, Ghalib, all these themes of mystic teaching!
What a saint we would have thought you if you had not been a drinker!²⁵

However flawed or odd the poem may sound in its English translation, there is no doubt that, in the original version which Bhagat Singh read, it deals explicitly and powerfully with the sorrows of life, betrayals of friendship, disappointments in love, notions of piety, and the character of religious and secular sainthood. Bhagat Singh's fondness for this poem greatly complicates our stock images of his life. For, what is one to make of Ghalib's opening line: *"Ye Na Thi Hamari Kismet"*? How does one combine political agency and the vagaries of human fate? Philosophers have wrestled with this question. Bernard Williams, for instance, has written on "moral luck": how life choices, autonomy, and actions are greatly constrained by social, economic, and political structures.²⁶ These impersonal structures – the tectonic plates of historical forces – can shift unexpectedly and at random constrict the arc of human agency, leading some moral philosophers to revisit the classical past and think of fate and the tragic nature of human life. Human agency may then begin to look like a glib assumption, and history can be seen to show the frequency with which the assumptions of autonomy and agency have been invalidated. Ghalib, in the intense and condensed form of verse, is raising some of the questions that moral philosophers such

---

²⁵ The translation of this ghazal is by Ralph Russell in *The Oxford India Ghalib*, pp. 339–40. For the Urdu original, see Mahmood, *Diwan-e-Ghalib*, p. 16. Unless otherwise stated, all the other translations of Urdu poems here are mine.
²⁶ See Williams, *Ethics and the Limits of Philosophy*. Also see Williams' classic, *Shame and Necessity*. A similar terrain is explored in Nussbaum, *The Fragility of Goodness*.

as Bernard Williams and Martha Nussbaum have raised in our own day.

The emotion and pathos of this first poem is nearly outdone by a second Ghalib poem that was close to Bhagat Singh's heart. The opening line here is *"Dil Hi To Heh"* (After all it is the heart) and the complete verse goes:

> The heart is not a pile of bricks or stones,
> Why would it not feel pain?
> I shall cry a thousand times
> For all of the uncalled torments the world sends my way
>
> I am to be found neither in the temple nor in the mosque
> Not even on a householder's threshold
> I simply wait for him on deserted pathways
> Why would anyone care about any of this?
>
> The human life and prison are in tandem
> Sorrow and life are bound together, like prison and prisoner
> What happens to the prisoner before he dies?
> Is he free of pain?
> He is not only an atheist
> But also notorious for being unfaithful in matters of love
> If you care so deeply for matters of faith and heart
> Why be so foolish and venture on to the path of one known for his lack of faith?
>
> In the absence of this wretched Ghalib
> Nothing in life comes to a halt
> Why complain? Why cry?
> Why wail? Why brood?[27]

This tragic poem exemplifies why Ghalib is not a poet for the faint of heart: he was never one to occlude shallow thinking,

---

[27] For the original Urdu poem, see ibid., pp. 8–10.

social hypocrisies, and human exigencies. By copying this poem on the rationed stationery available to him in the Lahore prison, Bhagat Singh seems to acknowledge Ghalib as a kindred soul. Some of the lines in this widely circulated poem closely echo Bhagat Singh's own situation on death row: "The human life and prison are in tandem/ Sorrow and life are bound together, like prison and prisoner// What happens to the prisoner before he dies? Is he free of pain?" If Bhagat Singh was in fact able to examine the tragic consequences of his actions with equanimity when facing the end of his life, it was in part because of the powers of persuasion in Ghalib's existential voice.

There were other Iqbal poems to which Bhagat Singh was attracted and would often recite in the company of his friends. One of them is titled, simply, *"Saqi"*, which roughly translated denotes a cup-bearer or, now, a bartender; a more elegant equivalent in our context might be "spiritual master" denoting the poet's alter-ego. *"Saqi"* is a short poem that uncoils with a punch:

> Yes, those who drink without limit can fall
> Yet, the real miracle occurs when those falling are saved
>
> The legendary wine-drinkers have all faded away
> What we need today is to discover new springs of immortality
>
> The entire evening and night was consumed by bouts of
>   drinking and noise
> But now as dawn approaches, let us remember God.[28]

It is the opening lines of this composition that Bhagat Singh found so compelling. And we can see why: it was his lifelong mission to help those who had stumbled or fallen. This was in line with what Iqbal says – that our focus ought not to be on the structures that cause the fall but rather on doing what we

---

[28] For the Urdu original see: http://iqbalurdu.blogspot.com/search?q=saqi+121, accessed on 14 August 2019.

can to assist those within our communities who have fallen or are vulnerable. While on the surface this does not seem to be an emancipatory poem – it has much to do with bouts of drinking and the resulting commotion, a common trope in Urdu poetry – it does suggest a progressive resolution to social dilemmas while being couched in the language of religion and imbued with a deeply messianic content. While it is hard to say exactly how Bhagat Singh may have deciphered this poem, to me it appears that he senses in this verse a call to help all those wounded by life, either by circumstance or the material realities of deprivation under colonial rule. And "new springs of immortality" seems to be signalling new ideologies, such as anarchism and fascism, which were in the air at the beginning of the twentieth century.

Not all of Iqbal's poems are as easy to decipher as the widely recited *"Saqi"* with its stock images from classical Persian and Urdu poetry. One of Iqbal's most complex poems, *"Masal-e-Pertu"*, attracted Bhagat Singh's close attention and once again we have him copying out large portions of it, demonstrating that he was by temperament open to nuanced and non-ideological readings of the cultural and religious realities encountered by his contemporaries. This is the poem:

> Wine drinkers are like shadows of a goblet,
> The same prayer is offered every evening
>
> Do not be foolish and think you are the only one who prays
> Stones and trees often pray to God
>
> May the light lead us to a new world
> For the indignities of the present one remain unbearable
>
> In some gardens silence is supreme
> Even the melodies go still
>
> All those who seek happiness in wine
> Do they simply forget about transgressions?

Who can say if I and the clergy will ever get along
For I am decreeing love to be the universal law

The saints even when clad in rags are full of aura and magic
The young find these miracle-workers irresistible

I tremble in front of those who gather daily to acquire fame
A fame that arises as they burn their own homes

May our motherland flourish for eternity
Our salutations, mother, as the ship departs your shores

When all those unaccustomed to pray assemble for prayer
How strange that of all people they summon Iqbal to be the prayer.[29]

As one reads through Iqbal's dense verse, a key question arises: What could have attracted Bhagat Singh to a poem that primarily addresses the nature of prayer? The answer, despite the poem's considerable complexity, is possibly simple. Iqbal offers a powerful critique of the nihilism that is inherent in capitalism. By deploying an alternative vocabulary made up of such categories as saints, aura, magic, silence, and prayer, he wants his readers not to be seduced by the goods on offer in the marketplace of colonial modernity. And he seems to be saying that, even if one were temporarily swayed by the instrumental rationality of colonial modernity, hope still remains. And the reason for this hope, Iqbal says, is to be found by looking around society and observing the truth that "When all those unaccustomed to pray assemble for prayer" the final triumph of capitalism is postponed. The poet's communitarian logic is enlarged when he notes sarcastically: "The saints even when clad in rags are full of aura and magic." He concedes that while colonial modernity has considerably impoverished Sufi saints and pirs and their role

[29] For the Urdu original see: http://iqbalurdu.blogspot.com/2011/04/bang-e-dra-091-masal-e-pertu-e-mei-tof.html, accessed on 14 August 2019.

in society, "the young find these miracle-workers irresistible". In other words, as Weber might have put it, the world is still far from being disenchanted. Saintly charisma holds, and the world of community and prayer still provides webs of meaning and interpretive salience.

In the last line of the poem Iqbal seems to allude to his own biography. He seems to be saying – Look at me as an exemplar; if one like me, educated at secular universities like Cambridge and Ludwig Maximilan in Munich, can be summoned to be a prayer leader, then there is indeed more to our lives than the deck of cards scattered by the project of modernity.

While Iqbal was in many ways a poet of sentiment, emotion, and communitarian values, he could be equally invested in ideological musings.

The final Iqbal poem that captured Bhagat Singh's heart – *March 1907* – reads like a political manifesto:

> Ours is an age without mystery, the beloved has no veil
> Secrets spill out in the open, the silence is shattered

> In the past those who drank wine did so in secret taverns
> Now in our age the entire world is a tavern, all drink unabashedly

> The people of the West ought to know, this God-created world is not merely a business
> Your standards of purity are counterfeit

> Western civilisation is launched on a path of self-willed destruction
> Nothing in this world survives without solid foundations

> When I told the birds that the free were acting like slaves
> The flowers in the garden said I must know the secret

> God, surely has millions of lovers but many are still haunted by the loneliness of forest-dwellers

As for me I shall only follow the One who cares for the
  people of God

Listen my heart, even the smallest of transgressions are sin
What then will be left of my honour if I am always anxious
  in this world

My goal is to leave with the caravan in the middle of the
  night
But beware even though I am tired I am still full of fire and
  sparks

Please do not inquire about the poet Iqbal's goals
He is weary of new tyrannies and thus awaits alone.[30]

Iqbal is here again offering a fusillade against capitalism, but this time polemically conflating imperialism, capitalism, and the West. He bemoans the loss of tradition, particularly gnostic modes of mysticism. He does not directly allude to saints and the bearers of esoteric knowledge, but with "secrets" and "silence" he draws our attention to a pre-modern world of learning and erudition where what was deemed truly valuable was not freely available within state schools and universities. The democratisation of knowledge under the aegis of capitalism and modernity irks Iqbal deeply. In his conservative worldview, what is precious ought to stay shrouded in mystery. True knowledge ought not to be available via mass instruction: this is what he means by the beloved needing to remain veiled; only a great master skilled in esoteric knowledge can unveil it to provide glimpses of eternal truths. Without this, "the silence is shattered" and with "secrets spilling out in the open" we get forms of knowledge that are remote from all context, which, when combined with modern mass movements, can then give rise to political tyranny. Given

---

[30] http://iqbalurdu.blogspot.com/2011/04/bang-e-dra-092-march-1907.html, accessed on 14 August 2019.

the anxieties of the new age, Iqbal implores readers to see that their only choice is to strike forward alone, preferably in some sort of mystical solitude. For if they do not, their community will, by mimicking the West, invite unwanton destruction. The ideological thrust and conservative zeal exhibited in *March 1907* make it simultaneously a poem that explores themes that can broadly be described as humanistic and concerned with interior spaces.

This reading of poems by Ghalib and Iqbal that were dear to Bhagat Singh is an attempt to suggest the core of what deeply touched Bhagat Singh. I choose the words "deeply touched" advisedly, for it is hard to say how these poems influenced him. They certainly provided him with what George Steiner calls "ontological astonishment".[31] Did such astonishment influence any of the political statements and communiqués that Bhagat Singh issued from the Lahore jail? I do not believe the question can be answered with any certainty. However, what is certain is that both Ghalib and Iqbal provided Bhagat Singh with rich existential resources throughout his short life. We get a good glimpse of how the full force of Urdu poetry worked in his mind in the final letter he wrote to his brother Kultar Singh on 3 March 1931, twenty days before he was hanged.[32] Although the letter is cryptic and full of ellipses, it seeks to transcend finitude and provide succour to all fearful of death:

My Dear Kultar:

I felt very sad on seeing tears in your eyes. There was so much pain in all that you narrated. I cannot bear to see tears in your eyes. I implore you to stay calm, continue with your studies and take care of your health. Please stay strong. What more can I say to you? . . . I would like to share a few couplets of poetry with you:

---

[31] Steiner, *No Passion Spent*, p. 272.
[32] Although the Urdu text of this last letter is widely available on vari-

> *Some are worried that they will miss latest updates on salacious gossip*
> *My passions, friends are different. I want to know when tyranny will end.*[33]
> *Why be disappointed with the world?*
> *Why complain to the master of the skies?*
> *For when injustices in the world mount*
> *We shall convene to oppose.*
> *We do not live for eternity*
> *The flame lit at dawn does not flicker through the night.*[34]
> *I shall saturate the air with my ideas,*
> *So what, if the body decays at the end, ideas live on.*
> *Stay happy, countrymen, we shall continue with our journey.*

Always have courage.
Namaste!
Your brother,

Signed: Bhagat Singh.

Conclusion

To now tie together the various threads – the books that Bhagat Singh read, his personal ruminations, the poets he admired, and his epic political struggles. Raymond Williams suggests that we are not born with an ability to read the world, we gradually learn to decode it: deciphering the world is a cultivated and cumulative skill. So, how is this skill of reading the world acquired? It is crucial to answer this large question, for only by doing so can we engage with our key questions: How did Bhagat Singh

---

ous internet sites, the text used here is based on Deol, *Sardar Bhagat Singh*, p. 149.

[33] Bhagat Singh cites this couplet from the Urdu poet Brij Narain Chakbast (1882–1926).

[34] This is a famous and widely cited couplet from Iqbal.

transform his "minimal self" – the fate of most of us – to a maximal self, which is a relatively rare event in human life? We have some insights at hand from disciplines such as psychology, philosophy, and sociology on how humans across cultures and time have gathered variegated resources, a sort of working knowledge that allows a minimal self to function in the larger world. Despite the master disciplines involved, the list of resources that have been identified for organising our thoughts and actions is fairly small. It includes language, mimesis (imitation), images, narratives, intuitions, emotions, experience, and deliberation.[35] "Each one of us," writes Williams,

> has to learn to see. The growth of every human being is a slow process of learning . . . the rules of seeing, without which we could not in any ordinary sense see the world around us. There is no reality of familiar shapes, colours, and sounds, to which we merely open our eyes. The information that we receive through our senses from the material world around us has to be interpreted, according to certain human rules, before what we ordinarily call reality forms. The human brain has to perform this creative activity before we can, as normal human beings see at all.[36]

In applying this theory of knowledge to Bhagat Singh, we could say that, initially, he acquired the art of seeing via his education in his natal home, the village school, and subsequently in metropolitan Lahore. In this he was no different from millions of other colonial subjects in the early part of the twentieth century. But most colonial subjects, having acquired the art of seeing, did not turn into revolutionaries or into the sorts of maximal self that Bhagat Singh did. What accounts for Bhagat Singh's remarkable transformation?

[35] I have arrived at this list by my reading of Williams, *The Long Revolution*; Damasio, *Descartes' Error*; and Kahneman, *Thinking Fast and Slow*.
[36] Williams, *The Long Revolution*, p. 17.

Once again, Williams is of help. He tells us that some individuals during certain epochs of human history find the given rules, justifications, commentaries, and given interpretations inadequate. They seek to reinterpret the world, create new rules, and provide us with alternative horizons.[37] And although Williams does not tell us why only certain individuals find the given rules and normative descriptions inadequate, based on what we have seen of the inner world of Bhagat Singh it seems possible to advance the argument that his quest to break the given rules and social codes of colonialism came in great measure from his vast reading. In one part of his library he found through Rousseau and Marx the ideas of freedom and revolution; in another through Ghalib and Iqbal he examined the idea of Kismet (fate), Yar (Friend), Dard (pain), and Naya Jahan (a new world).

This eclectic reading, which generated new vocabularies and intellectual horizons, suggests that Bhagat Singh ought not to be interpreted solely as a political leader. The enduring humanistic elements in his thought, aspirations, and praxis derive from an intellectual transformation, the creation of a maximal self virtually unknown among political thinkers of his social background. Bhagat Singh's maximal self has left us with a radically new language of being: secular, cosmopolitan, optimistic, rational, realist, and reflexive. Self-fashioning of this kind also means the ability to acknowledge that pain, suffering, and tragedy are integral to the human condition. Bhagat Singh's walk to the gallows on that fateful day in March 1931, without fear or trepidation, was the concrete expression of such a deeply ethical self.

---

[37] Ibid., pp. 16–19.

6

An Epic Without a Text: Imagining Indian Diasporas

> The true picture of the past flits by. The past can be seized only as an image which flashes up at this instant when it can be recognised and is never seen again . . . the state of emergency in which we live is not the exception but the rule. We must attain to a conception of history that is in keeping with this insight.
>
> **Walter Benjamin**

In the late 1980s, the Social Science Research Council in New York commissioned a well-known Indian novelist, Amitav Ghosh, to write a piece on the cultural connections between India and its diasporic populations. Ghosh came up with a rather dramatic hypothesis – that although we take it for granted that there is and should be an abiding relationship between India and its migrants, this relationship has been historically both peculiar and anomalous.[1] And how so? Ghosh sought to back up his provocative proposition by arguing that the links between India and its modern diaspora were not those of language, politics, religion, or economics.

Beginning with the linguistic register, he argued that Indian migrants – unlike the British or French or Chinese overseas – conceded all too readily to the languages of the new areas they

---

[1] See Ghosh, "The Diaspora in Indian Culture", pp. 73–8.

called home. Thus in Mauritius, an island where Indian migrants have a numerical preponderance over other communities, the dominant language is not Hindi but a French creole. Similarly, in Trinidad and Guyana, where the Indian diaspora is substantial, Indians speak a creole mixed with European and native languages rather than their indigenous Bhojpuri. Unlike other civilisations, in this argument, India did not export a language with its outgoing groups. Equally, when it came to the institutional or political framework of the subcontinent, India's dispersed populations had not appropriated anything from these structures either. In this sense the Indian diaspora was in Ghosh's view strikingly dissimilar to the diasporas of the Arabs, Turks, and Anglo-Saxons, who had borrowed heavily from the institutional and political paradigms of their respective mother countries.

Having sought to discredit the idea of linguistic and political affiliation among diasporic Indians and their country of origin, Ghosh went on to try dismantling notions of systematic connections in the religious and economic spheres. Both Hinduism and Indian Islam, he contended, are marked by systematic diversity, and as such do not possess either the uniformity of dogma or ritual practices to press their claims among those who had left and resettled in foreign shores. He cited the example of how Hindus in India can now barely recognise the religious practices of Hindus in the West Indies.[2] And finally, he downplayed the possibility of any significant economic links between India and its diaspora.

Instead of language, religion, politics, and economics, Ghosh argued that what connected India and its diaspora was largely the domain of the imagination, which he called an "epic relationship". But even in this limited bracketing he saw a massive hiatus; and, strangely enough – given that his argument for an

---

[2] A brilliantly humorous account of the distance between Hindu prayer rituals in India and their counterparts in British Guiana (Guyana) in the late-twentieth century can be found in Dhar, *Raga'n Josh*, pp. 353–61.

"epic relationship" was connected centrally with the imagination – no canonical text seemed to him visible as evidence of this epic relationship. Moreover, he argued that even if such a metatext were ever proposed or written, it would be a "shabby, bedraggled, melancholy kind of epic".[3] In sum, Ghosh seemed to celebrate the fact that an imaginary "epic relationship" exists without a unifying text. It seems to me that while these startling propositions put forward by Ghosh make for intriguing reading, anyone who follows the cartography of the South Asian diasporas knows that most of them are poorly formulated and, subjected to scrutiny, far from convincing.

One could cite scores of empirical examples and numerous case studies to question these propositions. For instance, if we examine the linguistic register, we know that Indians have not drowned in some ocean of heteroglossia. The province of British Columbia on the west coast of Canada experienced a long chain of Indian migration, extending over a hundred years, primarily from the Punjab region. Although it is true that, initially, when Indian numbers were very small in the region, much of the public discourse took place in English, as the demographics of the diaspora thickened the usage and visibility of Punjabi increased significantly. Members of the Punjabi migrant community set about purchasing printing presses from which they published newspapers, journals, novels, plays, and literary anthologies, and some of the plays they published in their vernacular were successfully staged. The dramatic growth in Punjabi print culture also laid the foundations for an interest in live broadcasts over both radio and television. In the 1980s a community drive led to the establishment of a chair in Punjabi language and literature at the University of British Columbia. This was followed by the provincial education ministry including instruction in Punjabi as part of the school curriculum from grade 1 to grade 12. Without

---

[3] Ibid., p. 76.

unduly exaggerating the importance of these materials – for there is no public culture in British Columbia informed by a minority language – what needs to be underscored is that one can cite solid examples of Indian diasporic communities taking the language question seriously and doing quite a lot with it.

What about political articulations, then – the second proposition on the peculiarities of Indian migrant communities? As a writer who has also been a social scientist Ghosh is well aware that it would be naïve to seek imprints of medieval Indian expansion, such as those of the Tamils who took Indian forms of kingship to South East Asia. In the absence of such spectacular linkages, he seems to conclude prematurely that "there are no significant political or strategic considerations in the links between India and her diaspora."[4] If one were to view communal consciousness quintessentially as an Indian contribution to modern political vocabulary, it is in fact far from difficult to document how this consciousness has come to heavily influence the politics of those who left the motherland. Else on what political grid could one position organisations such as the Babbar-Akalis, the Kashmir Liberation Force, and the Vishwa Hindu Parishad? These atavistic bodies have long been firmly tied to the politics of the subcontinent.

The disapora's economic sphere is also far more complex than Ghosh allows. Without venturing into the data on remittances and capital inflows from the newly minted fortunes of Indian engineers in California, a much more humble example can be cited. In the early 1900s it was Punjabi farmers who introduced rice farming to the United States. Today, rice cultivation is big business in the agricultural valleys of California. And finally, in the domain of religion it is now commonplace to suggest that both popular religiosity and official theologies are constantly replicated and renewed in the diaspora.

[4] Ibid., p. 75.

Despite my sceptical view of Ghosh's intervention, I think that as a creative writer he is on to something more credible when he proposes in passing that the massive migration from India has never been emplotted in a literary text of epic proportions. This seems to me a lacuna that, particularly in the context of Canada, bears thinking about. While some of the finest writers of English today in metropolitan centres like New York, London, and Toronto are of Indian origin, this fact has not translated into a body of literature that ties South Asians into what Benedict Anderson made famous as "imagined communities". These imagined communities are the result of commodified print culture and literary production, particularly the novel. Lisa Lowe, who has written extensively on Asian–American communities, is rather apt when she observes:

> In both England and the United States, the novel as a form of print culture has constituted a privileged site for the unification of the citizen with the imagined community of the nation, while the national literary canon functioned to unify aesthetic culture as a domain in which material differences and localities were resolved and reconciled. The bildungsroman emerged as the primary form for narrating the development of the individual from youthful innocence to civilised maturity, the telos of which is the reconciliation of the individual with the social order.[5]

With the emergence of the novel as a textual institution in the West, it became possible to spin foundational cultural fictions surrounding nationalism, gender privileges, class distinctions, the public and the private, and imperial mission. The entire project of modernity, particularly its normative doctrine of individualism and secularism, had to be radically inscribed on the minds and bodies of subjects who were often unwilling to

---

[5] Lowe, *Immigrant Acts*, p. 98.

let go of allegiances to older orthodoxies. The writings of Jane Austen, Charles Dickens, and Goethe, while providing entertainment to an ever increasing reading public, helped resolve the cultural contradictions resulting from new forms of activity and economic reorganisation. So my central question here is: What sort of literary institution can be said to perform the same role for the transnational communities of the diaspora? How are the ruptures, traumas, and contradictions of migrant communities resolved? If the nation is narrated by the novel, what sort of text narrates the diaspora?

My initial answer to these questions is influenced by the writings of Walter Benjamin. The textual archives of Indian migrant communities are then to be found in "flashes of memory" that are often explicated in "moments of danger".[6] These flashes of memory are not contained in any single genre and can take multiple forms: anecdotes, rumour, gossip, poetry, fiction, drama, memoirs, and literary fragments. Further, I argue that there is an intertextuality across these forms whereby the facts of fiction can equally be rendered as the facts of history. As such, it seems to me a grave error to look for these "flashes of memory" in the institutional arena of high culture alone, or within disciplinary boundaries.[7]

The most famous Indian writer currently living in Canada is Rohinton Mistry. Born to a Zoroastrian family in 1952, he went to school and college in Bombay. Soon after finishing his B.Sc. in 1974, he emigrated to Canada and made Toronto his home. While working in a bank, he again enrolled for post-secondary

---

[6] Walter Benjamin, "Theses on the Philosophy of History".

[7] An effort that I see as not dissimilar to mine here can be found in the work of the historian of modern India Joya Chatterji, who is keenly interested in issues of migration, resettlement, diasporic experience, and the reconstitution of citizenship by looking at the writings of Bengali migrants and refugees in elite literature as well as subaltern memoir. See, esp., Chatterji, "Migration Myths and the Mechanics of Assimilation", pp. 218–63.

education and got himself a degree in liberal arts from the University of Toronto (1984). Over this time he started writing short stories. His first story, "Auspicious Occasion", was set in Bombay and revolved around the quotidian life of the city's Parsi community. These two themes, the decaying environment of a post-colonial metropolis and the vicissitudes of Parsi life, became obsessions in Mistry's literary oeuvre. His first collection of eleven short stories, *Tales from Firozsha Baag* (1987) was followed by an ambitious novel, *Such a Long Journey*, which was awarded a long list of honours and distinctions.[8] He had similar success with *A Fine Balance*, a six-hundred page tale of Bombay and its inhabitants over an eight-year period starting in 1975.[9]

Who, one may ask, could be more qualified than Mistry to narrate the lived experience of Indians in Canada? He clearly has the stamina, distinction, and vision to weave a powerful tale on the triumphs and tragedies of diasporic Indians in the American continent. His twenty-five years in Toronto have only yielded two diasporic short stories: "Lend Me Your Light" and "Swimming Lessons".[10] Both are autobiographical texts, one explaining why the author left Bombay and what he finds in Toronto, particularly within its Parsi population, and the other a debriefing on the process of settlement and attendant fantasies. Thus, within a total literary production of over 1100 pages, Mistry has only 44 pages on the minutiae of immigration. Perhaps it is far easier to be the Dickens of domesticity in Bombay than to sketch the interior landscape of displacement, ghettoisation, and racialised labour sites.

---

[8] Commonwealth Writer's Prize for best book in 1991; the Canadian Governor-General's award; the Booker Prize shortlist.

[9] Once again the trophies rolled in. Alongside the Commonwealth Writer's Prize for best book, and a spot on the shortlist for the Booker Prize, Mistry received one of Canada's most prestigious literary awards, the Giller Prize, followed by the Los Angeles Times Book Prize for fiction.

[10] Mistry, *Tales from Firozsha Baag*.

What did Maluka Desire: A Redemption in Leaving?

Paradoxically, the first major novel on Indian immigration to Canada was written by someone who can in some ways be said to be almost unqualified to produce such a text, for he was not a professional writer or a master stylist. This semi-autobiographical text, entitled *Maluka*, published in 1978, is the work of Sadhu Singh Dhami.[11] Dhami was born in a dusty village of central Punjab in 1906. At the age of sixteen he moved to Canada and started working in a saw-mill. His older Punjabi co-workers, impressed by his intelligence, encouraged him to go to school and even promised to help subsidise his education. Around 1924 Sadhu Singh enrolled in John Oliver School in Vancouver. After finishing high school he went on to the University of British Columbia, and from there to the University of Alberta, the University of California at Berkeley, and the University of Toronto. From this last institution he received a doctorate in educational psychology in 1937. After working in the incipient trade-union movement he secured a job with the International Labour Organisation in Geneva and worked there until his retirement in 1966. In the 1960s he began to write the story of a young boy named Maluka, which is really in most part the life story of Sadhu Singh Dhami and his times. Much like Kipling's *Kim*, it is a coming-of-age script during the colonial regime, a crisis of identity embedded in alternative modernities and cultural confusions, and finally a decisive leave-taking.

The opening chapter is entitled "The Lumber Mill". This is apt, because when the first batches of young Punjabi men began to arrive in Canada in the early 1900s, the great majority of them found employment either in saw-mills or with the Canadian Pacific Railways. With the transcontinental railway line having

---

[11] Dhami, *Maluka*.

only recently been completed, and with the provincial economy opening out into a modern economy, there were substantial opportunities for employment. From immigration records we know that, between 1904 and 1908, 5000 men from India made British Columbia their home.[12] The bulk of them were from central Punjab and almost every one of them arrived in Vancouver the same way. First they took a train that transported them from their native village to Calcutta, a distance of approximately 1500 miles. From Calcutta they left by Japanese freighters for Hong Kong, a trip that could take anywhere from fifteen to twenty days. Kuldeep Bains, who undertook this journey, recalls that

> They gave you the bottom grade, the basement. That's the only place they had. Before we left we had to buy some groceries, portable beds, a stove and some coal. We prepared our own meals on the deck, we slept on the deck. There were no staterooms at all. There must have been over a hundred Sikhs staying on the deck. All night long and day long we stayed on the deck. If it rained, we would put up a little tent up there. We made our own meals there. There was a small dispensary, I think there was a doctor on board too, he gave me some pills. I got sick, I had never seen the ocean in my whole life.[13]

In the early days, unlike now, the Canadian government had no offices in India to process immigration papers. Many of the key immigration formalities such as a medical examination and interviewing were carried out in Hong Kong. The process could take several weeks, and once the paperwork was finished it took a month or so for the voyage from Hong Kong to Victoria or Vancouver.[14]

---

[12] Johnston, *The East Indians in Canada*, p. 6.
[13] Cited in Jagpal, *Becoming Canadians*, p. 40.
[14] I am indebted to Jagpal, *Becoming Canadians*, for my understanding of how the pioneers undertook the journey from India to Hong Kong with a stopover in Hong Kong.

Maluka quickly became enmeshed in this new community of migrants. He secured a job working on the green chain at the Dominion Lumber Mills. It was a life of perpetual motion securing and managing large booms of cedar logs, heavy iron machinery manipulated to the din of constantly shifting chains and roller systems, and the humming of an incredible variety of saws: head-saws, band-saws, rip-saws. But late in the evening, when all the activity had finally ceased, the men would retire to eat and drink in what were then revealingly called Hindu cook houses: in the eyes of Canadians all Indians – Sikh, Muslims, or otherwise – were simply Hindu. Sadhu Singh Dhami provides us with a graphic description of this hyper-masculine world:

> The "Hindu boys", as the Indian workers, mostly Sikh farmers from the Punjab, were called locally, ran their own co-operative kitchen, each paying his share of the food and a day's wage towards the cook's monthly salary. Over a hundred of them were employed by the mill . . . The cook house which had a pantry and the cook's room at the back, served as the kitchen, the dining hall and the club house. Most of the social life of the colony was lived in it, and hot tea was always on tap. Men walked in and out to relax and gossip, to argue and to quarrel, often merely to relieve boredom. Here they gathered to listen to the community leaders, who came from Vancouver, Victoria or other small settlements in the lumber mills on the Vancouver island, to collect money for a school or a Gurdwara, for a religious or political movement in the Punjab. Here the more gifted among them read aloud the Punjabi classics, recited poetry or sang familiar village songs stirring deep sentiments and powerful longings for the half-forgotten joys of old.[15]

And as for their living quarters, we have the following description:

---

[15] Dhami, *Maluka*, pp. 12–13.

Six long parallel sheds with tarred paper-roofs, each partitioned into small rooms with two bunks in each. They had been built on the marshy bank of the Fraser filled with mill refuse and covered over by soggy layers of saw-dust. With time, they had acquired a weatherbeaten dark-gray look, and had sunk almost a foot into sawdust. In the passage way of these sheds, on both sides, hung dirty working clothes, almost touching the rows of heavy working shoes and the black gum boots under them, and on the worn-out boards of the floor the nail heads stood bare and shiny.[16]

As these men lived their lives in the mills, cook houses, and bunk houses, with occasional forays into the world beyond, the primary reference for them remained India. They regularly read from Indian newspapers, kept up an extensive correspondence with their extended families, and if successful in accumulating capital often went back to buy land, get married, and build homes in the natal village. In all of their sensibilities, moorings, categories of thought, structures of feeling, cultural dispositions, and practices they had little inclination or desire to transgress the symbolic or cognitive universe of their origins. The Ghadar movement that sought to free India militarily from colonial rule was born in their midst.

Our protagonist Maluka, much like Kipling's Kim, was comfortable with his native world and fellow men. And the community solidarity and cultural bonds solidified as he used his elementary knowledge of English to translate and interpret the North American world for the benefit of his countrymen. What was mute or invisible acquired a voice and visibility through Maluka's ingenuity and linguistic interventions. He became the semiotic expert to domesticate the unknown world beyond the cook house. Beholden to his gracious assistance, and acknowledging the potential of his youth, all his mentors and friends

---

[16] Ibid., pp. 11–12.

encouraged him to abandon the hardships of a dead-end life in the saw-mill to pursue the goal of higher education, so that one day the community could have its own organic intellectual. Eventually, Maluka is persuaded. He first enrols in a local high school and then goes on to study at the university.

But this larger world of education, which Maluka initially found so hard to traverse, soon poses its routine terrors. His parochial loyalties, cultural nationalism, and male bonding are soon tested in the world of ideas, books, and changing moral codes. In high school Maluka falls in love with a classmate named Doris. She is everything he is not: white, Christian, and a domestic symbol of the Empire. We are talking here of the 1920s. Despite these differences the two embrace one another. Since Maluka is seen as the child prodigy of the community, this romantic liaison across racial and religious boundaries traumatises his sponsors. In turn, Maluka, the alter ego of Sadhu Singh, feels oppressed and claustrophobic. The censoring eyes and inquisitorial gaze of his countrymen lead him to yet another transgression: he abandons the historic symbols and ritual life of his religious tradition and stages a rebellious exit from his shack in the saw-mill, from the city which he had made his home, but above all from the community of his natural and emotional solidarity. Much like Stephen Dedalus in *A Portrait of the Artist as a Young Man*, Maluka breaches the boundaries of his community of affection to discover and learn about life beyond his home and "race". Leaving Vancouver behind, he goes on to live in Edmonton, San Francisco, Toronto, and Geneva. He is only fully redeemed by renouncing his primordial attachments to caste, ethnicity, and religion.

Maluka is a puzzling novel. Sadhu Singh Dhami is not famous as a man of letters. He has received no literary accolades for fictionalising the conditions and perils of migrancy. At best, he is deemed a minor writer. Yet he has to my mind persuasively succeeded in evoking some of the deepest sources of high modernism: the fragmentation of the self, unbelonging, and cultural ambivalence. His literary influences, life choices, intellectual citations, and ideological possibilities are hybrid. One day he goes to address the Theosophists on the Hindu *Upanishads*, and on another he trains trade-union leaders in Marxian economics. Although he constantly talks about the politics of Indian nationalism, is deeply aware of Gandhi, and corresponds with Nehru, as an adult he never participates in the national movement. His preferred politics are those of the international labour movement. When it comes to theological allegiances, he wants "to tear the mask from the face of religion".[17] The multicultural world that Maluka eventually creates cannot be compressed into "Sikh" or "Hindu" diasporas. As Adorno says in his memoir, *Minima Moralia*, subtitled *Reflections from a Damaged Life*: "The past life of emigrés is, as we know, annulled, because anything that is not reified cannot be counted and measured, ceases to exist."[18] The arrangements Maluka makes in the New World and the fundamental questions he poses can only be framed as those of cosmopolitanism. But more on this later.

Dilemmas of Iteration and Making a Fetish of Belonging

Iteration: repetition of an action or process; to do over again; to perform a second time; to repeat, to renew

Victor Turner, who was once widely cited, is now somewhat forgotten. His anthropological writings on pilgrimage and *communitas* remain, all the same, fecund for the study of comparative diasporas, because there are a lot of family resemblances between journeys of pilgrimage and the global mobility of diasporas. In a classic essay entitled "Liminality and Communitas", Turner

---

[17] Ibid., p. 302.
[18] Cited in Said, *Culture and Imperialism*, p. 333.

proposed that historically all societies need constant exchange and show a dialectical relationship between what he termed structure and anti-structure.[19] Through the structural dimension we get law, economic production, and morality. And the anti-structural formation, if it can be called that – perhaps this is the reason Turner much prefers the Latin word *communitas* – provides social systems with speculative thought, works of art, utopian solidarities, strains of rebellion – in short unbelonging. While Turner celebrates *communitas*, as a social scientist he is well aware that societies cannot do without the order and stability of structures. But when the time comes for renewal and change and the introduction of new vocabularies, societies look towards liminal figures: prophets, charismatic leaders, poets, artists, and those who are generally seen as living on the margins of society. Turner's reflections on liminality are worth quoting at length:

> The attributes of liminality or of liminal *personae* ("threshold people") are necessarily ambiguous, since this condition and these persons elude or slip through the network of classifications that normally locates states and positions in cultural space. Liminal entities are neither here or there; they are betwixt and between the positions assigned and arrayed by law, custom, convention, and ceremonial. As such, their ambiguous and indeterminate attributes are expressed by a rich variety of symbols in the many societies that ritualise social and cultural transitions. Thus liminality is frequently likened to death, to being in the womb, to invisibility, to darkness, to bisexuality, to the wilderness, and to an eclipse of the sun or moon.[20]

In short, liminality is dangerous, transgressive, and thus regenerative. Since it seeks to introduce something new into culture through an ensemble of critical interventions and unrehearsed

---

[19] The essay is in Turner, *The Ritual Process*.
[29] Ibid., p. 95.

peregrinations, it cannot be said to derive from iteration. From Turner's perspective, Sadhu Singh Dhami's protagonist would fit this typology of liminality. Maluka is a figure who begins from within a structure and then turns into a "threshold" person.

I would like now to examine an anti-type of Maluka: a person who is hardly ever assailed by self-doubt, is content to live within a structure and established cartographies, and is heroic enough to espouse a similar iteration for others. My material for this exercise is a memoir by Tara Singh Bains.[21]

Bains was born in 1923 in the medium-sized village of Sarhala Khurd in Hoshyarpur district, a region that has been staging ground for much of the modern immigration from India to Canada. He was certainly not the first in his family to make the journey to the west coast of Canada. In 1908 his father came to British Columbia and then moved to California. Ten years later he moved back to his birthplace and built a sprawling three-storey brick house that earned him the nickname *pakkianwala* (one who owns a brick house), as distinct from the great majority who lived in more humble mud-walled homes. Tara Singh Bains was four years old when his elder sister left for Canada. It was this sister who in 1953 sponsored the brother to come and settle in Canada. The first thirty years of Bains' life were lived in India. He received his early education in a village school, his later instruction in English was at the Khalsa High School in Mahalpur. While he does tell us a little about the subjects he studied, we get no insight into the sorts of books he read, nor do we know who his literary or cultural heroes may have been. In 1944 our young protagonist joined the Indian army with the rank of sergeant and moved to distant Jabalpur in central India. As in quite a lot of Indian autobiographies, we get very little information on Bains' inner life. However, from time to time we do get some insight into his emotions and joys:

[21] See Bains and Johnston, *The Four Quarters*. The following account of

Freedom of life, total glow of life, started with my army career. It was a total relief and total happiness and relaxation too. I was by nature a hard worker, god-gifted to perform my duty honestly and to the maximum of my strength. At the same time I was impregnated with religious orientation. Even when I was a little child I was attuned that way. I carried on my religious life very regularly, although not perfectly. I tried to get up before others, take my bath, complete my prayers, all before Sunrise.[22]

Much of the early section of the memoir is preoccupied with genealogy, family history, and questions of honour and public behaviour. We do not have here any of the early digressions, ambivalence, and secular openings of Maluka. The greatest rebellion in Bains' youth was against the authority of his father.

Stuart Hall, the founding figure of British cultural studies, says in one of his essays on identity that he left the Caribbean for England to get away from his possessive mother.[23] Tara Singh Bains seems to want to leave because of his father. Though his family had not kept in touch with the sister who left for Canada in the 1920s, Bains uses the larger family and village network to locate her and persuades her to help him move to Canada. In the early 1950s Canada's quota for migrants from India was very restricted, but the sister succeeded in persuading Canadian Immigration to let her brother in.

Like many before him, he reached Vancouver without his wife and children. One of the first episodes he narrates of his arrival calls for some interpretation, because psychologically it is a record of perhaps the most traumatic event in his displacement.

Tara Singh Bains is based on this autobiography recorded by the historian Hugh Johnston.

[22] Ibid., p. 17.

[23] Hall, "Minimal Selves", p. 44.

As mentioned earlier, Bains was a man of faith. He lived the life of a believer and as a baptised Sikh that meant he kept his hair unshorn, wore a turban, and maintained the other symbols of his religion. This inordinate commitment to an absolute God and his commandments was at odds with the lives being led by his local kinsmen. His sister's family, either because of its socialisation or more covert cultural positions, had long abandoned the external insignia of the Sikh code. And now Bains' clansmen insisted that his obvious physical and sartorial appearance would prove a considerable impediment for him in securing a comfortable future. Their arguments were antithetical to Tara Singh Bains' core sense of being: he refused to go along with the cultural diktat of his extended family. In private, he experienced a tremendous emotional upheaval and fear of the secular. Finally, sensing his great discomfiture, his brother-in-law and nephews left him alone.

There was to be no leave-taking from his origins for Bains. In Turner's terms, he had refused to be a "threshold" person. Here we see, literally and metaphorically, a post-colonial commitment to religious identity and cultural nationalism. Tara Singh Bains saw no regenerative potential in transgressive high modernity. There was nothing satisfying about stigmata or negative freedom. And yet, what signifies loss to Tara Singh was, as noticed earlier, seen as a gain by Maluka. Both emerge from the same environment and similar class backgrounds, but they arrive at radically different conclusions on how to face their future. It seems imperative to point out here that what to outsiders may appear a unified, monolithic, diasporic group is in fact based on the testimony of these two voices – fractured, the site of multiple identities and disparate hopes.

Tara Singh Bains initially found employment at a family farm, and soon after, like the bulk of his compatriots, secured a job at a saw-mill. Some of his recollections from this period of his life (the early 1950s) are worth quoting:

I started on Tuesday evening on the shift that went from 7:00 p.m. to 4:00 a.m., and I worked until Friday before I was told that I was not being paid for my first four shifts because they were considered a training period. That drove a wedge into my mind about the exploitative nature of the man we were working for, but I kept working. We were paid $1.45 an hour for eight hours, but when we did overtime, we worked for free. And it happened many times that we worked through our coffee and lunch breaks and for some time after our shift was over. If we did not work, the job would be on the line . . . The mill had two gang saws, and each shift these saws would cut fifty thousand or sixty thousand board-feet of moisture-laden hemlock or fir, heavy wood, with none of the lighter cedar as a relief . . . From the mill this lumber carried on to the green chain and down the green chain to the pull-off sections where we stood, two on each side, taking it as fast as it came and piling it according to size and order on wooden blocks, load by load, for removal by a carrier truck.[24]

Here the similarities with Maluka are striking. And, like Maluka, responding to exploitative work conditions and ghettoisation of the labour pool, Bains became active in the trade-union movement. He soon rose to be a vice president of his local sub-union and was elected as a delegate to attend the twelfth annual convention of the British Columbia Federation of Labour. But unlike the mature Maluka, Bains also took a close interest in the affairs of his own ethnic community. He routinely organised religious festivals in his home town of Port Alberni and took a prominent part in many fund-raising drives for cultural projects in India. In 1956 he served as a secretary-treasurer of the Canadian East Indian Welfare Society. The longing for things Indian comes out beautifully in the following passage:

[24] Bains and Johnston, *Four Quarters*, pp. 61–2.

In those days, because my family wasn't there, I read a lot. I was getting quite a few Punjabi monthlies from India – *Aatam Science*, from Calcutta, a very spiritual magazine, *Sant Sipahi* and *Gurmat*, two religious magazines from Amritsar, and *Amar Kahanyan*, with stories emphasising Indian moral values, social discipline, and creating a better sensitivity of living. In English I read the *Vancouver Sun* every day, *Life* magazine every week, and *Reader's Digest* monthly, and I would also read the odd magazine from the market, like *Time*. I also read *The Sikh Review*, from Calcutta, every month in English, and after I came to Port Alberni I started the weekly airmail edition of *Hindustan Times*.[25]

In 1960, because of a serious illness in the family, Tara Singh Bains returned first to his own village in the Punjab and later settled at his wife's natal place. Once again he became active in local and family affairs: setting up schools, starting new businesses, and getting family members married. After a six-year stay, he returned to Canada in 1966. This time round he was to stay put for over a decade and for the first time brought along his wife, three sons, and a daughter. The Indo-Canadian community in Canada was now beginning to grow rapidly in numbers and Bains was to play a significant role in its campaigns for self-representation through ethnic newspapers, cultural organisations, and political activism. But something always stayed amiss for him in Canada and in his memoirs he, at one point, makes an incredible confession: "So British Columbia looked to me like a desert place with only scattered oases."[26] In the early 1900s his father had gone back to India after a short sojourn in California; likewise his son, once he had retired in 1987, was to spend increasing time in India. This shuttling back and forth between India and Canada became a marked feature of his life. One can only wonder what lay behind this constant shuttling.

[25] Ibid., p. 79.
[26] Ibid., p. 112.

Heidegger believed that the locus of the self is a place or habitat. There are, he states, authentic and inauthentic spaces.[27] For close to eighty years now, Bains identifies India and his village as the authentic place for him to be in. It is this archetypal mobility that has perhaps made some in metropolitan societies theorise that immigrant groups have no sense of place.

Conclusion

To go back to the novelist Amitav Ghosh, with whom I began. It can in fairness perhaps be said that his was a preliminary statement on the study of the modern Indian diaspora. Many of the publications and materials available now did not exist in 1989 when he ventured his hypothesis. And a considerable amount of work still needs to be done before we can begin to speak authoritatively of the cultural sociology of India's diasporic populations. One way of advancing the research agenda is by examining narratives, in terms of both plot (story) and discourse (ideology).

It troubles me, as an academic of Indian origin settled in Canada, that a distinguished writer like Mistry has shown little interest in spinning out a grand allegory out of all the material available on Indian migration to Canada and the West more widely over the past century and more. Yet, there are consolations: even without sophisticated literary interventions of the variety I assume Mistry can provide, we do still manage to arrive at a number of insights into the experience of migration. For we can always fall back on what Benjamin termed *flashes of memory*. Perhaps Lyotard is also relevant here in arguing that the epoch of grand narratives is over and we have moved into the age of small narratives. I have looked at two such small narratives in this here, one suggestive of what has come to be known as cosmopolitanism (unbelonging), the other an instance of what may be described as cultural nationalism, or simply nationalism (belonging).

---

[27] Heidegger, *Being and Time*.

Bibliography

Ahluwalia, M.M., *Kukas: The Freedom Fighters of the Punjab*, Bombay, 1965.

Ahmad, Aijaz, *In Theory: Classes, Nations, Literatures*, London, 1992.

Alam, Muzaffar, *The Languages of Political Islam in India 1200–1800*, Ranikhet and Chicago, 2004.

Alam, Nidhan Singh, *Jug Paltau Satguru*, Delhi, 1947.

Amin, Shahid, *Event, Metaphor, Memory: Chauri-Chaura 1922–1992*, Delhi, 1995.

Anderson, K., *Lenin, Hegel and Western Marxism*, Urbana, 1995.

Asif, Manan Ahmed, *The Loss of Hindustan: The Invention of India*, Cambridge, 2020.

Auer, Blain, "Persian Historiography in India", in John Perry, ed., *Persian Literature from Outside Iran*, London, 2018.

Bains, T.S., and H. Johnston, *The Four Quarters of the Night: The Life Journey of an Emigrant Sikh*, Montreal, 1995.

Bajwa, Fauja Singh, *Kuka Movement: An Important Phase in Punjab's Role in India's Struggle for Freedom*, Delhi, 1965.

Ballantyne, Tony, *Between Colonialism and Diaspora*, Durham, 2006.

Barooah, Nirode, *Chatto: The Life and Times of an Anti-Imperialist in Europe*, New Delhi, 2004.

Bayly, C.A., "Orientalists, Informants and Critics in Benares, 1790–1860", in Jamal Malik, ed., *Perspectives of Mutual Encounters in South Asian History 1760–1860*, Leiden, 2000.

Bayly, C.A., *Empire and Information*, Cambridge, 1999.

Bayly, C.A., *Recovering Liberties: Indian Thought in the Age of Liberalism and Empire*, Cambridge, 2011.
Benjamin, Walter, "The Task of the Translator", in Hannah Arendt, ed., *Illuminations*, New York, 1969.
Benjamin, Walter, "Theses on the Philosophy of History", in Hannah Arendt, ed., *Illuminations*, New York, 1973.
Berlin, Isaiah, *The Crooked Timber of Humanity*, New York, 1991.
Bhadour, Attar Singh, *Sakhi Namah; Sakhee Book, or the Descriptions of Gooroo Gobind Singh's Religion and Doctrines*, Benares, 1873.
Bhadour, Attar Singh, *The Rayhit Nama of Prahlad Rai, or the Excellent Conversation of the Duswan Padsha and Nand Lal's Rayhit Nama, or Rules for the Guidance of the Sikhs in Religious Matters*, Lahore, 1876.
Bhadour, Attar Singh, *Travels of Guru Tegh Bahadur and Guru Gobind Singh*, Lahore, 1876.
Bhatnagar, V.S., annotated and trans., *Kanhadade Prabandha*, New Delhi, 1991.
Bhattacharya, Neeladri, "Predicaments of Secular Histories", *Public Culture*, vol. 20, 2008.
Breazeale, Daniel, ed., *Untimely Meditations*, Cambridge, 1997.
Brown, Emily C., *Hardayal: Hindu Revolutionary and Rationalist*, Tucson, 1975.
Brown, W.N., "The Sanctity of the Cow in Hinduism", *Economic Weekly*, 16, 1964.
Browne, James, *India Tracts*, Blackfriars, 1788; rpntd in Ganda Singh, ed., *Early European Accounts of the Sikhs*, Calcutta, 1962.
Buchignani, Norman, and Doreen Indra, *Continuous Journey: A Social History of South Asians in Canada*, Toronto, 1985.
Bulmer, Ralph, "Why is the Cassowary Not a Bird? A Problem of Zoological Taxonomy Among the Karam of the New Guinea Highlands", *Man* (N.S.), 2, 1967.

Caveeshar, S.S., "Gurdwara Rikabganj da Jhamela", in Ganda Singh, ed., *Punjab 1849–1960*, Ludhiana, 1962.

Chakrabarty, Dipesh, "The Public Life of History: An Argument out of India", *Postcolonial Studies*, vol. 11, 2008.

Chatterji, Joya, "Migration Myths and the Mechanics of Assimilation: Two Community Histories from Bengal", in idem, *Partition's Legacies*, Ranikhet and Albany, 2019.

Chatterjee, Elizabeth, Sneha Krishnan, and Meghan Eaton Robb, "Feeling Modern: The History of Emotions in Urban South Asia", *Journal of Royal Asiatic Society*, vol. 17, 2017.

Chatterjee, Partha, *The Nation and Its Fragments*, Princeton, 1993.

Cheema, M.S., "Sir Attar Singh and His Bhadaur", *The Tribune*, 17 December 2000.

Choudhary, Sukhbir, *Growth of Nationalism in India*, New Delhi, 1973.

Clifford, James, *The Predicament of Culture*, Cambridge, 1988.

Cole, Peter, David Struthers, and Kenyon Zimmer, eds, *Wobblies of the World*, London, 2017.

Crooke, William, *Religion and Folklore of Northern India*, Oxford, 1926.

Dalmia, Vasudha, "Sanskrit Scholars and Pandits of the Old School: The Benares Sanskrit College and the Constitution of Authority in the Late Nineteenth Century", *Journal of Indian Philosophy*, vol. 24, 1996.

Damasio, Antonio, *Descartes' Error: Emotion, Reason and the Human Brain*, New York, 1994.

Dard, Hira Singh, *Merian Kuchh Itihasak Yadan*, Jullundur, 1955.

Davidson, H., *Report on the Revised Settlement of the District of Ludhiana*, Lahore, 1859.

Davis, N.Z., "The Rites of Violence: Religious Riot in Sixteenth Century France", *Past and Present*, 59, 1973.

Deol, G.S., *Sardar Bhagat Singh: The Man and His Ideology*, Nabha, 1978.

Deol, G.S., *Shaheed Bhagat Singh*, Patiala, 1969.
Deol, G.S., *The Role of the Ghadar Party in the National Movement*, Jullundur, 1969.
Deshpande, Prachi, *Creative Pasts: Historical Memory and Identity in Western India, 1700–1960*, Ranikhet, 2006.
Dhami, Sadhu Singh, *Maluka*, Patiala, 1997.
Dhar, Sheila, *Raga'n Josh: Stories from a Musical Life*, Ranikhet, 2005.
Dharamvira, *Lala Har Dayal*, New Delhi, 1970.
Diener, Paul, Donald Nonini, and Eugene E. Robkin, "The Dialectics of the Sacred Cow: Ecological Adaptation Versus Political Appropriation in the Origin of India's Cattle Complex", *Dialectical Anthropology* 3, 1978.
Dirks, Nicholas B., "Colonial Histories and Native Informants: Biography of an Archive", in Carol A. Breckenridge and Peter van der Veer, eds, *Orientalism and the Postcolonial Predicament*, Philadelphia, 1993.
Domin, Dolores, *India in 1857–59: A Study in the Role of the Sikhs in the People's Uprising*, Berlin, 1977.
Douglas, Mary, *Implicit Meanings*, London, 1975.
Douglas, Mary, *Purity and Danger*, London, 1966.
Dumont, Louis, *Homo Hierarchicus*, London, 1972.
Dumont, Louis, and David F. Pocock, "Pure and Impure", *Contributions to Indian Sociology*, 3, 1959.
Elam, J. Daniel, "The 'Arch Priestess of Anarchy' Visits Lahore: Violence, Love, and the Worldiness of Revolutionary Texts", *Postcolonial Studies*, vol. 16, 2013.
Eliade, M., *Patterns in Comparative Religion*, London, 1958.
Falcon, R.W., *Handbook on Sikhs for Use of Regimental Officers*, Allahabad, 1896.
Fischer-Tine, Harald, *Shyamji Krishanvarma: Sanskrit, Sociology and Anti-Imperialism*, New Delhi, 2015.
Freitag, Sandria B., "Sacred Symbols as Mobilizing Ideology: The North Indian Search for a Hindu Community", *Comparative Studies in Society and History*, 22, 1980.

Ghose, Loke Nath, *The Modern History of the Indian Chiefs, Rajas, Zamindars*, pt II, Calcutta, 1879.
Ghosh, Amitav, "The Diaspora in Indian Culture", *Public Culture*, vol. 2, 1989.
Giddens, Anthony, *Modernity and Self-Identity*, Cambridge, 1991.
Gilmartin, David Paul, "Tribe, Land and Religion in the Punjab: Muslim Politics and the Making of Pakistan", PhD thesis, University of California, Berkeley, 1979.
Glasgow, R.D.V., *The Minimal Self*, Wuzburg, 2017.
Goldman, Emma, "Psychology of Political Violence", in idem, *Anarchism and Other Essays*, New York, 1910.
Gough, K., "Indian Peasant Uprisings", *Bulletin of Concerned Asian Scholars*, vol. 8, 1976.
Gould, Harold, *Sikhs, Swamis, Students and Spies*, New Delhi, 2006.
Grewal, J.S., H. Puri, and Indu Banga, eds, *The Ghadar Movement*, Patiala, 2013.
Grewal, P.M.S., *Bhagat Singh: Liberation's Blazing Star*, New Delhi, 2007.
Griffin, Sir Lepel, *Rajas of the Punjab*, London, 1873.
Griffin, Sir Lepel, *Ranjit Singh*, Oxford, 1892.
Guha, Ranajit, ed., *Subaltern Studies I: Writings on South Asian History and Society*, Delhi, 1982.
Guha, Ranajit, ed., *Subaltern Studies II: Writings on South Asian History and Society*, Delhi, 1983.
Guha, Sumit, "Speaking Historically: The Changing Voices of Historical Narration in Western India, 1400–1900", *The American Historical Review*, vol. 109, 2004.
Gulati, K.C., *Akalis Past and Present*, Delhi, 1974.
Gupta, Akhil, "Globalization and Difference: Cosmopolitanism Before the Nation-State", *Transforming Cultures*, vol. 3, 2008.
Gupta, Manmathnath, *Bhagat Singh and His Times*, n.p., 1977.
Habermas, Jürgen, *The Philosophical Discourse of Modernity: Twelve Lectures*, trans. Fredrick Lawrence, Cambridge, 1990.

Habib, S. Irfan, *Inquilab*, New Delhi, 2018.
Hall, Stuart, "Minimal Selves", in Lisa Appignanesi, ed., *Identity*, London, 1987.
Hardayal, Lala, "India and the World Movement", *Modern Review*, vol. 13, 1913.
Hardinge, Lord, *My Indian Years 1910–16*, London, 1948.
Harris, Marvin, "India's Sacred Cow", *Human Nature*, I, 1978.
Harris, Marvin, "The Cultural Ecology of India's Sacred Cattle", *Current Anthropology*, 7, 1966.
Hasan, Mushirul, "Nehru: The Writer, the Historian", *The Hindu*, 13 November 2014.
Heehs, Peter, *The Bomb in Bengal: The Rise of Revolutionary Terrorism in India*, Delhi, 1993.
Heidegger, Martin, *Being and Time*, New York, 1962.
Hershman, Paul, "Virgin and Mother", in Ioan Lewis, ed., *Symbols and Sentiments*, London, 1977.
Higgins, Kathleen Marie, "An Alchemy of Emotions: Rasa and Aesthetic Breakthroughs", *Journal of Aesthetics and Art Criticism*, vol. 65, 2007.
Hoare, Quintin, and G.N. Smith, eds, *Selections from the Prison Notebooks of Antonio Gramsci*, London, 1973.
Hobsbawm, Eric, *Primitive Rebels*, Manchester, 1959.
Howes, Jennifer, *Illustrating India: The Early Colonial Investigations of Colin Mackenzie*, London, 2010.
Ingalls, Daniel, Jeffery Mason, and M.V. Patwardhan, trans., *The Dhavanloka of Anandvardhana with the Locana of Abhinavagupta*, Cambridge, 1990.
Iqbal, Muhammad, *Javid-Nama*, trans. Arthur Arberry, London, 1966.
Irwin, Robert, *For Lust of Knowing*, London, 2006.
Jagpal, Sarjit Singh, *Becoming Canadians: Pioneer Sikhs in Their Own Words*, Madiera Park, 1994.
Jan, Ammar Ali, "A Study in the Formation of Communist Thought in India, 1919–1951", PhD dissertation, University of Cambridge, 2018.

Jensen, Joan M., *Passage from India*, New Haven, 1988.
Jeyaraman, Bala, *Periyar: The Political Biography of E.V. Ramasamy*, Delhi, 2014.
Johnston, Hugh, *The East Indians in Canada*, Ottawa, 1984.
Johnston, Hugh, *The Voyage of the Komagata Maru: The Sikh Challenge to Canada's Color Bar*, 1989; rpntd Vancouver, 1995.
Josh, Sohan Singh, *Akali Morchian da Itihas*, Delhi, 1970.
Josh, Sohan Singh, *Baba Sohan Singh Bhakna: Life of the Founder of the Ghadar Party*, New Delhi, 1970.
Josh, Sohan Singh, *My Tryst With Secularism: An Autobiography*, New Delhi, 1991.
Joshi, S.N., "Circumstances Leading to the Rise of the Akali Movement", *Proceedings, Punjab History Conference*, Third Session, Patiala, 1969.
Juneja, M.M., "Bhagat Singh Used to Literally Devour Books", *Times of India*, 22 March 2011.
Kahneman, Daniel, *Thinking Fast and Slow*, New York, 2011.
Kaviraj, Sudipta, *The Invention of Private Life*, Ranikhet, 2015.
Ker, James, *Political Trouble in India*, 1917; rpntd Delhi, 1973.
Kerr, Ian J., "British Relationships with the Golden Temple, 1849–90", *The Indian Economic and Social History Review* 21, 1984.
Kessinger, Tom, *Vilyatpur 1848–1968: Social and Economic Change in a North Indian Village*, California, 1974.
Khan, N., *Egyptian–Indian Nationalist Collaboration and the British Empire*, London, 2011.
Kurosawa, Akira, *Something Like an Autobiography*, New York, 1983.
Lal, Chaman, *The Bhagat Singh Reader*, Noida, 2019.
Lal, Gobind Behari, "Detailed Account of the Ghadar Movement", in T.R. Sareen, ed., *Select Documents on the Ghadar Party*, New Delhi, 1994.

Lanternari, Vittorio, *The Religions of the Oppressed*, New York, 1965.

Lasch, Christopher, *The Minimal Self: Psychic Survival in Troubled Times*, New York, 1984.

Laursen, Ole Birk, "Anarchist Anti-Imperialism: Guy Aldred and Indian Revolutionary Movement, 1909–14", *The Journal of Imperial and Commonwealth History*, vol. 46, 2018.

Leach, Edmund, "Anthropological Aspects of Language: Animal Categories and Verbal Abuse", in Erik H. Lenneberg, ed., *New Directions in the Study of Language*, Cambridge, Mass., 1964.

Leach, Edmund, *Culture and Communication*, Cambridge, 1976.

Leigh, M.S., *The Punjab and War*, Lahore, 1922.

Leitner, G.W., *History of Indigenous Education in the Panjab*, 1883; rpntd Patiala: Languages Department, Punjab, 1971.

Leonard, Karen, *Making Ethnic Choices: California's Punjabi Mexican Americans*, Philadelphia, 1992.

Lévi-Strauss, Claude, *The Savage Mind*, Chicago, 1966.

Lowe, Lisa, *Immigrant Acts*, Durham, 1996.

Macauliffe, M.A., "The Sikh Religion Under Banda", *The Calcutta Review*, vol. lxxiii.

Macauliffe, Max Arthur, *The Sikh Religion*, Oxford, 1909.

Mackenzie, W.C., *Colonel Colin Mackenzie, First Surveyor-General of India*, Edinburgh, 1952.

Maclean, Kama, *A Revolutionary History of Interwar India*, London, 2015.

Mahmood, Khwaja Tariq, *Diwan-e-Ghalib*, Delhi, 2000.

Maine, Henry, *Ancient Law*, London, 1861.

Majithia, Sunder Singh, *Gurdwara Rikabganj*, Amritsar, 1914.

Major, Andrew J., "Return to Empire: The Sikhs and the British in the Punjab 1839–1872", PhD thesis, Australian National University, Canberra, 1981.

Malcolm, Lieutenant-Colonel, *Sketch of the Sikhs*, London, 1812.

McLane, John R., *Indian Nationalism and the Early Congress*, Princeton, 1977.

McLeod, W.H., "The Kukas: A Millenarian Sect of the Punjab", in G.A. Wood and P.S. O'Connor, eds, *W.P. Morrell: A Tribute*, Dunedin, 1973.

McLeod, W.H., *Guru Nanak and the Sikh Religion*, Oxford, 1968.

McLeod, W.H., *Sikhs of the Khalsa: A History of the Khalsa Rahit*, Delhi, 2003.

McLeod, W.H., *Textual Sources for the Study of Sikhism*, Manchester, 1984.

Merriman, John, *The Dynamite Club: How a Bombing in Fin-de-Siecle Paris Ignited the Age of Modern Terror*, Boston, 2009.

Metcalf, B.D., ed., *Moral Conduct and Authority*, California, 1984.

Metcalf, Thomas, *Imperial Connections: India in the Indian Ocean Arena, 1860–1920*, Berkeley, 2007.

Mishra, Satish Chandra, "Commercialization, Peasant Differentiation and Merchant Capital in Late Nineteenth-Century Bombay and Punjab", *Journal of Peasant Studies*, 10, 1982.

Mistry, Rohinton, *A Fine Balance*, New York, 1995.

Mistry, Rohinton, *Such a Long Journey*, New York, 1991.

Mistry, Rohinton, *Tales from Firozsha Baag*, Toronto, 1987.

Mittal, S.C., *Freedom Movement in the Punjab*, Delhi, 1977.

Modern Asian Studies (Special Issue), "Knowledge in Circulation in Early India", vol. 44, 2, 2010.

Moffat, Chris, *India's Revolutionary Inheritance: Politics and Promise of Bhagat Singh*, Cambridge, 2019.

Mukherjee, Tapan K., *Taraknath Das: Life and Letters of a Revolutionary in Exile*, Calcutta, 1998.

Nabha, Kahn Singh, *Gursabad Ratankaar Mahan Kos*, 1930; rpntd Patiala, 1960.

Naidis, Mark, "Propaganda of the Ghadar Party", *Pacific Historical Review*, vol. 20, 1951.

Nair, Neeti, "Bhagat Singh as 'Satyagrahi': The Limits to Non-

Violence in Late Colonial India", *Modern Asian Studies*, vol. 43, no. 3, 2009.
Nandy, Ashis, *The Intimate Enemy*, Delhi, 1989.
Nayar, Kuldip, *Without Fear: The Life & Trial of Bhagat Singh*, Delhi, 2007.
Nehru, Jawaharlal, *The Discovery of India*, New York, 1946.
Nussbaum, Martha, *The Fragility of Goodness: Luck and Ethics in Greek Tragedy*, Cambridge, 1986.
O'Hanlon, Rosalind, "Recovering the Subject: Subaltern Studies and Histories of Resistance in Colonial South Asia", *Modern Asian Studies*, 22, 1988.
Oberoi, Harjot, *The Construction of Religious Boundaries*, Chicago, 1994.
Pinney, Christopher, *Photos of the Gods: The Printed Image and Political Struggle in India*, London, 2004.
Pollock, Sheldon, "Sanskrit Literary Culture from the Inside Out", in idem, ed., *Literary Cultures in History*, Berkeley, 2003.
Pollock, Sheldon, ed., *A Rasa Reader: Classical Indian Aesthetics*, New York, 2016.
Pollock, Sheldon, ed., *Literary Cultures in History*, Berkeley, 2003.
Puri, Harish K., "Ghadar Movement: An Experiment in New Patterns of Socialisation", *Journal of Regional History*, vol. 1, 1980.
Puri, Harish K., *Ghadar Movement: Ideology, Organisation, & Strategy*, Amritsar, 1983.
Puri, Harish K., "The Influence of the Ghadar Movement on Bhagat Singh's Thought and Action", *Journal of Pakistan Vision*, vol. 9, 2008.
Purser, W.E., *Revised Settlement of the Jullundur District*, Lahore, 1892.
Ramnath, Maia, "Two Revolutions: The Ghadar Movement and India's Radical Diaspora, 1913–1918", *Radical History Review*, vol. 92, 2005.

Rao, V.N., David Shulman, and Sanjay Subrahmanyam, *Textures of Time: Writing History in South India 1600–1800*, Delhi, 2001.

Richards, J.F., James R. Hagen, and Edward S. Haynes, "Changing Land Use in Bihar, Punjab and Haryana, 1850–1970", *Modern Asian Studies*, 19, 1985.

Rocher, Rosane, "British Orientalism in the Eighteenth Century: The Dialectics of Knowledge and Government", in Carol A. Breckenridge and Peter van der Veer, eds, *Orientalism and the Postcolonial Predicament*, Philadelphia, 1993.

Rose, H.A., *A Glossary of the Tribes and Castes of the Punjab and North-West Frontier Province*, vol. 1, Lahore, 1911.

Russell, Ralph, *The Oxford India Ghalib: Life, Letters and Ghazals*, Delhi, 2003.

Sachau, Edward, ed. and trans., *Alberuni's India*, 1888; rpntd Lahore, 1962, 2 vols.

Sagar, Sabinderjit Singh, *Historical Analysis of Nanak Prakash: Bhai Santokh Singh*, Amritsar, 1993.

Sahani, Ruchi Ram, *Struggle for Reform in Sikh Shrines*, Amritsar, 1965.

Said, Edward, *Culture and Imperialism*, New York, 1993.

Said, Edward, *Orientalism*, New York, 1978.

Sanehi, Swaran Singh, "Kukas as They Live", in John C.B. Webster, ed., *Popular Religion in the Punjab Today*, Delhi, 1974.

Sareen, T.R., ed., *Select Documents on the Ghadar Party*, New Delhi, 1994.

Scott, James C., *The Moral Economy of the Peasant: Rebellion And Subsistence in Southeast Asia*, New Haven, 1976.

Scott, James C., *Weapons of the Weak: Everyday Forms of Peasant Resistance*, New Haven, 1985.

Sen, Amartya, *The Argumentative Indian*, London, 2005.

Sharma, Shalini, *Radical Politics in Colonial Punjab*, Abingdon, 2014.

Shastri, Raja Ram, *Amar Shahidan Dian Yadan*, Barnala, 2004.

Shastri, Raja Ram, Oral Interview Transcripts in Hindi, Nehru Memorial Museum and Library, New Delhi.

Siderits, Mark, Evan Thompson, and Dan Zahavi, eds, *Self, No Self*, Oxford, 2011.

Singh, Bhagat, "To Young Political Workers (1931)", in S. Irfan Habib, *Inquilab: Bhagat Singh on Religion and Revolution*, Delhi, 2018.

Singh, Bhagat, "Why I am An Atheist", in S.C. Verma, ed., *Bhagat Singh on the Path of Liberation*, Chennai, 2007.

Singh, Bhagwan, *Jang Aur Azadi*, San Francisco, 1915.

Singh, Dhian, *Sri Satguru Bilas*, Bhaini Sahib, 1942.

Singh, Fauja, "Early European Writers: Browne, Polier, Forster, and Malcolm", in idem, ed., *Historians and Historiography of the Sikhs*, New Delhi, 1978.

Singh, Ganda, *A Brief Account of the Sikh People*, Patiala, 1956.

Singh, Ganda, ed., *Early European Accounts of the Sikhs*, Calcutta, 1962.

Singh, Ganda, *Kukian di Vithia*, Amritsar, 1944.

Singh, Ganda, ed., *Punjab 1849–1960*, Ludhiana, 1962.

Singh, Giani Gian, *Pustak Khalsa Dharam Patit Pavan Bhag*, Amritsar, 1903.

Singh, Harbans, ed., *The Encyclopedia of Sikhism*, Patiala, 1992.

Singh, Harbans, *The Heritage of the Sikhs*, Bombay, 1964.

Singh, Joginder, *Kuka Movement: Freedom Struggle in Punjab*, New Delhi, 1985.

Singh, Joginder, "The Sikh Gentry and Its Politics in the Post-World War I Period", *Proceedings of the Indian History Congress*, vol. 53, 1992.

Singh, Jvala, "Sourced Sikh History", https://www.youtube.com/watch. Talk in a series hosted by UK Punjab Heritage Association, retrieved 9 August 2020.

Singh, Kahan, *Gursabad Ratanakar Mahan Kos*, 1930; rpntd Patiala, 1960, 2nd edn.

Singh, Khushwant, *A History of the Sikhs*, Princeton, 1966.
Singh, Khushwant, and Satindra Singh, *Ghadar 1915: India's First Armed Revolution*, New Delhi, 1966.
Singh, Kirpal, *An Historical Account of Bhai Vasti Ram and Bhai Ram Singh*, Amritsar, n.d.
Singh, Malvinder, series ed., *Bhagat Singh's Jail Note-Book*, ed. and intro. Harish Jain, Chandigarh.
Singh, Mehar, *Sikh Shrines in India*, New Delhi, 1975.
Singh, Mohinder, *The Akali Movement*, Delhi, 1978.
Singh, Nahar, *Goroo Ram Singh and the Kuka Sikhs*, 3 vols: vol. 1, New Delhi, 1965; vol. 2, New Delhi, 1966; vol. 3, Sri Jiwan Nagar, 1967.
Singh, Nahar, *Namdhari Itihas*, Delhi, 1955.
Singh, Niranjan, *Jiwan Vikas*, Delhi, 1970.
Singh, Pashaura, *Life and Work of Guru Arjan*, New Delhi, 2006.
Singh, Sahib, *Sri Guru Granth Sahib Darpan*, vol. 1, Jullundur, 1962.
Singh, Sangat, *Freedom Movement in Delhi*, Delhi, 1972.
Singh, Santokh, "Satgur Bilas", unpublished, available in the private library of Nahar Singh.
Singh, Sardar Attar (of Bhadaur), *Sakhee Book or the Description of Goroo Gobind Singh's Religion and Doctrines*, Benares, 1873.
Singh, Sohan, *Jiwan Sangram*, Jullundur, 1967.
Singh, Trilochan, *Historical Sikh Shrines in Delhi*, Delhi, 1972.
Smith, Vincent A., *Akbar the Great Mogul: 1542–1605*, Oxford, 1919.
Srivastava, Harindra, *Five Stormy Years*, New Delhi, 1983.
Steel, Mrs F.A., "Folklore in the Punjab", *The Indian Antiquary*, 11, 1882.
Stein, M.A., trans. & ed., *Kalhana's Rajatarangini*, 1900; rpntd Delhi, 1989, vol. 1.
Steiner, George, *No Passion Spent*, New Haven, 1996.
Taylor, Charles, *Sources of the Self: The Making of Modern Identity*, Cambridge, 1989.

Temple, R.C., "Honorific Class Names in the Punjab", *Indian Antiquary*, 11, 1882.
Thapar, Romila, "The Image of the Barbarian in Early India", *Comparative Studies in Society and History*, 13, 197.
Thapar, Romila, *The Past Before Us: Historical Traditions of Early North India*, Ranikhet and Cambridge, 2013.
Thucydides, *The Peloponnesian War*, ed. Robert Strassler, New York, 1998.
Trumpp, Ernest, *The Adi Granth, or The Holy Scripture of the Sikhs*, London: W.M.H. Allen & Co.
Turner, Victor, *The Ritual Process: Structure and Anti-Structure*, Ithaca, 1987.
van den Dungen, P.H.M., "Change in Status and Occupation in Nineteenth Centuty Punjab", in D.A. Low, ed., *Soundings in Modern South Asian History*, Canberra, 1968.
Verma, Shiv, ed., *Bhagat Singh on the Path of Liberation*, Chennai, 2007.
Verma, Archana, *The Making of Little Punjab in Canada*, New Delhi, 2002.
Wagner, Kim, *Amritsar 1919: An Empire of Fear and the Making of a Massacre*, New Haven, 1919.
Walker, Benjamin, *The Hindu World: An Encyclopedic Survey of Hinduism*, vol. I, New York, 1968.
Walker, T. Gordon, *Chiefs and Families of Note in the Punjab*, vol. I, 4th edn, rvsd G.L. Chopra, Lahore, 1940.
Walker, T. Gordon, *Final Report on the Revision of Settlement 1878–83 of the Ludhiana District*, Calcutta, 1884.
Waraich, Malwinder Jit Singh, and Harish Jain, eds, *Bhagat Singh Jail Notebook*, Chandigarh, 2016.
Waraich, Malwinder Jit Singh, *Bhagat Singh: The Eternal Rebel*, Delhi, 2007.
Weber, Max, *Charisma and Disenchantment: Vocation Lectures*, ed. Paul Reitter and Chad Wellmon, trans. from the German by Damion Searls, New York, 2020.

Williams, Bernard, *Ethics and the Limits of Philosophy*, Harvard, 1985.
Williams, Bernard, *Shame and Necessity*, Berkeley, 1993.
Williams, Raymond, *The Long Revolution*, New York, 1961.
Worsley, Peter, *The Trumpet Shall Sound: A Study of Cargo Cults in Melenasia*, New York, 1978.
Yang, Anand A., "Sacred Symbol and Sacred Space in Rural India: Community Mobilization in the 'Anti-Cow Killing' Riot of 1893", *Comparative Studies in Society and History*, 2, 1980.

Index

actions 2, 16–17, 44, 49, 54, 63, 109–10, 116, 118, 128, 130, 135, 137–8, 147, 165, 168, 171–2
  autonomy of 165
  direct 128
  emotive 17
  inspirational 17
  political 135, 153
Adi Granth, The 82, 96, 99
administration xviii–ix, 31, 52, 54–5, 61, 67, 85, 88, 110, 117–18, 169
  British 55, 110
  colonial xviii, 85, 88, 169
  English 55
  local 67
  provincial xix
aesthetics 8, 15–17, 28, 102
  Indic theory of 15
  rasa 17, 28
Africa xvii–viii, 114
agitation 104–7, 111, 114, 121
agrarian unrest of 1907 104
Ajaib Singh 97–8
Akali movement 104–6, 120, 123
Akalis 109, 118, 120, 189
Alam, Muzaffar 40, 92
Al-Biruni 19–20
Aldred, Guy 129, 136
All India Sikh League 103
Ambala 30–1, 67, 69–72

America 130, 158, *see also* United States
Amritsar xix, 43, 49–50, 60–1, 63, 68–70, 72–4, 99–100, 110, 112–13, 115, 118, 140, 204
Amritsar 1919 115
Anandpur 72–3
Anandvardhana (theoretician of Sanskrit aesthetics) 8, 9
Anarchism 127, 130, 134, 143–4, 147–52, 155, 158, 178
  global 134, 148
  Indian 144, 158
Anglo–Sikh War, First 56
Anglo–Sikh war of 1845 41
annexation 32, 64–5, 119
anthology 43, 74, 139, 155
anti-Kuka policies 31
antiquity 23–4, 87
aristocracy 97, 111
Aristotle 21, 23
armed
  resistance 128, 138
  revolution 125
  struggle 128, 133, 138, 156
  struggles 129
  uprising 120
Arora, Budh Singh 97, 98
Asia xvii–viii, xxi, 6, 9, 16, 18, 25, 78, 87, 126, 151, 160–1, 170, 189
Asiatic Society of Bengal 88

aspirations 9, 81, 185
attitudes 55–6
autonomy 93, 97, 130, 144, 162, 165, 175

Bakunin 136–7, 148–50, 152, 154, 171
Bakunin Institute in Oakland 137
Banda Bahadur (warrior-king) 5, 83–4
Barkatullah, Maulvi Mohammad 131, 139
Batada (Rajput warrior) 11–12
battles xix, 11, 32, 38, 146
Bayly, C.A. 81, 86–7, 102, 170
beef-eating 62
behaviour 17, 33, 46, 54, 77–8, 163, 201
beliefs xix, 2, 25, 34–5, 41, 44, 48–9, 55, 57, 59, 62, 70, 74, 76–7, 101, 139, 148, 152, 163–4, 171
  folk 34
  Oriental 55
  religious 25, 139
  unshakeable 49
Benares 81, 86, 90, 132–3
Bengal xvii, 88–9, 132, 143, 157
Bengal Philharmonic Society 89
Benjamin, Walter 90, 97, 168, 186, 191, 205
Bhadour, Sir Attar Singh 28, 74, 79, 81–3, 85–6, 89, 91, 93–5, 97, *see also* Attar Singh
Bhagavad Gita 135
Bhaini 30–1, 40–2, 44, 46–7, 69–71, 73, 78
Bhais 5, 36–42, 47, 61, 66, 72–4, 76–7, 89, 100–1, 113–14
  Bagarian 39

characteristics of 42
concept of 37
tradition of 36–7, 39, 72
Bhujangi Singh Sabha 111
Big Four (Britain, France, the United States, and Italy) xvii
biography xv–vi, 9, 81–2, 85, 88, 102, 126, 136, 140, 180
blessings 38, 39
Bombay 64, 191–2
bomb-throwing episode 138, 147–8, 153
Boria, Kavelli Venkata 80–1, 101
Bose, Rash Behari 132–3
boundaries xvii, 49, 51–2, 60, 69, 87, 121, 191, 197
  caste 87
  ethnic xvii
  national xvii
  religious 87
Bradlaugh Hall, Lahore 115
Breazeale 22
Britain xvii, 130
British
  annexation of the Punjab 64
  army 65, 98
  authorities 36, 56, 60, 103, 117
  colonial administration 85
  colonialism 25, 133
  colonial state 143
  imperialism 32
  judicial system 63
  official documents 31
  officials 30, 32, 35, 54, 61, 63, 111–12, 118
  oppression 32
  policy xv, 107, 110, 114
  Raj 54, 61
  rule xv, 32, 104, 115, 119
British Empire xvii, 157

brotherhood 30, 48, 76, 137
Browne, James 97–8
Brown, Emily C. 55, 98, 126, 129, 137, 141
Buddha, Bhai 37
bureaucracy xxiii, 88, 146
Burma 76, 109
butchers 30, 49–51, 54, 56, 60–1, 63, 76

Calcutta 25, 81, 99, 108, 131, 194, 204
Canada 28, 115, 125–6, 131, 188, 190–4, 200–1, 204–5
Capital Committee 108
capitalism xxii, 102, 123, 179, 181
castes 10, 18, 39, 42, 47–8, 59–60, 62, 66, 70–1, 80, 87, 119, 126, 140–1, 160, 197
  boundaries 87
  commercial 119
  distinctions 140
  hierarchy 48
  high 62, 126
  low 66, 70
  system 47–8
Caveeshar, Sardul Singh 100, 103–5, 113–19, 122
Central Asia 6, 87
Central Sikh League 115
challenges xxi, 2–3, 34, 119–20, 164, 169, 171
chanting 75–6
charities 13–14, 39
Chatterjee, Partha 142, 158
Chattopadhyaya, V. 127
Chauri-Chaura 145–6
Chief Commissioner's Office Home Proceedings (CCOHP) 103, 108–13, 116, 120

Chief Khalsa Diwan 106, 111–13, 115, 117–18
China 109, 138
choices 9, 17, 27–8, 126, 153, 155, 175, 182, 198
  dilemmas of 27
  historiographical 27
  individual 28
  strategic 126
Christians 26, 54, 87, 92–3, 119, 197
  missionaries 54, 92, 119
Christianity 95, 102
chronicles 6, 18, 27, 29, 37, 129
civil courts 51
civilisations 15, 54, 62, 180, 187
civil society 32, 35, 51, 165
colonial
  administration xviii, 85, 88, 169
  archive 80–1
  authorities 30, 49, 61, 95
  conquest 26
  convention 85
  education 160
  institutions 81
  knowledge 80–1, 87, 96, 100–1
  language 90
  modernity xix, xxii, 27, 100–1, 122, 160, 179
  oppression 138
  policy 110
  rule xv, 54, 64, 127, 178, 196
  societies 119, 160
  suspicion 31
  war 65
colonial India 77, 104, 125, 133, 157, 161, 171
colonialism 25, 79, 97, 133, 172, 185
communism 144, 149, 152

community
  diasporic 133, 189
  migrant 189, 191
  millenarian 30, 63–4, 67
compositions 20, 24, 37, 40, 74–5, 82, 156, 177
conduct 35–6, 45, 83, 139
confrontation 11, 78, 116, 118
consciousness 15, 18–19, 23, 33, 41, 46, 50, 118, 133, 162, 189
  anti-imperialist 50
  historical 19, 23
  public 18
  social 118
  structures of 33
conventions 9, 14, 52, 55, 62, 85, 90, 96, 121, 199, 203
  colonial 85
  Indic 14
  political 55
  sophisticated 9
conversations 6, 15, 84, 96, 150
cosmopolitanism 139–40, 142, 198, 205
  alternative 139, 140
  pre-colonial 140
cows 10, 28, 46, 50–1, 54–61, 63, 68
  importance of 58, 60
  killing of 56, 68
  reverence for 46
  sacrality of 28
  sacred 55
  slaughter of 55–6, 60–1, 63
    ban on 61
    executions for 56
  symbolism 55
  veneration of 56
  worship 59

cow-protection movements 68
crimes 3, 4, 50, 60
Cripps Mission xviii
cultural
  code 51, 77
  dignity 127
  hegemony 28, 136, 170
  nationalism 26, 197, 202, 205
  practices 9, 139
  references 41, 55
  traditions 6, 57, 64
culture xix, 9, 15–16, 18, 27, 36, 42, 47, 54–5, 57–8, 77, 80, 86, 88, 133, 164, 184, 188–91, 199
  Indian 88
  Indic 9, 18, 36
  indigenous 54
  print 188, 190
  public xix, 86, 189

Dard, Hira Singh 120, 185
Defence of India Act 133
Delhi 5, 10, 28, 31, 61, 88, 98, 103, 105, 107–9, 111, 113, 115–18, 120–1, 126, 147, 153–4
Delhi Administration Archives (DAA) 103, 108–13, 116, 120
De Montmorency 105, 109–13
Dera Baba Nanak 73
desire 14, 16, 22
  salvific 14
dharma 10, 91
Dirks, Nicholas 80, 81
disaffection 33, 64
discrimination 125, 134
disenchantment xxii, xxiii, 145
Diwan-e-Ghalib 175

doctrines 36, 52, 54, 137
domesticity 17, 192
Douglas, Mary xxiv, 30, 42–3, 57
drama 15, 22, 191
Dumont, L. 44, 48, 59, 60

East Asia xvii, 6, 189
Eastern Punjab 94
East India Company 98
economic
  disaffection 64
  dislocation 64, 67
  reorganisation 191
economics xvi, xxiii, 21, 164, 186–7, 198
  behavioural xvi
  modern 21
economy 65–7, 125, 172, 194
  agrarian 66–7
  provincial 194
  rural 65
ecumene xv, 86–7, 102
  Christian-Greek 87
  cosmopolitan 102
  north Indian 86, 102
  traditional xv
education 21, 40, 85–6, 126, 140, 160, 163, 169, 184, 188, 192–3, 197, 200
  colonial 160
  indigenous 85
education curriculum 84
elephants and horses 12, 31, 73
emotional
  aesthetic force 16–17
  drives 28
  intensity 17
  outreach 8
emotions 15–16, 18, 21–5, 27–8, 35, 170, 176, 180, 184, 200
  deconstruction of 27
  overabundance of 24
  physical element of 16
  raw 22, 23
  role of 28, 170
Empire
  Austro-Hungarian xvii
  British xvii, 157
  Slavic xvii
England 67, 113, 127–9, 190, 201
English–Punjabi dictionary 92
Enlightenment 16, 24, 27, 81, 165, 169
epic xvi, 5, 9, 16–18, 21, 24, 75, 159, 163, 183, 187–8, 190
  Indian 9, 17
  poetic 16
  relationship 187–8
ethnicity 141, 197
Europe xvii–viii, 100, 114, 130
exigencies xvi, 113, 177
expression 17, 48, 58, 115, 185

facts xxi, xxiii, 1, 3, 7–9, 19, 26–7, 191
  empirical 19
  historical 8–9, 19
faith 37, 41, 52, 69, 141, 145, 164, 176, 202
  interiorisation of 52
  Sikh 37, 69
famine 33, 67
  of 1860–1 67
  of 1869–70 67
fear 15, 54, 145, 185, 202
feelings xx, 16, 25, 56, 61, 124, 165
  Hindu 56
  public 61
Ferozepore 41, 47, 49, 68–9, 132

festivals 31, 72, 76, 140
　Baisakhi 73
　Bhakna Hola 140
　Diwali 72, 73
　Holi 72
　Lohri 31
　Maghi 76
　multi-cultural 140
　multi-religious 140
　traditional 31
folklore 27, 57
Forsyth, T.D. 31, 72
Fort of Malodh 31
Fort William at Calcutta 81
France xvii, 68
freedom 23, 32, 104–5, 120–1, 130, 135, 137–8, 149, 151, 165, 185, 202
　political 130, 135, 138
　subjective 165
　war for 32
freedom struggle 104, 120–1, 151
Freud 7, 21, 24, 170

Gandhi, Mahatma xv, 17, 135, 144–6, 150–1, 156, 161, 170, 172, 174, 198
　life of 17
gau dan 58
gau mata 58
gender 17, 190
genealogy 91, 124, 133, 153, 169, 201
　Indo-Persian 91
German Foreign Office, Berlin 130
German–Hindu Conspiracy Trial 143
Germany 130, 133, 159

Ghadar
　activists 135, 139, 148, 158
　agenda 137
　archives 138
　emissaries 132
　history 142, 148, 158
　ideologues 135, 155
　leadership 130, 131, 158
　plans 132
　radicals 143
　uprising 115
Ghadarites 130–5, 137–9, 141–2, 156–7
Ghadar Movement 28, 104, 124–5, 130, 132–5, 138–40, 142–4, 148, 156–7, 196
　expansion of 134
　history of 125
　ideologue of 138
　leadership of 132
Ghadar (or Revolutionary) of India 129
Ghadar Party 114, 125–6, 131, 133–4, 138–41, 144, 150–1, 156
　ideologues 144
Ghadar political formation 134
Ghalib, Mirza 166, 172–7, 182, 185
ghettoisation 192, 203
Ghosh, Amitav 86, 186, 205
Gita, the 135, 141
Golden Temple, Amritsar 43–4, 55–6, 61
Goldman, Emma 153, 155, 169
Government of India Act of 1919 115
Government of India Proceedings 114
grain riots 77

grammar 90, 93
Great Rebellion of 1857 129
Griffin, Lepel 74, 85–6
Guha, Sumit 18, 77
Gujarat 10, 11
Gupta, Akhil 139
Gurdas, Bhai 37, 39
Gurdwara Rikabganj Movement 103–12, 114, 117–23
  British Policy and 110, 114
  chronological account of 105
  functioning of 106
  implications of 107
  neglect of 104
  protest meetings and 113
  social character of 107, 118
Gurdwara Rikabganj Wall 107, 109, 111–13, 115–16, 118, 122
  demolition of 107
  issue of 112, 115
  reconstruction of 115, 118, 122
gurdwaras 103–4, 106–14, 117, 119–20, 122–3, 195
Gurmat 204
Gurmukh Singh 38, 89
Guru Amar Das, third Sikh Guru 43
Guru Gobind Singh 36, 75, 82–3, 86, 89, 94–5, 97, 107
Guru Granth Sahib 36–7, 40, 74–5, 82
  compilation of 37
  eternal future Guru of the Sikhs 36
Guru Hargobind 39
Guru Nanak 37, 74, 111
gurus 37, 39, 75
  honorific 40

teachings of 37
wisdom of 37
Guru Tegh Bahadur, the ninth Sikh Guru 82, 86, 94–5, 97, 107

hadis 95
Hailey, W.M. 105, 108, 110–11
Hamlet 2, 22, 63
Hardayal, Lala 126–30, 136–9, 141–2, 148, 150, 153
  education 127
  ideas of 138
  six-step programme 138
  writings 150
Hardinge, Lord 108, 132
Hegel, G.W. xxii, 1, 9, 21, 25, 165, 169–70
hegemony 14, 28, 119–20, 136, 160, 170
  Brahmanic 14
  cultural 28, 136, 170
  imperial 119
Herodotus 6, 23
heroism 15, 171
Hershman, Paul 58–9
Hindi Association of the Pacific Coast 125
Hindoo/Hindu 19–20, 42–3, 48–50, 52–3, 55–6, 60–2, 68–87, 98, 116, 119, 121, 126–7, 140, 143, 187, 189, 195, 198
  community 61
  feelings 56
  nationalism 127
  orthodox 62
  tradition 43
Hinduism 55, 187
Hindu and Sikh 50, 56, 61

Hindustan Republican Association
  (HRA) 145, 164
historians xv, xxi, 4–8, 10–11,
  13, 18–21, 23, 25–9, 32, 40,
  50–1, 77, 80–1, 84, 97, 104,
  142, 150, 157, 160, 167,
  191, 201
  British 19
  canonical 6
  classical 6
  court 18
  cultural 28
  Graeco-Roman 6
  Indic 6
  Kashmiri 6
  modern 19, 25
  nationalist 32, 50
  professional 25, 27
  Roman 21
historical
  agents 13
  assumptions 19
  consciousness 19, 23
  fidelity 19
  methodology 10
  narration 25
  narrative 9, 14, 24
historiography
  critical 25
  Graeco–Roman 6
  Indian xvi, xxiv, 20–1, 24–5
  Indian nationalist 33, 151
  Islamicate 6
  marxist 65
  modern xix, xxi, 25–6, 28
  nationalist 63, 104, 151
  Orientalist 81
  Persian 18
  positivist 9
  rasa-infused 26

Sinic 6
strains of 22
trends in 6
truth and persuasion in 1
world 20
history
  academic xix
  analytical xvi, xix
  as passion 26
  as personal grand strategy xviii
  as poetry 6
  authentic 5
  confessional 27
  contemplation of 1
  disciplinary xix, xxi, xxiii
  dry-as-dust 28
  efficacy of xvi
  evolutionary xix
  exhaustive 5
  human 21, 185
  impassioned 26
  Indian 26, 31, 62
  in prose 6
  institutional 25, 125
  in verse 21
  Kukas 35
  making of 28
  modern 26
  monumental 6
  myth as 26
  of appropriation 92
  of the imperium 9
  Persian 18
  poetic 9, 24
  poetical 8
  prose 18, 20
  rasa-laden 19
  regional 6
  resistance to xix
  royal lineages 85

secular 7
Sikh xxii, 84
South Asian xxiv, 15, 19, 78
writing of xix, 6, 21, 22
holiness 34–5, 38, 41–2, 47, 49, 77
  common sense of 35
  defence of 49
  personal 42
  principles of 49
  standards of 35
holy order 35, 76
Home Judicial Proceedings 61
Hong Kong 109, 131, 194
honour 2, 10, 116, 135, 146, 171, 181, 201
Hoshyarpur 68–9, 200
human
  affairs 23, 77
  agency 22, 175
  history 21, 185
  mind xx, 35
  nature xx, 173
  society xxiii, 57
  will 22, 130

iconoclasm 52, 141
identity xv, xviii, 50, 59, 119, 136, 141–2, 159–60, 193, 201–2
  cultural 119
  independent 50
  parochial 141
  religious 119, 202, 136, 142
ideology xix, 28, 36, 46–7, 54–5, 62, 68, 78, 89, 106, 123, 126–7, 135, 142, 144, 155, 166, 178, 205
  comprehensive 46
  counter-hegemonic 78

Ghadar 135, 155
hybrid 127, 142
insurrectionary 123
Kuka 47
political 166
racist imperial 55
religious 28
revolutionary 106
secular 28
urban 68
Iliad, The 21
illusions and errors xx, xxii, 48, 95, 101, 107, 171
imagination 8, 19, 135, 156–87, 188
  intellectual 156
  secular 135
immersion 14, 43
immigrants 125–6, 132
immigration 192–4, 200
Imperial Assemblage, Delhi 88
imperial darbar 89
Imperial Delhi Committee 117
imperialism 32, 79, 144, 181
imperium 9, 21
India
  1937 elections xviii
  British colonial rule in xv
  freedom struggle 104
  histories of 18, 26
  liberation of 128, 129
  partition of xv
  peninsular 13
  revolution in 124, 130
India House, London 127
Indian
  aesthetic theory 15
  anarchism 144, 158
  attitudes to cattle 55
  culture 88

diaspora 142, 158, 186–7, 205
epics 9, 17
historiography xvi, xxiv, 20–1, 24–5
history 31, 62
intellectuals 15, 26
Islam 187
militancy 156–7
nationalism 25, 33, 127–8, 134, 142, 151, 158, 198
nationalists 136, 138
politics 150–1
Indian National Congress xviii, 103, 128, 134–5, 156
Indic
  conventions 14
  historical methodology 10
  theory of aesthetics 15
individualism 123, 165, 190
industrial revolution xxi
Industrial Workers of the World 129
initiation 44–5
innovation 2, 62
insurgents 31, 34, 51, 77, 89
  Kuka 34, 77
  nationalist 51
insurrection 50, 75, 78
intellectual
  agility 98
  autonomy 97
  debt 86, 96, 98
  grid 99
  imagination 156
  life xxiii, 166
  peripatetic 134
  tensions xxi
  traditions 99
International Anarchist Congress 128

interpretations 36, 42, 70, 148, 185
Iqbal, Muhammad 159, 161, 172–4, 177–83, 185
Islam 35, 91–2, 187
  Indian 187
  moral order in 35

Jagpal 126, 194
Jajmani system 66
Jallianwala Bagh massacre of April 1919 104, 145
Jalor 10, 11
Japan 5, 133
Japji 74
Jatheras 52
Jat Sikhs 70
Jensen 131, 157
Jinnah xv–xvi, xviii
  separatist agenda xvi
Johnston, Hugh xxiv, 115, 126, 194, 200–1, 203
Josh, Sohan Singh 105, 116, 118, 120, 140, 150, 187
  views on Rikabganj movement 105
judgments xix, xxi, xxiv, 16, 77, 93
Jullunder/Jullundur 58, 69, 72, 105, 110, 112
justice 7, 32, 162, 167–8, 171
  English 32
  social 162

Kahneman, Daniel xix–xxi, 184
Kalhana (Kashmir historian) 6–10, 18, 21, 24
Kanhadade, Raval (Rajasthan ruler) 10–11, 14
Kashmir 6, 9, 56, 73, 189
Kashmir Liberation Force 189

kavya 6, 8–9, 14, 26
Kenner, Hugh 79
Kerr, Ian 55
Khalsa Diwan 89, 106, 111–13, 115, 117–18
Khan, Ali Ibrahim 81, 101, 128
Khilji, Allaudin 10–11
King Lear 2
kingship 17, 189
knowledge
  claims 160
  colonial 80–1, 87, 96, 100–1
  constructions 98
  deep 26
  emotions of 28
  encyclopaedic 100
  form of 19
  gathering 98, 101
  modes of 102, 160
  Orientalist 96
  research 26
  systems of 19, 79–80, 87, 101, 160
Komagata Maru 115, 126
Kropotkin, Peter 136, 148, 150, 152
Kuka movement 28, 32–3, 35, 64, 68, 70–1, 76–7
  interpretations of 76
  striking similarities of 33
Kukas 28, 30–6, 39–40, 42, 45–54, 56, 60–4, 66–78, 89, 94
  actions 32, 35, 50–1, 56
  as a marginal sect 36
  conviction of 72
  cosmology 36
  evolution as a "sect" 35
  expression of pure/impure marks 48

  garments and turbans 47
  history of 35
  ideology 47
  insurgents 34, 77
  interpretation of actions 32
  movement 28, 32–3, 35, 64, 68, 70–1, 76–7
  notions of purity 47
  principles 73
  sacrilege and violence 51
  Sikhs and 36
  struggle 32
  symbolic structure 48
  verbal and physical attacks 50
  views on nature of the Raj 54
  zealots 31, 53
Kuka Sikhs 28, 30–1, 34, 36, 39–40, 46–7, 49–53, 60–1, 68–71, 74–5, 77
  attack the state of Malerkotla 31
  lives of 28
  protest actions of 51
Kuka uprising 94
Kurosawa, Akira (Japanese film-maker) 1–4

labour/labourer xxii, 58, 67, 115, 117, 130, 134, 141, 147, 192, 198, 203
  agricultural 130
  daily-wage 141
  dignity of 130
  exploitation 134
  farm 58
  grievances of 134
  immigrant 134
  indentured system 115

racialised 192
rural 67
Lahore xviii–xix, 38–9, 42, 49, 54, 56, 65, 68–9, 82–4, 89, 98, 100, 103, 110, 113, 115, 127, 132–3, 143–4, 148–50, 153–4, 158–9, 161, 163, 166, 169, 177, 182, 184
Lahore Conspiracy Case Proceedings 143, 159
Lahore Resolution of 1940 xviii
Lahore Singh Sabha 89
Lahore state 38, 42, 54, 65
Lahore tribunals 143
Lal, Bhai Nand 37, 83, 95
land 5, 64, 122
    agrarian 5
    revenue system 64
    tax 64
langars 39, 42
languages
    Arabic 6
    Bhojpuri 187
    Braj 6
    circulation of 87
    classical 86
    colonial 90
    English 32, 37, 43, 54–5, 60–3, 74, 77, 83, 85–6, 90, 92, 94–6, 99, 126–7, 129, 143, 149, 154, 169, 175, 188, 190, 196, 200, 204
    Gujarati 10, 139
    Gurmukhi 82–5
    Hindi 37, 92, 125, 149, 155, 187
    Indian 80
    Kanarese 80
    native xx
    ordinary 8
    Persian 6, 18, 38, 84, 86–7, 89, 91–2, 95, 97–8, 140, 159, 178
    political 147
    Punjabi xviii, 6, 37, 40, 56, 58, 65, 84–6, 90, 92, 94, 96, 129, 134–5, 139–40, 145, 155, 188–9, 193, 195, 204
    Rajasthani 10
    Sanskrit 6, 8–9, 20, 36, 38, 80–1, 84, 86–7, 89, 91, 139
    symbolic 34
    Tamil 80
    Telugu 80
    Urdu 40, 85–7, 89, 122, 125, 129, 139–40, 172, 175–9, 182–3
Lawrence, Henry 56, 60
Leach, Edmund 51, 57
learning 16–17, 38, 62, 87, 89, 92, 95, 100, 181, 184
legitimacy 40, 54, 72–4, 76, 165
Leitner, G.W. 84–6
liberty 118, 124, 135, 138
liminality 44, 76, 199–200
logic 51, 77, 86, 102, 138, 179
Lord of Sambhar 10
love 7, 15, 128, 172–3, 175–6, 179, 197
Ludhiana 30–1, 39–40, 52, 66–7, 69–70, 76, 87–9, 92, 110
Lyallpur 109–11, 121–2
Lytton, Lord 88

Macauliffe, Max 5, 19, 83–4, 86, 100–1
Macbeth 2
Mackenzie, Colin 80–1

INDEX

Macnabb, J.W. 30, 32, 71
Mahabharata, 9, 17, 24
mahants 119–20
Maharaja of Patiala 31, 86
Majithia, Sunder Singh 111–12
Malcolm, John 81, 98–9
Malerkotla 31–2, 34, 50, 54, 61, 63, 67, 69, 75–6, 78
  attack on 31
  parade ground 32, 34
Malodh 31, 34, 76
Malwa 39, 69, 85, 94
manuscripts 5, 84, 94, 97–8
  Gurmukhi 84
  Persian 84, 97
  Punjabi 94
  Sanskrit 84
markets 21, 66
marriages 17, 47–8, 59, 128, 137
martyrs 28, 74, 103, 115
Marx 21, 144, 152, 166, 169–71, 185
mastanas 75–6
maulvis 81, 101
McAndrew, Lieutenant Colonel G., Memorandum by 63, 72–3
McLeod, W.H. 32–3, 45, 74–5, 93
Memorandum on Ram Singh and Kukas 30
memory xv, 4, 49, 107, 155, 168, 191, 205
metaphors 1, 33, 75, 171, 174
metaphysics 28, 135, 137, 139, 141
metres (poetic) 5, 13, 20–1
Middle East xvii–viii
migration 133, 188, 190–1, 205
militancy 129, 137, 152, 156–7

militants 127, 132–3
  organisations of 141, 156
millenarian 68, 89
Mill, James 18, 21, 81
mimesis 21, 184
"Minimal Selves" 201
miracles 37, 41–2, 77
mirasis 122
mleccha 12, 46, 61–2, 75, 94
modernism 139, 142, 198
modernity xix, xxii, 27, 91, 100–2, 122–3, 142, 160–1, 164–6, 172, 179–81, 190, 193, 202
  colonial xix, xxii, 27, 100–1, 122, 160, 179
  revolutionary 172
  secular 91
Montagu-Chelmsford Reforms 147
moral
  code 35, 48
  framework of holiness 49
  indignation 34, 51
  order 35
  repulsion 61
  rules 47
  superiority 76
  values xxiii, 204
Mountbatten, Lord xv
movements
  anti-colonial 134
  causes of 33
  composite 142
  diasporic 142
  indigenous 156
  Kuka 28, 32–3, 35, 64, 68, 70–1, 76–7
  limited 106, 121
  mass-based 138
  millenarian 39, 63

national 106, 198
overlapping 134
peasant-based 69
political 195
"pragmatic" aspects of 33
reform xv
regional 104
religious 119, 195
revolutionary 106, 121
social 32
Mughals 25, 56, 73
Mukti-Puris 14
munshis 81, 101
music 75, 86–8, 102, 173
Muslim League xvi, xviii
Muslims xvi, xviii, 19, 31, 52–3, 56, 60–2, 78, 116, 121, 140, 159, 173, 195
  Indian 56
  principality 31, 78
  Punjabi xviii
mysticism 87, 141, 181
myth/mythology 25–7, 34, 168

Nabha, Kahn Singh 62, 69, 100, 113
narratives xv, xxi–ii, 1, 9, 13–14, 16, 20, 22, 24–5, 75, 84, 86, 99, 142, 151, 157–8, 162, 171–2, 184, 205
  emotively charged 25
  hegemonic 162
  historical xxi–ii, 9, 14, 20, 22, 24
  metaphoric 75
  nature of 1
  poetic-historical 14
national
  boundaries xvii
  mood xviii
  movement 106, 198

  politics 150–1
National Archives of India 61, 114
nationalism 25–6, 33, 56, 101–2, 127–8, 134, 136, 142–6, 151, 156, 158, 190, 197–8, 202, 205
  cultural 26, 197, 202, 205
  Gandhian 143
  Hindu 127
  hybrid 127
  Indian 25, 33, 56, 127–8, 134, 142, 151, 158, 198
  moderate 127, 146
  Palestinian 101
  radical 144
nationalist
  historiography 63, 104, 151
  insurgents 51
Naujawan Bharat Sabha 145–6
Nau Nihal Singh 38, 40
Naurasnama 18
Nehru, Pandit Jawaharlal 25, 144, 151, 161, 168–71, 174, 198
Nietzsche 1, 21–4, 27, 159, 170
nihilism 2, 179
Non-Cooperation movement 103, 145, 163
non-violence 145
norms xxiii, 54, 162
North America 130, 158
North India 51, 56, 62, 68, 77, 146
North Western Provinces 64

Odyssey, The 21
O'Hanlon, R. 78, 101
"On the Uses and Disadvantages of History for Life" 22
"On Truth and Lies in an Extra-Moral Sense" 1
oppression 32, 138

Orientalism 79, 81, 96, 101
"Orientalists, Informants and Critics" 81
orthodoxies 32, 191

Padmanabha 10–11, 14–15, 21
Pal, Bipin Chandra 135
pamphlets 105, 109–10, 112
pandits 81, 101, 141
Panjab University 84
panth 36–7, 43, 47, 68, 71
  history of 43
  Nanak- 36
  Sikh 47, 68, 71
Paris Peace Conference xvii
Partition xv–vii, xix
  lexicon xvii
  prospects of xvi
  tool of xvii
  tragedy xv
passions 16, 21–7, 87, 95, 124, 168, 173, 183
  history as 26
  human 25
  unrestrained 21
past
  distortions of 25
  excavations of 25
  narratives of 25, 157
  research knowledge of 26
  ways of studying 26
  writing on 26
Patiala 31, 60, 69, 71, 86, 90, 100, 110
peasant 35, 51, 65, 67, 69, 71, 77
  jacqueries 51
  property 65
  rebellions 77
  societies 35
peasantry 33, 64–5, 67–8, 73, 114
  discontented 33

Punjab 64
  Sikh 65, 67–8, 73
personhood 159, 162, 168
philosophy xvi, 1, 23, 86–7, 102, 128, 148, 160, 164–6, 170, 172, 175, 184, 191
  classical 23, 160
  Oriental 164
pilgrimages 13–14, 30, 43, 70, 73, 198
Plato xix, 19, 23–4
plebiscites xvii
Pocock, David F. 44, 48
poet-historians 7–8, 10–11, 13, 18, 28
poetry 1, 6, 8–10, 15, 18–19, 21, 26, 28, 88, 92, 94, 129, 139, 141, 161, 166, 172–4, 178, 182, 191, 195
  as knowledge 10
  history as 6
  revolutionary 129
  vernacular 28
policies xv, 31, 54, 56, 61, 102, 113, 115
  anti-Kuka 31
  bomb and pistol 138
  British 107, 110, 114
  colonial 110
  colonial state 102
  government 111
  of divide and rule xv
  state 56
political
  actions 135, 153
  affiliations 101, 187
  campaigns 28
  conventions 55
  dynamics 33
  exclusion 125
  formation 134

freedom 130, 135, 138
ideology 166
language 147
legitimacy 54
mentor 39
movement 195
power 28, 135
radicalism 134
rebels 30
risks 54
sentiments 121
thought 127, 150
"Political Suggestions, Information and Other Services of Sir Attar Singh K.C.I.E., Chief of Bhadaur" 90
politics xvi, 17–18, 30, 38, 119, 123–34, 141, 144, 150–1, 156, 164, 170, 186–7, 189, 198
  agitational 123
  confessional 141
  Indian 150, 151
  municipal 134
  national 150–1
  South Asian 18
Pollock, Sheldon 7–9, 15–17
  assertion of *rasa* 17
  "force" aspect of trinity 16
  gloss 16
pollution 43, 47–8, 51, 54
power xv, xviii–ix, 7, 16, 28, 31, 34, 40–1, 53, 55, 59, 107, 123, 135, 138
  creative 7
  equations 55
  military 31
  political 28, 135
  political-military 31
  spoils of xviii

"Predicaments of Secular Histories" 26
Presbyterian missionary activities 92
Press Sedition Bill 147
primordialism 142
princely state 5
principality 31, 54, 75–6, 78
  Muslim 31, 78
  Sikh 31
propaganda 27, 125, 127, 133, 147
property 65, 124, 128, 136–7
  peasant 65
  private 128, 136–7
prose xxiv, 6, 18, 20–1, 92
  histories 18, 20
  history in 6
prostitution 137
protocols xvi, 8, 26–7, 160
  interpretive 8
  post-Enlightenment 27
  verification 26, 160
Proudhon, Pierre-Joseph 136–7, 149, 152
psychology xvi, xix, xxi, xxiii, 162, 184, 193
  cognitive xvi, xix, xxi, xxiii
  knee-jerk group xxi
public
  affairs 87, 89
  consciousness 18
  culture xix, 86, 189
  feelings 61
  opinion 87
  sentiment xix
Public Safety and the Trade Disputes Bill 147
punishment 56, 62

Punjab
  central 39, 44, 64, 66, 68–9, 193–4
  developments in 104–5, 107, 120
  early-colonial 65
  early-modern 5
  economy 65–6
  legislature xviii
  nineteenth-century 41, 57–8, 90
  political developments in 105
  undivided xviii
Punjab Congress 103
Punjabis 28, 50, 54, 57–8, 60, 88, 132
Punjab school of administration 31, 54
Punjab University College 89
punth 94
punya 14
Puranas 13
purificatory
  immersion 43
  rites 57
Puri, Harish K. 125, 133–4, 148

Queen Victoria's jubilee celebrations 89

radical
  nationalism 144
  organisations 132
  student organisation 145
Radical Club 136
radicalism 134
ragas 13
Rahit-nama 45, 47, 83, 95–6
Raikot 50, 61, 63
Rai, Lala Lajpat 145, 161

Rajputs 10–12
Ramayana, 8–9, 17, 24
Ramnath 133, 134, 135
rasa 8–9, 15–19, 24–8
  aesthetics 17, 28
  eight 15
  flavourings of 18
  in South Asia 18
  Pollock's assertion 17
  reliance on 25
  theory 15, 19, 24
  use of 15
  uses and regulations of 16
  workings of 17
Rashomon 3, 4
rationality xxii, xxiii, 24, 41, 179
  critique of 24
Rawalpindi xviii, 110
  riots xviii
reality xviii, 9, 62, 81, 178, 184
  empirical 81
  historical 9
  social 62
Rebellion of 1857 129
rebellions 30, 33, 64, 77, 89, 91–2, 125, 129, 157, 199, 201
  Kuka civil 89
  peasant 77
  political 30
reforms
  electoral 134
  gurdwara 106
  movements xv
religions xxii–xxiii, 5, 19, 34, 42–3, 48, 55–6, 63, 74, 79, 82, 84, 88, 90–2, 94–100, 104, 119, 128, 137, 141, 156, 178, 186–7, 189, 197–8, 202
  Brahmanic 55

category 91–2, 95
concern of 34
histories of 42
importance of 91
role in resistance 34
Sikh 48, 84, 88, 94, 119
world xxiii, 79
religious
 beliefs 25, 139
 blessings 39
 boundaries 87
 chauvinism 135
 communities 50
 culture 55
 heritage 44
 identity 119, 136, 142, 202
 ideologies 28
 instruction 39
 leadership 142
 liminality 44
 mentor 39
 merit 39, 41, 63
 movements 119, 195
 norms 54
 practices 96, 139, 187
 protest 103
 reformers 30
 riot 68
 rituals 140
 sentiments 110, 121
 separatism xv
 temples 120
 thinking 43
 traditions 107, 159–60, 197
 violence 68
Republic (Plato) 24
research xxiii, 5, 26, 72, 81, 88, 90, 93, 104, 205
 conception of 26
 historical 81, 88, 104
 knowledge 26

resistance xix, 10, 34, 77–8, 104, 120, 128, 138
 armed 128, 138
 indigenous 77
 modes of 77
 passive 120
 stiff and glorious 10
restrictions 30, 46, 60
 administrative 60
 diet 46
revelation 90, 151
revolution xxi, 121, 124–5, 130, 132–3, 137, 146–8, 158, 171, 185
 armed 125
 spontaneous 137, 158
revolutionary 106, 121–2, 125, 128–34, 136–8, 149, 153–4, 158, 164–5, 170–2, 184
 activities 133
 amateur 125
 anarchist 154
 modernity 172
 poetry 129
 process 136
 Russian 128
 thinking 165
 war 138
right of inheritance 137
riots xviii, 61, 68, 77–8, 110, 154
 grain 77
 Kanpur 110
 Rawalpindi xviii
 religious 68
rites/rituals 30, 39, 44, 52, 57, 59, 62, 68, 75–8, 140, 187
 acts 44
 all-night 76
 bathing 45
 cluster of 44
 concerns 42

initiation 44
occasions 59
purificatory 57
purity 43, 45, 47–8, 57, 60, 62
religious 140
standing 55, 57, 74
suicide 4
village 52
ritual purity and impurity 30, 36, 42–9, 51, 54, 57, 59–60, 62, 90, 180
  boundaries of 49
  concept of 43, 47
  conceptual 90
  concern for 47
  dangers of 44
  ideas and notions of 42–4
  intrinsic 60
  maintenance of 43
  material 43
  notions of 43, 47, 57
  rules of 45
  spiritual 43
rivers 13, 14, 39, 69
  Beas 69
  Ganges 13, 43
  Godavari 14
  Gomati 14
  Narbada 13
  Sutlej 39, 69
romance 24, 152
Rousseau, Jean-Jacques 166, 170, 185
Rowlatt Satyagraha 104
rumours 35, 61, 191

sacred xxiii, 14, 28, 35, 39, 45–6, 48–52, 54–8, 60, 62, 68, 73, 75, 77, 103, 139, 142
  ancestral sites 49
  animals 56
  scriptures 45–6
  sites 14, 51
  spots 51–2
  symbol 50
  symbolic order 55
sacredness 34, 36, 53, 55, 74
sacrifices 55, 118, 130
  heroic 130
  Vedic 55
sacrilege 51, 53, 109
Said, Edward 79, 98, 101, 152, 198
salvation 14, 34, 173
sanctity 41, 55
"Science as a Vocation" xxii
Scott, James 35, 78
scriptures 36–7, 40, 42, 45–6, 90, 96
  sacred 45, 46
  Sikh 37
secularism 92, 97, 190
self-identity 159–60
self-interest 4, 96
sensorium 14, 16
sentiments xix, 24–5, 41, 56, 110, 121, 151, 180, 195
  political 121
  public xix
  religious 110, 121
  Sikh–Hindu 56
sermons 52
Settlement Report 66–7, 70, 72, 76
Shahidi Jatha 115–16, 118–19
Shakespeare 2, 166
Shastri, Bapu Deva 81, 101
Shastri, Raja Ram 154, 155
shrines 36, 43–4, 49, 51–2, 60, 94, 107–8, 111, 115, 121

ancestral 51
demolishing, and destroying 49
village 49
Sikh code of conduct 45
Sikh Educational Conference, Jullundur 105
Sikhism 5, 39, 42–3, 52, 86, 96–7, 119
  early 5
  history of 5
  propagation of 39
  purity in 43
  systematisation of 97
Sikh League 103, 115
Sikh movement 36, 42–3
  interpretations of 42
Sikh Raj 55
Sikhs
  chieftains 38
  conceptual structure 48
  eternal future Guru of 36
  faith 37, 69
  feudatories 38
  "heroic" tradition 31
  history and xxii, 84
  Kukas and 36
  low-caste 71
  orthodox 52
  panth 47, 68, 71
  preceptor 38
  principality 31
  religious practices of 96
  scriptures 37
  shrines 43–4
  society 36
  superior status 32
  tradition 30–1, 35–6, 38–9, 42, 73
Silk Trade Routes 6
Singh, Atma 99

Singh, Attar 28, 43, 74, 79, 81–98, 101–2
  biography of 88, 102
  financial assistance of 89
  findings 86
  intellectual influence 84
  intellectual vision and technical prowess 91
  knowledge of the Sikh religion 88
  linguistic abilities 92
  member of the Asiatic Society of Bengal 88
  Persian and Urdu 89
  private library 84–5, 88
  Royal Asiatic Society, London 88
  scholarly writings 96
  scholarship of 82–5, 92
  title of *Mahamahopadhyaya* 89
  title of *Mulaz-ul-ulama-o-ul-Fazal* 88
  translations 96
  way of thinking 94
  writings 83, 97
Singh, Bhagat xxiv, 28, 134, 144–56, 158–9, 161–80, 182–5
  inner life of xxiv, 161, 163, 172
  life of xxiv, 159, 161
  role in national politics 150–1
  writings 171
Singh, Bhagwan 100, 131, 138
Singh, Bhai Balak, Ram Singh's mentor 40, 42, 45–6
Singh, Bhai Bir 38, 41, 61, 71
Singh, Bhai Dit 89, 100
Singh, Bhai Ram 38, 40, 47, 66, 72–4, 76, 89

Singh, Bhai Santokh 5–6, 13, 18–19, 21, 24, 40
Singh, Daljit 105, 111–13
Singh, Fauja 72, 97
Singh, Ganga, Maharaja of Bikaner xvii
　works of 98
Singh, Giani Gian 59, 60
Singh, Harbans 25, 86, 90, 104
Singh, Harchand 105, 109, 112, 114–15, 121–2
Singh, Joginder 32, 123
Singh, Kahan, Sardar 47, 100
Singh, Khushwant 104, 109, 125, 131–2, 141
Singh, Maharaj 38, 41
Singh, Malvinder 150, 152
Singh, Mangal 71, 120
Singh, Master Tara 113, 122
Singh, Mohinder 106
Singh, Mota 115, 122
Singh, Nahar 30, 40, 42, 44, 47–9, 52–3, 61, 63, 69–74
Singh, Niranjan 121, 122
Singh, Ram (leader of the Kuka Sikhs) 30, 32–3, 36, 38–47, 52, 63, 66, 70–4, 76, 89
　early life of 40
　education 40
　leadership of 32
　letter to his disciples 33
　teachings 42, 43
　visit to Anandpur Sahib 36
Singh, Randhir 114, 122
Singh, Ranjit, Maharaja 32, 38, 40, 85, 86
　biography of 85
　death of 32

Singh, Ripudaman, Maharaja of Nabha 113
Singh Sabha movement 89, 119
Singh, Sangat 105, 106, 121, 122
Singh, Sher, Maharaja 38
Singh, Sir Daljit (Raja of Kapurthala) 105, 111
Singh, Sohan, Bhakna 129, 140
Singh, Sunder, Lyallpuri 122, 123
Singh, Teja, Samundri 115, 122
skills xxi, 17, 38, 71, 90–1, 93, 123
　cognitive xxi
　linguistic 90
　media 123
　reflexive 91
　technical 90, 91
slaughterhouses 30
smoking 46
social
　association 45
　behaviour 46, 54
　change xxii
　classes 121, 142
　composition 156
　concerns 57
　conditions 33
　consciousness 118
　developments 121
　discontent 115
　expectations 64
　imaginaries 130
　interests 119
　justice 162
　mobility 160
　movements 32–3, 157
　practices 139
　protest 119
　reality 62
　relations 140

relationships 48
rules 57
standing 39
structures 57
transitions 199
upheaval xxiii, 95
socialism 127, 144, 148–9
Social Science Research Council in New York 186
societies xvi, 35, 119, 139, 162, 165, 199, 205
  agrarian 45
  civil 32, 35, 51, 165
  colonial 119, 160
  contractual 143
  human xvi, xxiii, 57
  Indian 62
  local 35, 54
  metropolitan 139, 205
  modern 162
  peasant 35
  principle of 43
  Sikh 36
sociology xxiii, 137, 139, 184, 205
soldiers xviii, 12, 42, 65, 114, 119, 124
solidarity 36, 75, 128, 196–7
Somnatha 11, 14
Soratha 10–11
"Sourced Sikh History" 5
South Asia xxi, 6, 9, 16, 18, 25, 78, 151, 160–1, 170
South Asian diaspora 125, 144, 158
South-East Punjab 67
South India 13
Sri Bhaini Sahib 46
Sri Gur Pratap Suraj Granth 5
struggles 32, 63, 75, 78, 104, 120–1, 126, 128–9, 133, 138, 144, 151, 156, 163, 183
  anti-imperialist 63
  armed 128–9, 133, 138, 156
  Kuka 32
Suraj Prakash 5; *see also* Singh, Bhai Santokh
surveillance 16, 30, 149
"Swimming Lessons" 192
Syndicalism 127

tale-telling 20
Tarn Taran 60, 110
taxonomy 57, 79
testimonies xv, 3–4, 27
theology 34, 139
thinking xvi, xix–xxi, 17, 19, 43, 51, 61, 77, 94, 128, 152, 156, 163, 165, 167, 176, 190
Thornton, T.H. 49, 52, 70, 72, 96–7
Thucydides 23–5
Tilak, B.G. 136, 141
"To Make the Deaf Hear" 147
Toork/Turk 10–11, 94, 187
Town Hall, Amritsar 112
"To Young Political Workers (1931)" 156, 171
trade and agriculture xxii–iii, 10, 64–6, 71, 193, 198, 203
  commercialisation of 65
  international 10
traditions
  antique 80
  Bhai 36, 37, 39, 72
  classical 7, 166
  cultural 6, 57, 64
  expressive 35
  heroic 119
  Hindu 43
  historiographic 13

Indian 35
intellectual 99
martial 12
orthodox 36
pre-colonial 18
rasa history 19
religious 107, 159–60, 197
Sikh 30–1, 35–6, 38–9, 42, 73
tragedies 21, 192
translations 33, 43, 52, 74–5, 82–3, 90–4, 96, 98–9, 149, 154–6, 175
travelogue 79
treaty between British government and Lahore 39
Treaty of Versailles xvii
trials 3, 31, 36, 53, 143, 154, 159
Trumpp, Ernest 81–3, 86, 96, 99
truth xvi, xix, 1–5, 10, 18, 23–4, 27, 101, 118, 156, 160, 164, 179
  conceptual 27
  elusiveness of 2
  eternal 160, 181
  nature of 1, 2
  primordial 160
  "twice-born" 47

United States xvii, 28, 109, 125, 130–1, 133–4, 140–1, 143, 189–90
Universal Brotherhood 137
universalism 142
Untimely Meditations 22
untouchability 140
Upanishads 198
Uprising of 1857 42, 64–5, 114
uprisings 33, 42, 64–5, 77, 94, 114–15, 120, 130–1, 132
  armed 120

Kuka 94
millenarian 33
tribal 77

Valmiki 7, 18
values xxiii, 27, 35, 90, 133, 156, 164, 173, 180, 204
  egalitarian 133, 156
  moral xxiii, 204
Vedas 8, 62, 141
"Virgin and Mother" 58–9
Venice International Cinema Festival 3
verse 5, 21, 24, 36, 159, 161, 173–6, 178–9
  history in 21
Viceregal Palace 103, 108–9
violence 50–1, 54, 61, 68, 138, 145
Vishwa Hindu Parishad 189
Vohra, Bhagwati Charan 146, 150, 158

Walker, T. Gordon 39, 56, 66–7, 70, 72, 76
  Ludhiana Report 39
Waraich, Malwinder Jit Singh 144, 152, 155, 166, 170, 172
warriors 2–3, 5, 11, 12
"Why I Am An Atheist" 152, 156, 163
womanhood/women 10, 14, 44, 58–9, 137, 162
  freedom of 137
workers 129–30, 154, 179–80, 193, 195
World War, First 114
worship 52–3, 59, 142

Yagnas 13
Yugantar Ashram 129

www.ingramcontent.com/pod-product-compliance
Ingram Content Group UK Ltd.
Pitfield, Milton Keynes, MK11 3LW, UK
UKHW041933140426
5217IPUK00014B/459